THE ESSENTIAL ROBERT INDIANA

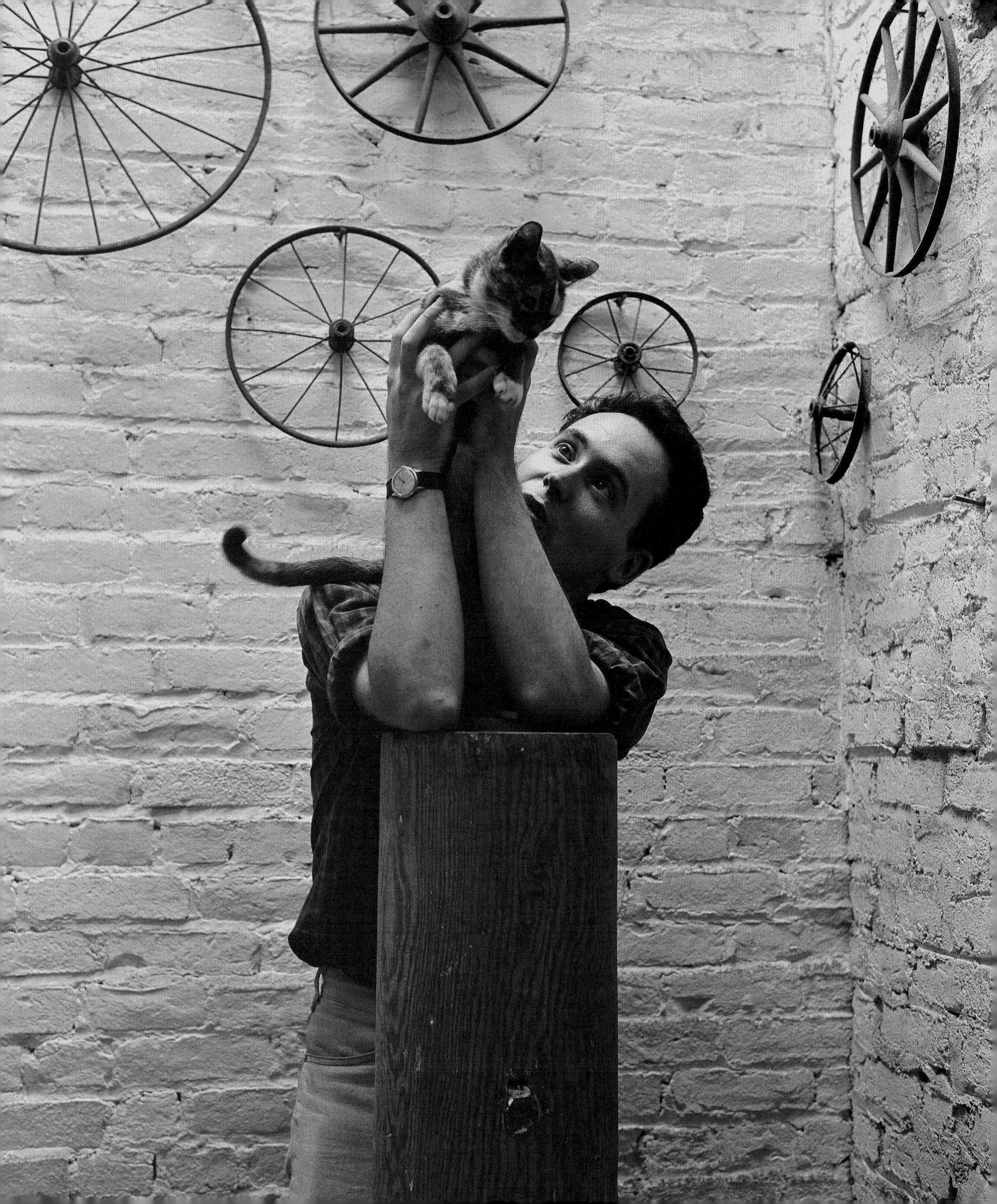

THE ESSENTIAL ROBERT INDIANA

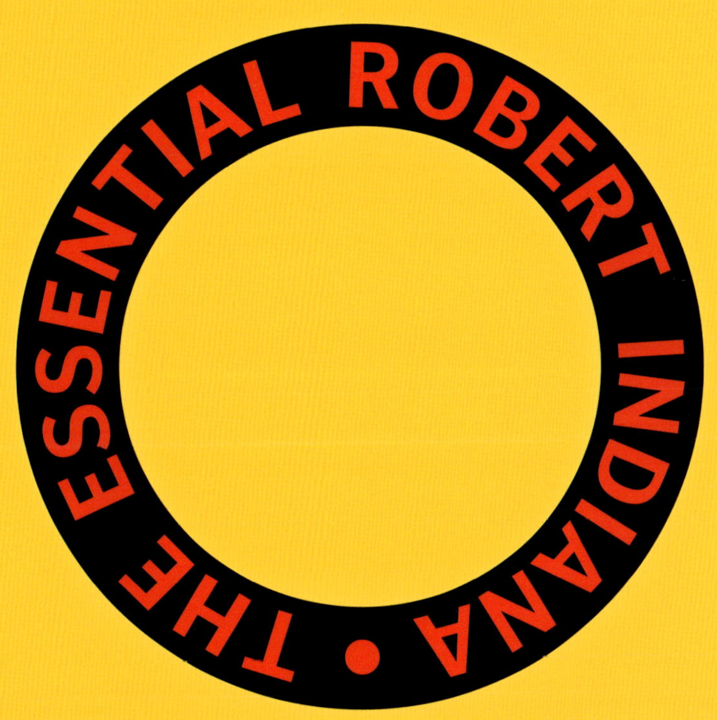

MARTIN KRAUSE
JOHN WILMERDING

INDIANAPOLIS MUSEUM OF ART

DELMONICO BOOKS • PRESTEL
MUNICH LONDON NEW YORK

Published on the occasion of the exhibition *The Essential Robert Indiana*, organized by the Indianapolis Museum of Art, May 24–August 18, 2013.

We would like to thank Morgan Art Foundation for their support in this exhibition.

Published by the Indianapolis Museum of Art and DelMonico Books, an imprint of Prestel Publishing.

Prestel, a member of Verlagsgruppe Random House GmbH

Prestel Verlag
Neumarkter Strasse 28
81673 Munich
Germany
Tel: 49 89 41 36 0
Fax: 49 89 41 36 23 35

Prestel Publishing Ltd.
4 Bloomsbury Place
London WC1A 2QA
United Kingdom
Tel: 44 20 7323 5004
Fax: 44 20 7636 8004

Prestel Publishing
900 Broadway, Suite 603
New York, NY 10003
Tel: 212 995 2720
Fax: 212 995 2733
E-mail: sales@prestel-usa.com

www.prestel.com

Indianapolis Museum of Art
4000 Michigan Road, Indianapolis, Indiana 46208-3326
www.imamuseum.org

ISBN: 978-3-7913-5258-9

Front cover: *Decade: Autoportrait '74, HURRICANE* (detail), from *Vinalhaven Suite*, 1980 (Plate 35)

Back cover: Robert Indiana standing in the plant room at his Coenties Slip studio, 1964

Library of Congress Cataloging-in-Publication Data:
The essential Robert Indiana / Martin Krause,
John Wilmerding.
pages cm
Published on the occasion of the exhibition *The Essential Robert Indiana*, organized by the Indianapolis Museum of Art, May 24–August 18, 2013.
Includes bibliographical references.
ISBN 978-3-7913-5258-9 (hardback)
1. Indiana, Robert, 1928-—Exhibitions. I. Krause, Martin F. II. Wilmerding, John. III. Indiana, Robert, 1928- Prints. Selections. IV. Indianapolis Museum of Art.
NE539.I53A4 2013
769.92—dc23
2012043172

Managing editor: Emily Zoss

Director of publishing and media: Rachel Craft

Manager of photography and publications:
Tascha Horowitz

Assistant photo editor: Julie Long

Permissions: Anne Young

Designer: Roy Brooks, Fold Four, Inc.

Copy editor: Michelle Piranio

Indexer: Cheryl Lemmens

Separations: GHP Media

Printing and binding: Midas Printing

Printed in China

CONTENTS

FOREWORD

During his teenage years, Robert Indiana was introduced to his first art museum: the John Herron Art Institute, as the Indianapolis Museum of Art was then known. The encounter furthered the young student's love of art and initiated a long-lasting relationship that continues to this day.

The IMA recognized the significance of Indiana's work early in his career, acquiring one of his first *LOVE* paintings in 1967, followed by the original monumental Cor-ten steel *LOVE* sculpture in 1970. His presence in the collection was further solidified by the acquisition of the polychrome aluminum *Numbers*, which were commissioned by Melvin Simon and Associates in 1980 and donated to the Museum in 1988. For his part, Indiana has been involved with the IMA on a multitude of levels. He worked with the Museum to design a poster for the reopening of the campus in 1970, has given periodic lectures over the years, and has generously donated a number of prints to the institution's collection.

Though forming an important area of focus for the artist since his student days at the School of the Art Institute of Chicago, Indiana's graphic works are often overshadowed within the larger scope of his oeuvre. Thanks to the perseverance of Martin Krause and John Wilmerding, this has been rectified through the organization of *The Essential Robert Indiana*, a remarkable exhibition and corresponding catalogue of the artist's prints. This presentation explores the personal history embedded in his prints in a way that is appropriate for an institution so interwoven with his roots. None of this could have been accomplished without the willingness and candor of the artist himself, who opened his home to both scholars and shared not only his works of art, but also the memories that inspired their creation.

It has been nearly twenty years since the IMA presented a monographic exhibition of Robert Indiana's work. I am pleased to welcome our friend back to the museum of his youth, and I thank all those who worked so hard to make it happen.

DR. CHARLES L. VENABLE
The Melvin & Bren Simon Director and CEO
Indianapolis Museum of Art

ACKNOWLEDGMENTS

No book springs to life fully formed. Rather, it follows a long and hopefully straight path from conception to publication, with the authors joined along the way by many fellow travelers. My coauthor, John Wilmerding, was this project's pathfinder and has proven to be a most companionable guide and mentor from the outset. Three years ago, John broached the concept of this long-overdue retrospective of Robert Indiana's graphic work to his former student, Maxwell L. Anderson, then The Melvin & Bren Simon Director and CEO of the Indianapolis Museum of Art, who embraced the idea, and it has been carried to fulfillment by his successor, Charles L. Venable. This work is richer for the contributions of Robert Indiana, who generously granted us unrestricted access to his collections and his recollections. Simon, Marc, and Emeline Salama-Caro have shown constant goodwill by providing images and their rights of usage for publication through the Morgan Art Foundation, which is also a generous lender of works to the exhibition, joining the artist and the Taglialatella Galleries in New York. The candid portraits of Robert Indiana by William John Kennedy that embellish the book, including several that are published here for the first time, appear courtesy of KIWI Arts Group through the good offices of Ilana Vardy and Rhonda Long-Sharp.

We were ably supported in this venture by our partners at DelMonico Books • Prestel, including Mary DelMonico and Karen Farquhar; our sympathetic editor, Michelle Piranio; and our sensitive designer, Roy Brooks. The coordination of the publication process at the Indianapolis Museum of Art was handled with usual aplomb by manager of publications Tascha Horowitz, editor Emily Zoss, photographer Tad Fruits, photo editor Julie Long, and our rights and reproductions expert, Anne Young. The increasingly important role of new media in this project was guided by director of publishing and media Rachel Craft, with video producers Emily Lytle-Painter and Daniel Beyer joining me on a memorable pilgrimage to Indiana's studio on the island of Vinalhaven, Maine. Brittany Minton, registrar for exhibitions, made the same trek to secure the works for the exhibition, which was administered by deputy director for collections and exhibitions Katie Haigh and manager of exhibitions Kayla Tackett. The loans were ministered to in the museum by my colleagues Kelly Griffith-Daniel, print room manager, and Claire Hoevel, paper conservator. Deb Lorenzen, my administrative assistant, who is capable of so many tasks of which I am incapable, and who kept this project on the straight and narrow, has recently migrated to coastal Maine, just as Robert Indiana did many years ago.

MARTIN KRAUSE
Curator of Prints, Drawings, and Photographs
Indianapolis Museum of Art

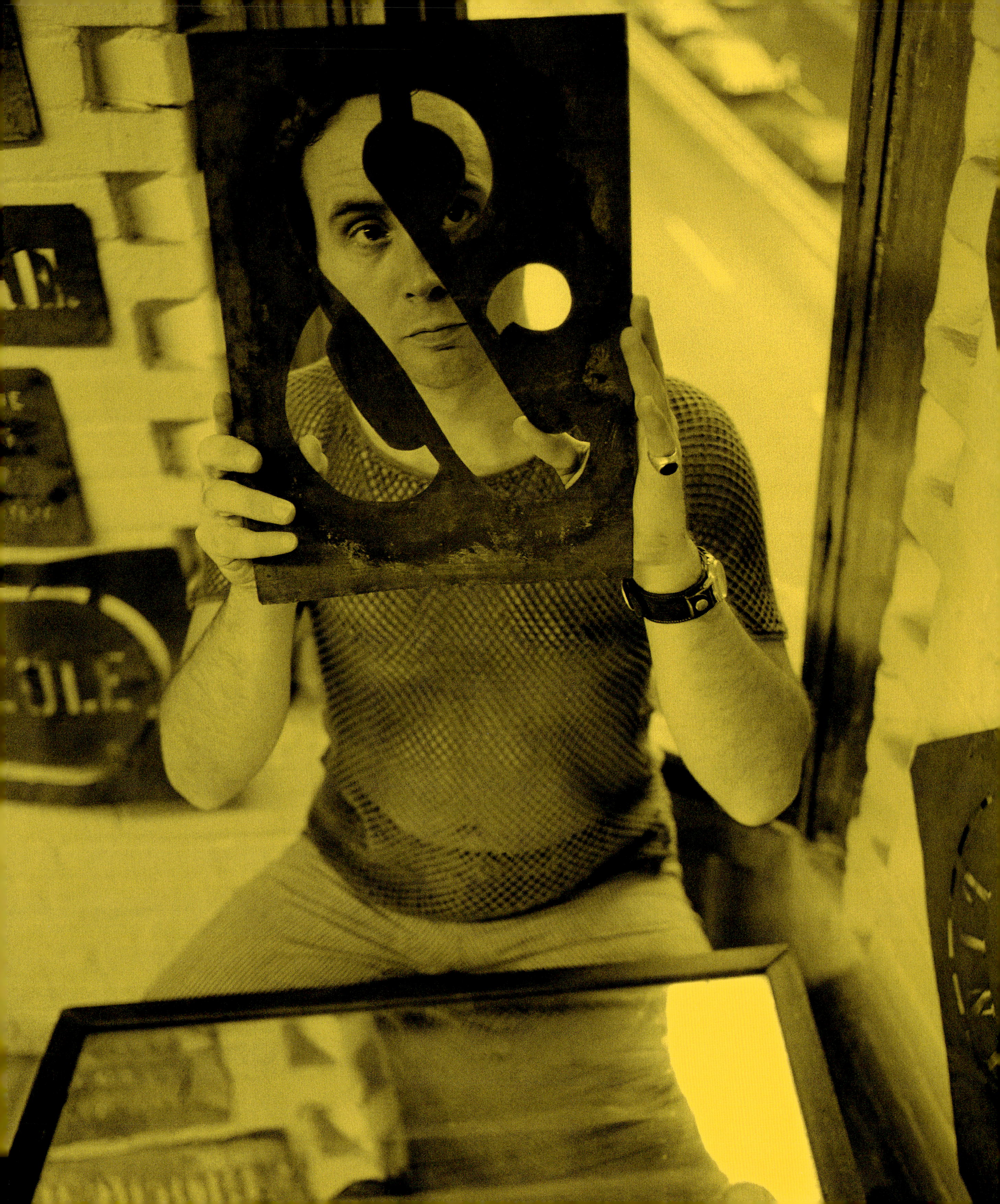

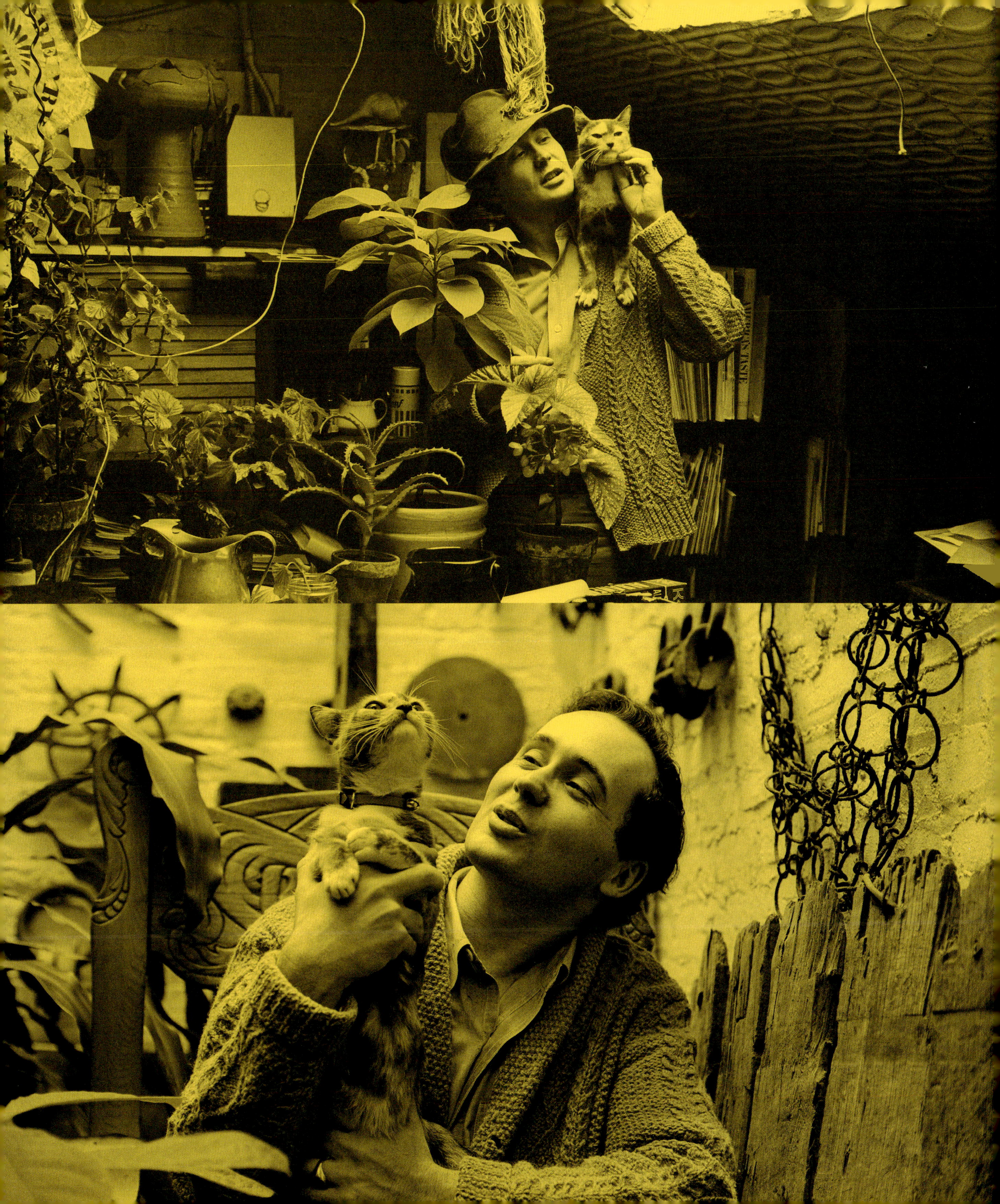

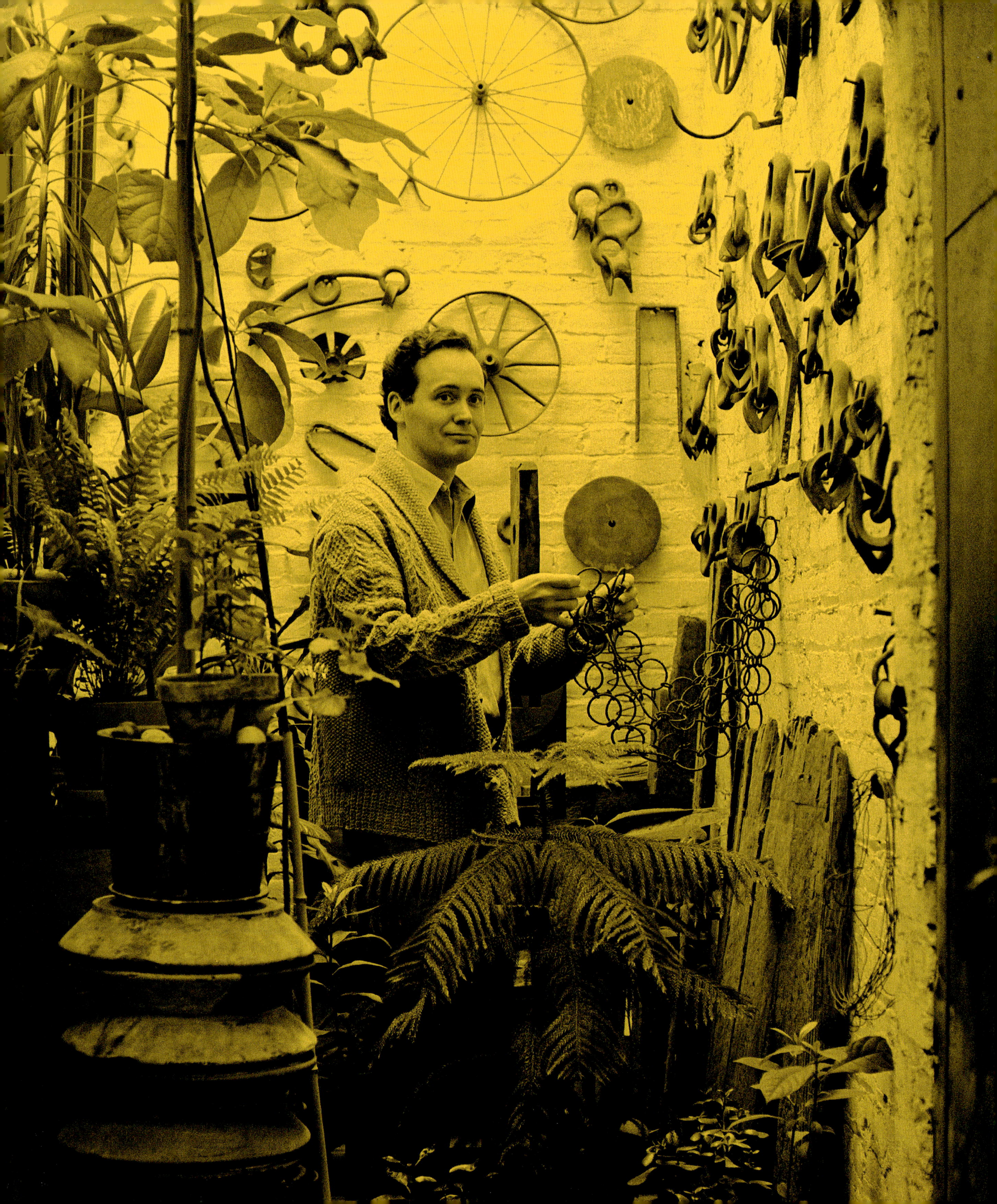

INTRODUCTION: ESSENTIALLY ROBERT INDIANA

MARTIN KRAUSE

Superficially, Robert Indiana's paintings and related prints since 1960 are the quintessence of clarity. With implacable surfaces, unnuanced colors, definite edges, and terse and declarative words, they speak with the authority and directness of the humble highway signs that were their progenitors—a familial link made explicit when Indiana famously described himself as "an American painter of signs charting the course . . . a people's painter as well as a painter's painter."[1] As was clear from the beginning, Indiana's images were more than paeans to the American road or homages to the rudimentary geometry, primary colors, and graphic design of roadside signs. They use a similar psychological attractability, but their messages are different. Too organized and too perfect to be simply informational, they result from thoughts that have been patiently refined and distilled to a desired essence. And though the images are crystal clear, there is much that remains obscured and ambiguous. ● This was sensed by critics early on. Gene Swenson, reviewing Indiana's show at the Stable Gallery, New York, in the summer of 1964, observed that "it is as if the artist were masked, or hiding behind a scrim of perfection and flippant irony."[2] Similarly, Mario Amaya generalized in his 1965 study *Pop Art . . . and After*:

> [Indiana's] huge "signs" resembling highway directions, which order one to EAT, ERR, or DIE, although they have a slick surface attraction, possess something deep and troubling beneath their road-sign simplicity. The words themselves transmit a psychological and emotional jolt and the artist appears to want them to gnaw into the subconscious and to come to terms with associations, past and present.[3]

Only later did Indiana reveal publicly that those "associations, past and present" had concrete ties to his own life, observing, "Most of my work is very autobiographical in one way or another."[4] Most of those associations were from his childhood in Indiana, and that childhood was remembered as bleak. It was the Great Depression, and the Clark family (Indiana's actual surname) was more rootless than John Steinbeck's Joads. By his count, Indiana lived in twenty-one houses in and around Indianapolis before he graduated from high school. Because he was an only child, his only reliable companions were his mother and father, Carmen and Earl; the omnipresent family car was a more lasting structure in his life than were any of his temporary residences. Numbers, as in his ever-morphing street addresses, became signifiers for him, as did words and colors. His most vivid recollection, he first reported in a 1963 interview, was a round green-and-red Phillips 66 gasoline station sign, the company for which his father worked. "My painting is that Phillips 66 sign," Indiana stated emphatically.[5] When asked if his fascination arose from the design or from his father's association with it, Indiana replied, "Both." ● Indiana revealed other autobiographical links within his images in lengthy descriptions of his paintings that were published in the catalogue for his first traveling museum exhibition in 1968,[6] as well as in his decodings of one painting after another in subsequent interviews and publications. The title of his 1966 painting *USA 666*, for instance, came from various sources: Phillips 66, "Use 666" (from yellow-and-black signs advertising a patent medicine that festooned the rural roadsides), and US 66, the route his father took to California after leaving the family. EAT (never DINE) was the impolite invitation to roadside diners, including those in which his divorced mother worked to keep the family fed. When coupled with DIE, as it often has been in Indiana's work, EAT was meant to evoke the last word his mother spoke to him in 1949 before she died. Even *LOVE*, Indiana's impish graphic icon, was autobiographical. According to the artist, its green and red came from the Phillips 66 sign and the blue from the Indiana sky against which it was silhouetted: "[My father's] sign; my sign," Indiana wrote in 1966.[7] ● Even when his images were not strictly rooted in autobiography, they were inspired by (or at least explained as arising from) coincidences that linked Indiana to outwardly unrelated people or events. The

1. Susan Elizabeth Ryan, *Robert Indiana: Figures of Speech* (New Haven: Yale University Press, 2000), 93.

2. G. R. S. [Gene Swenson], "Robert Indiana (Stable)," *Art News* 63, no. 4 (Summer 1964): 13.

3. Mario Amaya, *Pop Art . . . and After* (New York: Viking Press, 1965), 79.

4. Barbaralee Diamonstein, *Inside New York's Art World* (New York: Rizzoli, 1979), 153.

5. Oral history interview with Robert Indiana by Richard Brown Baker, September 12–November 7, 1963, Archives of American Art, Smithsonian Institution, Washington, DC, online at http://www.aaa.si.edu/collections/interviews/oral-history-interview-robert-indiana-12936.

6. *Robert Indiana* was organized by the Institute of Contemporary Art of the University of Pennsylvania, Philadelphia (April 17–May 27, 1968), in collaboration with the Marion Koogler McNay Art Institute, San Antonio (July 1–August 15, 1968), and the John Herron Art Institute, Indianapolis (September 1–29, 1968).

7. *Kunst Licht Kunst* (Eindhoven: Stedelijk van Abbemuseum, 1966), unpaginated.

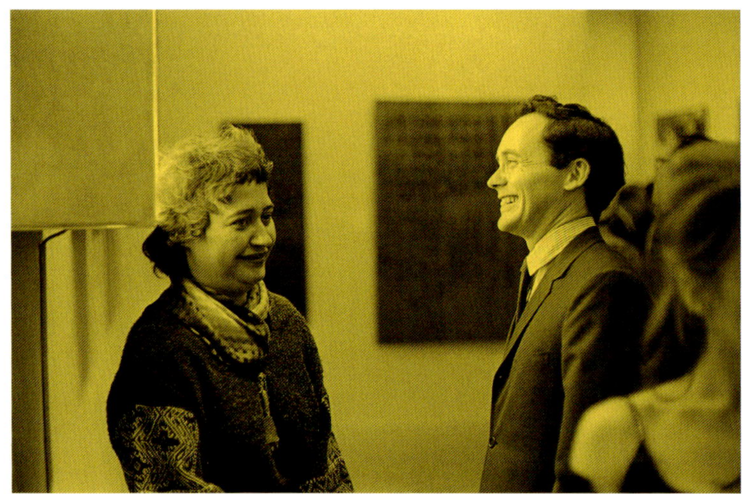

stylized image of Marilyn Monroe that figures in his 1967 painting *The Metamorphosis of Norma Jean Mortenson* came from a girlie calendar that happened to have been printed in his home state of Indiana. *THE FIGURE FIVE*, 1963, was Indiana's translation into his own idiom of Charles Demuth's 1928 painting *I Saw the Figure 5 in Gold*. Indiana felt a natural kinship with this early American modernist who, as Indiana did, built his image with numbers and words; but, equally important, the date of Demuth's painting was coincident with the year of Indiana's birth. Another forebear in the painting of cryptic symbolic portraits, Marsden Hartley, came into Indiana's focus only after he had settled on the island of Vinalhaven, where Hartley, a Mainer, had summered. Such coincidences provided Indiana with a spiritual as well as a professional link to these historical figures, and they remain a fascination to him. ● All of this backstory is encrypted into the symbolic colors, shapes, and single-syllable words that make up Indiana's visual vocabulary. But in spite of his paintings' superficial legibility, their meanings are not truly grasped or even intelligible until explained verbally by the artist. Such explanations allow us to see behind the mask that Swenson had so astutely perceived and that Indiana tacitly admitted to in 1977 (in reference to Picasso): "Of course, he who changes his name is wearing a mask."[8] But Indiana allows us to see only what he chooses to reveal. Conversations with the artist, beginning in 1963 and continuing today, run up against certain aspects of his private life that are out of bounds; he controls the narrative and, one supposes, the mask is never completely off. ● Indiana has always assumed the role of "curator" of his life, amassing, sorting, storing, and caring for biographical mementos. But can a life so curated be unexpurgated? When *LOVE* began its journey as a 1965 Christmas card design for the Museum of Modern Art, New York, was the red, green, and blue color scheme already a conscious homage to his father, or merely the electric combination of the most charged colors on his palette, as he has said elsewhere?[9] When the word EAT made its first appearance in 1961 on one of Indiana's "herms"—old beams that were carved, embellished, painted, and set upright by the artist as contemporary versions of

8. Diamonstein, *Inside New York's Art World*, 163.

9. "Introduction," in *Robert Indiana* (Philadelphia: Institute of Contemporary Art of the University of Pennsylvania, in association with the Falcon Press, 1968), 29.

ancient Greek signposts of the same name—were his mother's last words on his mind, or was it a Pop-arty statement on American consumerism, reduced to a three-letter, one-syllable word that suited his preference at the time for terse declarations? He offered both possibilities in 1977.[10] He has explained the license plate—IND 27—appearing on the Ford Model T in his *Mother and Father* diptych of 1963–67 as representing the year and possible site of his conception, yet such information can be only speculative given the fact that he was adopted at birth by Earl and Carmen Clark, which he does not talk about. ● Indiana's life, as he chooses to reveal it, is self-determined. "I'm fascinated by the lives of artists," he said in a 1991 interview, "and have tried to design my own life so that it is a little bit more interesting than my mother and father's, shall we say."[11] In other words, he sees himself as self-made. He pursued art in a family that had no artistic interests. He left his mother's home to move into the district of the high school he wished to attend in Indianapolis. He turned down a scholarship from the local art school and joined the Army Air Corps in 1946, at age seventeen, to avail himself of the GI Bill so he could attend the School of the Art Institute of Chicago. He never looked back. When he settled in New York in 1955, he was alone in the world. Finding his given name, Clark, too common to be memorable, he renamed himself after his native state in the manner of Renaissance artists who were known by the towns of their origin. He was renascent. But his past always remained as the foundation, informing the writings and works that now constitute the artist's signposts to his own history. ● Conjured up from the artist's most indelible recollections, the evocative and iconic images that are included in the current volume constitute the Indiana canon. The choice to present them in their printed form, though most of them reproduce paintings, is deliberate, as they are not only the most democratic manifestation of the work of this self-described "people's painter" but also the most refined. The prints—almost exclusively screenprints since the early 1960s—might be dismissed as hand-me-down images were it not for screenprinting's innate enhancements of the hard edges, flat surfaces, and luminous colors that Indiana aims for in his canvases. The further tempering of the printing process represents a perfection of a working method that Indiana has described as a progressive distillation of an image down to "the bare bones."[12] Legible and intelligible in their broad outlines, these works—like the artist—present an opaque façade that is carefully organized and controlled. What remains obscured beneath the simple words, numbers, shapes, and colors are the memories and signifiers of his life. These are the essentials that this book strives to elucidate.

10. See Diamonstein, *Inside New York's Art World*, 158.

11. Susan Sheehan, *Robert Indiana Prints: A Catalogue Raisonné, 1951–1991* (New York: Susan Sheehan Gallery, 1991), 14.

12. "Conversations with Robert Indiana," in *Robert Indiana* (Austin: University Art Museum, University of Texas, 1977), 36.

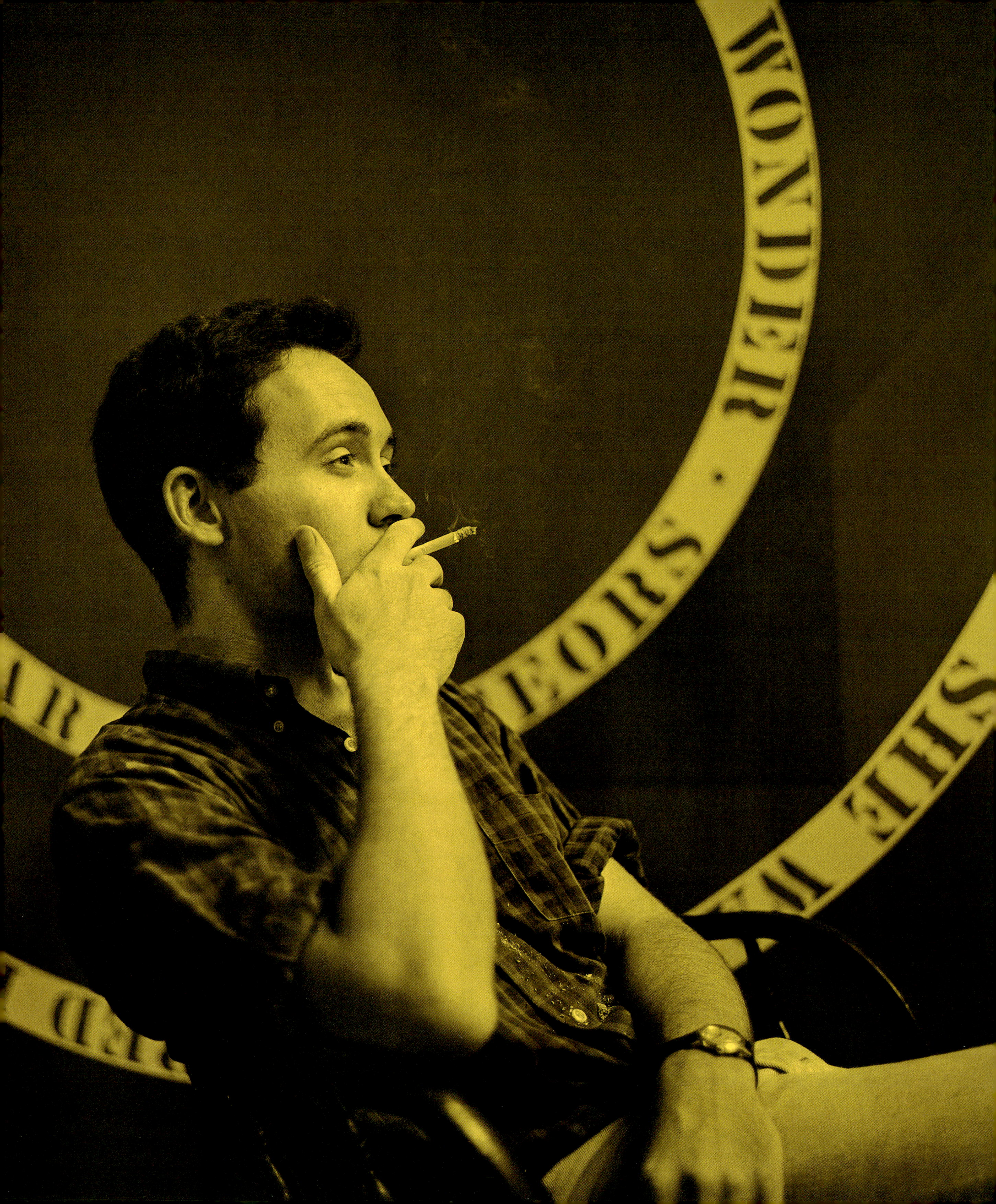

THE FORMALITIES OF ROBERT INDIANA

JOHN WILMERDING

Robert Indiana has established a position as one of the master printmakers in modern art. His career spans more than six decades, with strong connections to the Pop movement that emerged in the 1960s. At the same time, the content and style of his art soon found an individual expression that went beyond pure Pop to embrace conceptual and literary elements as well as aspects of optical and minimal art of the same period. Following in the wake of abstract expressionism, Indiana rejected the exuberant gesturalism and emotional self-projection of that earlier dominating style, in favor of severe planarity and hard-edged design inspired in large part by contemporary advertising signage. Although some artists of that earlier generation, such as Robert Motherwell, were important printmakers as well as painters, their aesthetic called for an outsized scale and primarily spontaneous execution that they could explore best on canvas. For many of the Pop artists, by contrast, the rigor and flatness of the printing process perfectly suited their new, essentially graphic style. ● As a consequence, within Indiana's production, as was true with most of his colleagues as well, the prints have usually matched in technical purity and visual power his generally larger output of paintings. He has regularly worked on sheets that are comparable in size to their corollary compositions on canvas, most extraordinarily in the oversized *Hartley Elegies* of his later career—tours de force of meticulous execution and emotional expression in their own right. In fact, one can argue that the major body of printmaking produced by the diverse range of artists associated with Pop has greatly broadened the field, instilling the medium with new inventiveness, vigor, and wit. Indeed, in several instances, notably in the work of Andy Warhol, the graphic arts have significantly influenced and transformed the making of both painting and sculpture, blurring the boundaries between traditionally defined media. ● Several major figures tied to the Pop movement, including Warhol (FIGURE 1), Roy Lichtenstein, Claes Oldenburg, and Alex Katz, have catalogues documenting their graphic output, which constitutes a substantial independent achievement in the career of each artist.[1] Not surprisingly, the total of Warhol's printed works, including unpublished editions, adds up to some 785 images, by far the largest production among his peers. Lichtenstein's catalogue lists 311 sheets, plus a large number of posters.[2] Oldenburg has produced more than 265 prints, and Katz over 146. Tom Wesselmann's prints have not been fully catalogued, but his estate estimates that close to one hundred exist. Robert Rauschenberg was a prodigious printmaker, and Jasper Johns and James Rosenquist, both still actively at work today, have been equally prolific; full catalogues for them have yet to be published. ● For Indiana's graphic output, we are fortunate to have a catalogue that covers the first two-thirds of his career, up to 1991. In addition, a volume published in conjunction with an exhibition of his *Hartley Elegies* documents the ten large-scale prints he made from the bigger group of paintings.[3] In the late 1980s, Indiana produced twenty-two canvases in this series over a period of several years—the first dozen as vertical rectangles, another six as diamond compositions, and four tondos—before he felt he had exhausted his formal possibilities. The printed *Elegies* followed in the early 1990s, and were limited to the vertical and diamond format designs. During the last two decades, Indiana has published another three dozen prints, with G & S Editions in New York, that include variations of *THE FIGURE FIVE*, the *Decade: Autoportraits*, half a dozen *Marilyns*, and a similar number of *LOVE*s and *LOVE* wall arrangements. These and other miscellaneous prints add up to more than 150 graphic images. ● Indiana (then Robert Clark) studied printmaking as an art student at the Art Institute of Chicago in the 1950s, working in woodcut, linocut, wood engraving, etching, and aquatint. He also had access to the museum's art library, an opportunity that brought him in direct contact with original master prints by Rembrandt and Dürer. The aspiring artist then completed a BFA at the University of Edinburgh in Scotland. After he moved to New York in 1955, he changed his name to Robert Indiana, after the state in which he was born and raised. Settling into a loft on Coenties Slip in lower Manhattan's east-side waterfront area, he met a

1. See Frayda Feldman and Jorg Schellmann, *Andy Warhol Prints: A Catalogue Raisonné, 1962–1987*, 4th ed. (New York: Ronald Feldman Fine Arts, 2003); Mary Lee Corlett, *The Prints of Roy Lichtenstein: A Catalogue Raisonné, 1948–1997* (New York: Hudson Hills Press, 2002); Richard H. Axsom and David Platzker, *Printed Stuff—Prints, Posters, and Ephemera by Claes Oldenburg: A Catalogue Raisonné, 1958–1996* (New York: Hudson Hills Press, 1998); and Klaus Albrecht Schroder et al., *Alex Katz Prints* (Ostfildern, Germany: Hatje Cantz, 2010). It should be noted that the first two are complete, while Oldenburg is still alive and producing. The Katz publication was generated in conjunction with a retrospective print exhibition at the Albertina in Vienna.

2. Some artists have been active in designing posters and other ephemera, which they have considered a part of their graphic production. Indiana has regularly been involved in poster production for exhibitions of his work, designing or approving dozens of compositions over the course of his career. But he has stated that he does not consider this category to be an official part of his graphic oeuvre. It does, however, constitute work that at some point should be examined and catalogued.

3. Susan Sheehan, *Robert Indiana Prints: A Catalogue Raisonné, 1951–1991* (New York: Susan Sheehan Gallery, 1991); and Susan Elizabeth Ryan, *Robert Indiana: The Hartley Elegies* (Lewiston, Maine: Bates College Museum of Art, 2005).

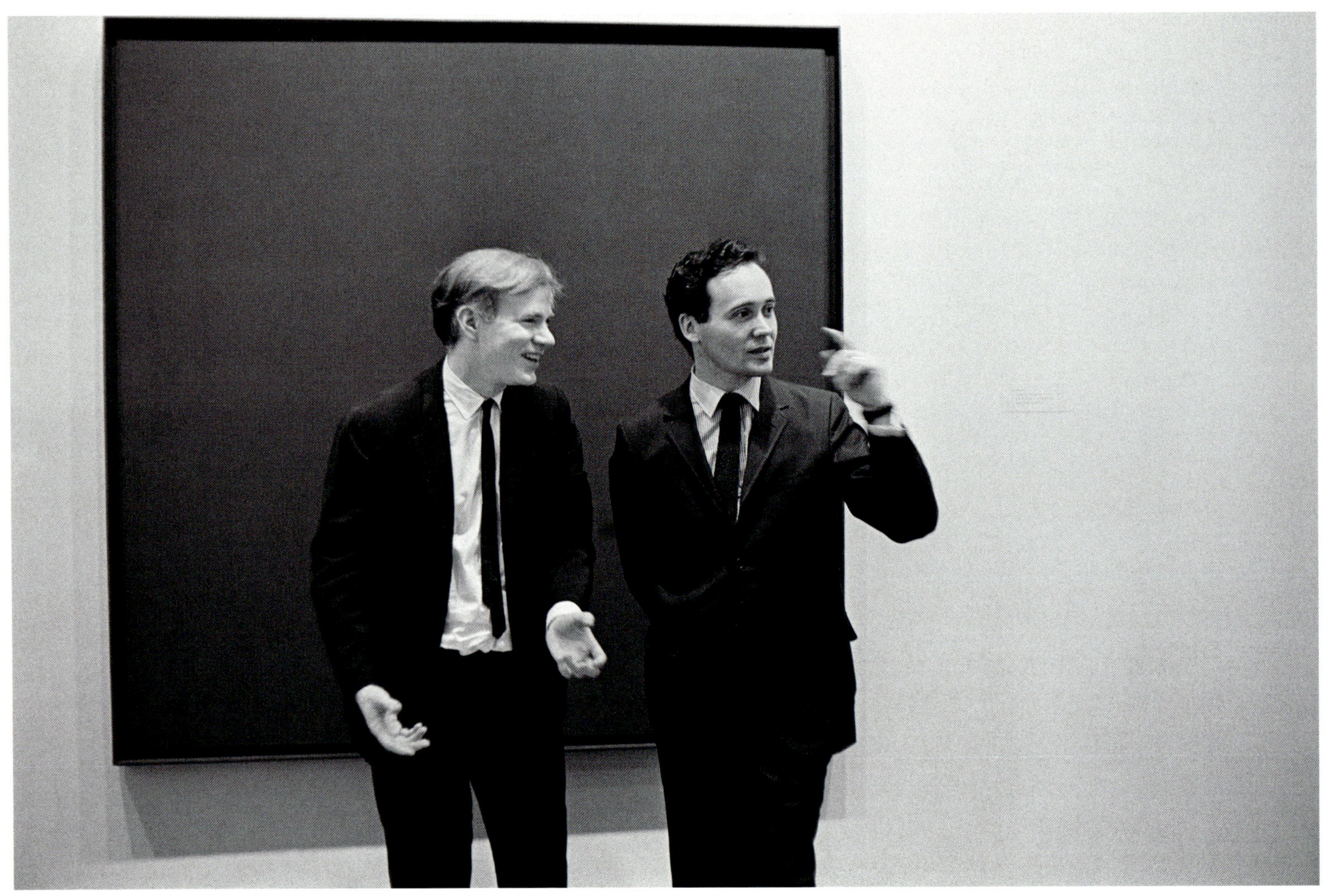

FIGURE 1

William John Kennedy, *Andy Warhol and Robert Indiana at the* Americans 1963 *exhibition at the Museum of Modern Art, New York*, 1963 (printed 2010)

silver gelatin fiber print

16 × 20 in. (40.6 × 50.8 cm)

© 2010 William John Kennedy, kiwiartsgroup.com

number of other young artists working there, among them Agnes Martin, Jack Youngerman, and Ellsworth Kelly.[4] Johns and Rauschenberg were also nearby in warehouse studios. Kelly in particular was an important influence in forming Indiana's visual vocabulary at this time, which took on new flatness, geometric simplicity, and hard-edged definition of forms. (After a couple of years, however, the two artists would part ways over Indiana's retention of lettering in his compositions and would go on to pursue separate but parallel minimalist styles.) At this time, Indiana also began experimenting with the popular new medium of silkscreen printing, recently exploited with great energy and imagination by Rauschenberg and soon taken up by Warhol. This process involves cutting a design into a stencil, which is fitted to a finely meshed screen. One then forces ink through the open areas onto a surface for printing. ● In his career, Indiana has made use of lithography, a printing process invented at the end of the eighteenth century. Unlike earlier printmaking methods such as woodcut, engraving, etching, and aquatint that required cutting, gouging, or biting with acid into hard wood blocks or metal plates, lithography involves drawing on blocks of polished stone and inking them in one or more colors. In screenprinting and lithography, each color to be printed calls for a different stencil or stone, demanding the most meticulous care to achieve the clean registration of adjacent colors in a composition. Lithography and screenprinting appealed most to Indiana. The processes were easier, quicker, and cheaper; they allowed for much larger print surfaces and were well suited to the insistent planarity he desired. By applying ink smoothly and evenly, he could achieve a sharp, machine-made look in the manner of modern billboards, posters, and signage. (This of course was the opposite of the conscious smearing, blurring, and off-register images sought by Warhol, who soon carried over his printmaking techniques into the execution of his paintings.) A great range of surface treatments was now available to artists and contributed to a flourishing new age in the graphic arts. It was at this juncture that Indiana declared himself to be "an American painter of signs," a characterization that can be applied to his work as a printmaker as well.[5] ● With his new identity and style came increased momentum in his artistic production as well as in recognition (and sales) of his work. One of Indiana's earliest sales, the 1961 painting *The American Dream, I* (FIGURE 2), was to the Museum of Modern Art, New York, a decisive step in securing his reputation. Over time, as other paintings were bought by private collectors or public institutions, Indiana felt their loss keenly and found that making a print of the departing canvas was a satisfying compensation. Thus developed a pattern throughout his career of producing prints of works that were leaving his hands.[6] Even so, the prints offer their own direct evidence of Indiana's original modes of composing images and language of expression. ● Once Indiana began producing paintings and prints in his classic Pop style, he soon settled on several basic shapes that would endure throughout his work. Although his art occasionally touches on figuration or illustration, Indiana overwhelmingly prefers to design with classic core geometries, namely the circle, the square, its variant the diamond, the rectangle, and, less frequently, the triangle. How he uses and mixes these configurations can vary greatly, from large spare patterns to more complicated combinations of fragmented parts and multiple repetitions within a single frame. Indiana's colors usually complement such variations, from the simple juxtapositions of two colors to a mix of several hues, mostly primaries, integrated with segments of black and white. Together these formal aspects often have suggestive visual or psychological associations and give resonant meaning to his images. Numbers, letters, words, and phrases appear frequently, but we find them contained and enhanced by the artist's bold geometric outlines. Indiana is an avid reader and an occasional writer of poetry, and these activities have assumed key roles in his playful but calculated balancing in his art of the verbal and the visual, of text and design. ● Because Indiana's prints tend almost exclusively to replicate his paintings, they are best examined together as part of a larger coherent career. The circle is a dominant motif and, arguably, from its repetition, the artist's favorite geometric form. There are only a few paintings executed as actual tondos—those coming at the end of *The Hartley Elegies* series, his great masterworks of

4. For a summary of these early years in New York and Indiana's first efforts at printmaking, see Poppy Gandler Orchier, "Introduction," in Sheehan, *Robert Indiana Prints*, 7.

5. Susan Elizabeth Ryan, *Robert Indiana: Figures of Speech* (New Haven: Yale University Press, 2000), 93.

6. This explains why many of the major paintings still in the artist's collection, or in the collection of the foundation that holds much of his estate, have no graphic counterparts.

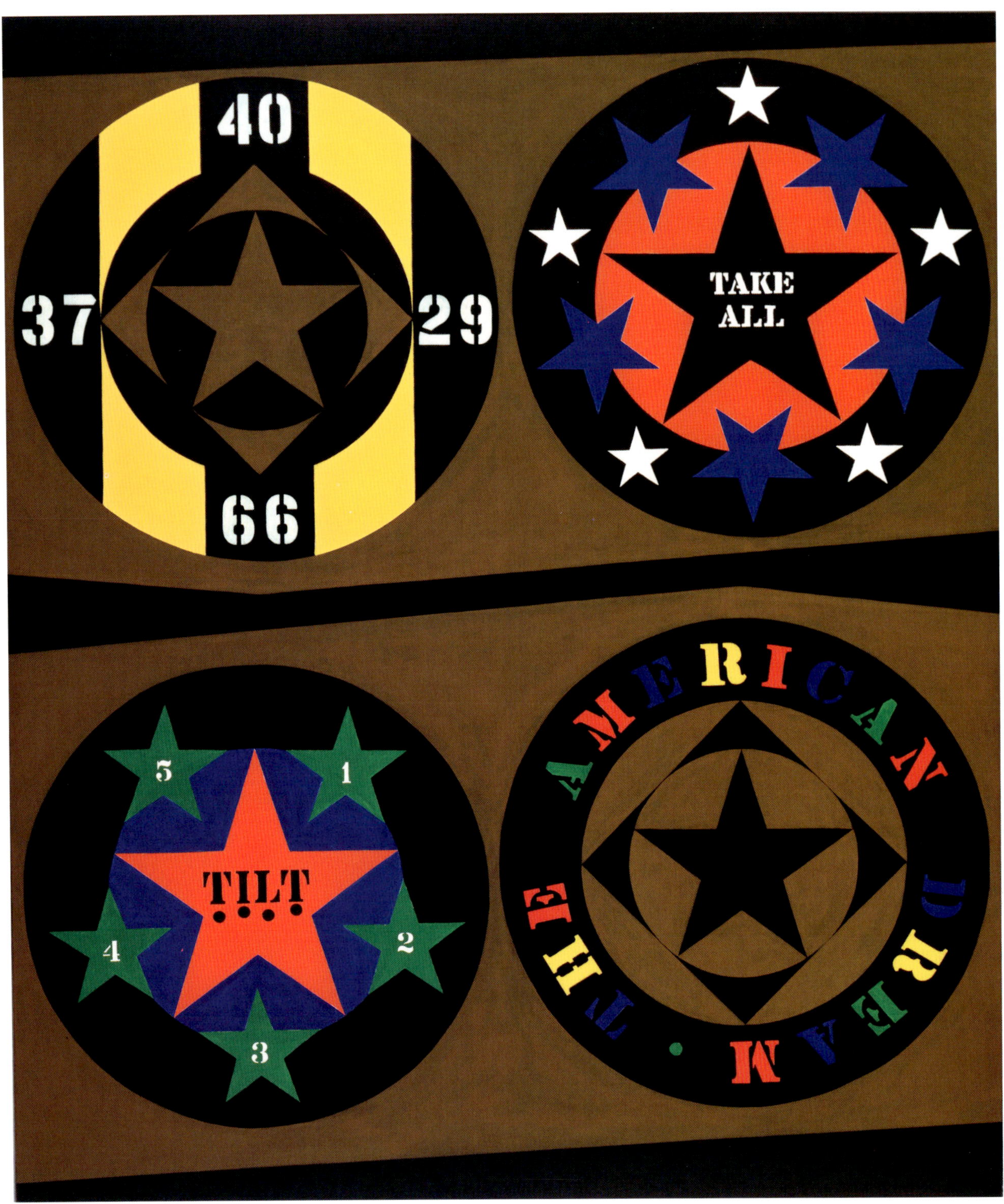

FIGURE 2

Robert Indiana, *The American Dream, I*, 1961

oil on canvas

72 × 60 ⅛ in. (182.9 × 152.7 cm)

The Museum of Modern Art, New York,
Larry Aldrich Foundation Fund

Photo: Courtesy of Morgan Art Foundation

the later years in Maine. Indiana says he found them challenging to compose, stretch, and frame. Most often, the circle fits within a vertical rectangle that allows for a word or words to appear across the lower edge as a title. Typical examples among the prints are *1962 YIELD BROTHER* (PLATE 5), *1963 THE FIGURE FIVE* (PLATE 6), *1965 MISSISSIPPI* (PLATE 8), and *1967 PARROT* (PLATE 10), all from the *Decade* suite of 1971; *PICASSO*, 1974 (PLATE 30); *THE BRIDGE*, 1983 (PLATE 41); and *MOTHER OF EXILES*, 1986 (PLATE 42). We can readily see that *1969 TERRE HAUTE No. 2*, 1971 (PLATE 12) makes use of a semi-circle in the same format. In a few instances, the bottom strip of space is left wordless, notably *EAT/DIE*, 1990 (PLATE 1), and *HIGH BALL on the REDBALL MANIFEST*, 1997 (PLATE 15). Other circles occupy perfect or nearly square frames, such as *1961 THE CALUMET*, 1971 (PLATE 4), *AMERICAN DREAM #5*, 1980 (PLATE 14), the *Decade: Autoportraits* from the *Vinalhaven Suite*, 1980 (PLATES 31–40), and the later *Decade: Autoportraits* from 2001 to 2009 (PLATES 17–26). Variants of course exist, with the square turned to hang as a diamond, enclosing a circle or circles within, as in *1964 The Brooklyn Bridge* (PLATE 7) and *1966 USA 666* (PLATE 9), both 1971; *THE AMERICAN DREAM #2*, 1982 (PLATE 13); the last half of *The Hartley Elegies: The Berlin Series (KvF VI, VII, VIII, IX,* and *X*; PLATES 48–52), all 1991; and *The Metamorphosis of Norma Jean Mortenson*, 1998 (PLATE 16). ● *THE CALUMET*, 1961, was one of Indiana's first paintings in his signature style, part of a group of canvases inspired by his reading of literary masters from the American Renaissance of the mid-nineteenth century—key figures in the establishment of a national culture whose works rose to the heights of international fame during the first decades of the twentieth century. Indiana was settled now in lower Manhattan, in the very area where Walt Whitman and Herman Melville had worked, looking out on the Brooklyn Bridge, the East River as it flows out to New York Bay, and Staten Island. From the empty and abandoned warehouses facing the old piers, Indiana salvaged rusted flywheels, posts and tie beams, and other relics from the earlier age of New York shipping traffic and commerce that he incorporated into his first wood assemblages. But it was from the rich literary tradition of America that he drew ideas for paintings. ● Henry Wadsworth Longfellow's *The Song of Hiawatha*, 1855, was the inspiration for *THE CALUMET*. The painting's title, the Indian names inscribed in the inner circles, and the sentence fragments running around the larger circumference all come from the epic poem. Phrases such as "tribes of men" and "mountains of the prairie" summon up the early nineteenth-century imagery of George Catlin, whose mission was to paint the existing Indian tribes in their native landscapes before their removal and disappearance. The containment of the inner rings within the outer circle suggests an encampment, with the tribal tents formally arranged for habitation or ceremony. Indeed, we can readily imagine how the evenly spaced names and rhythmic alignment of shapes are the visual embodiment of native chants and communal dances. Later, when the artist revisited the theme of Native Americans in other works, he would note how his taken name was "Indian" with just one letter added.[7] ● Two major related paintings, also from 1961, make use of similar circular formats to convey their meaning. *YEAR OF METEORS* takes its title and its text from an 1859–60 poem from Whitman's *Leaves of Grass* and refers both to a particular year of meteor showers witnessed in New York and, in the encircling line "The Great Eastern Swam up My Bay," to one of the great clipper ships passing in the river. Here the concentric circles remind us of the island of Manhattan and Staten Island framing the expanse of New York Harbor, reinforced by the painting's use of green and dark blue to signify the adjacency of water, earth, and sky. In turn, *Melville Triptych* (FIGURE 3) consists of three rectangular canvases hung side by side, with a circle inside each bearing phrases from the opening paragraphs of what is often considered America's greatest novel, Melville's *Moby Dick*, 1851. Indiana's palette of stark black and white captures, of course, the opposition of Ahab and the white whale. The place names he stenciled beneath each circle tie Melville and Indiana together across time. To describe Ishmael going to the waterfront to begin his cosmic seagoing voyage, the writer repeatedly employs images of circularity, just as the painter uses contiguous circles to create a visual motion across the three canvases. Melville's language is highly evocative:

7. Robert Indiana in conversation with the author, July 2011.

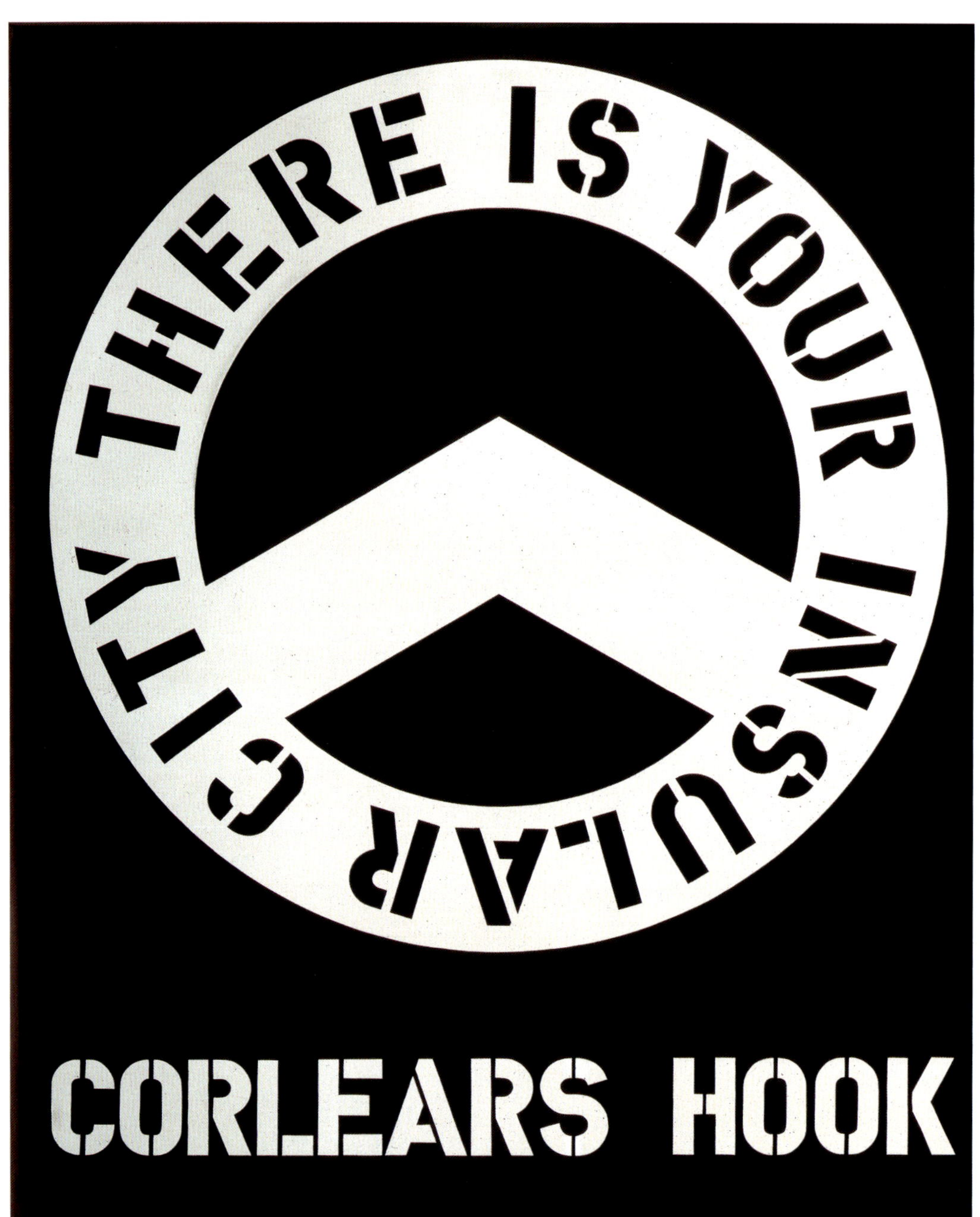

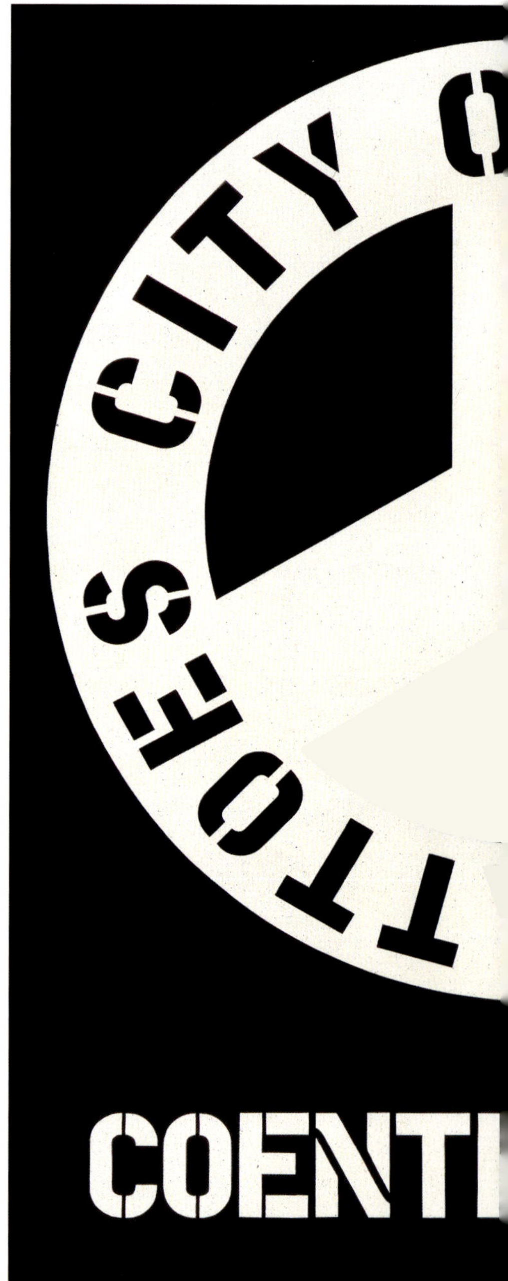

FIGURE 3

Robert Indiana, *Melville Triptych,* 1961

oil on canvas

60 × 150 in. (152.4 × 381 cm)

Courtesy of Morgan Art Foundation

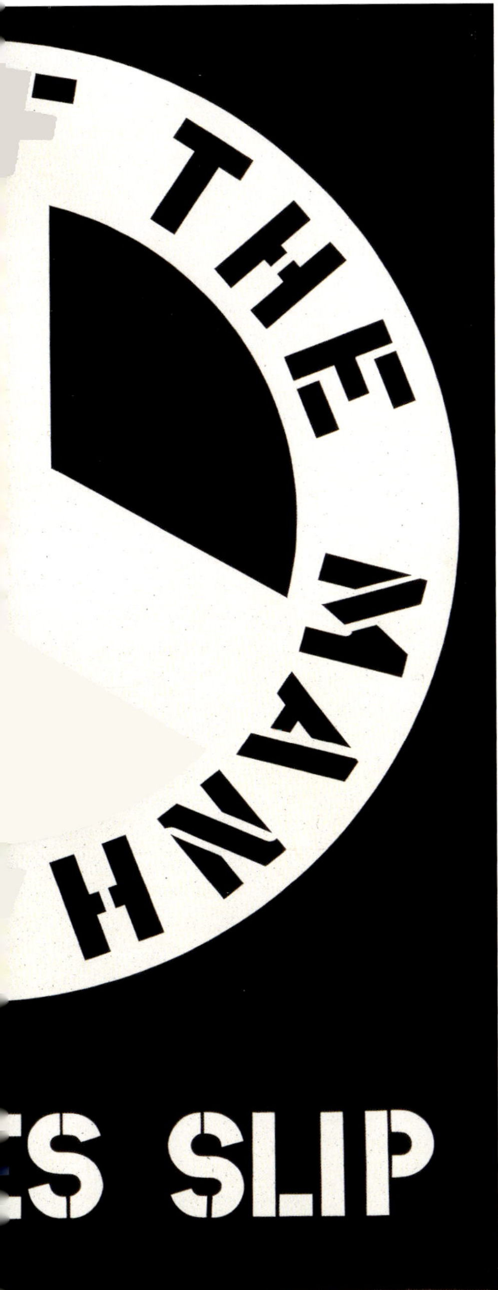
THE MANH
ES SLIP

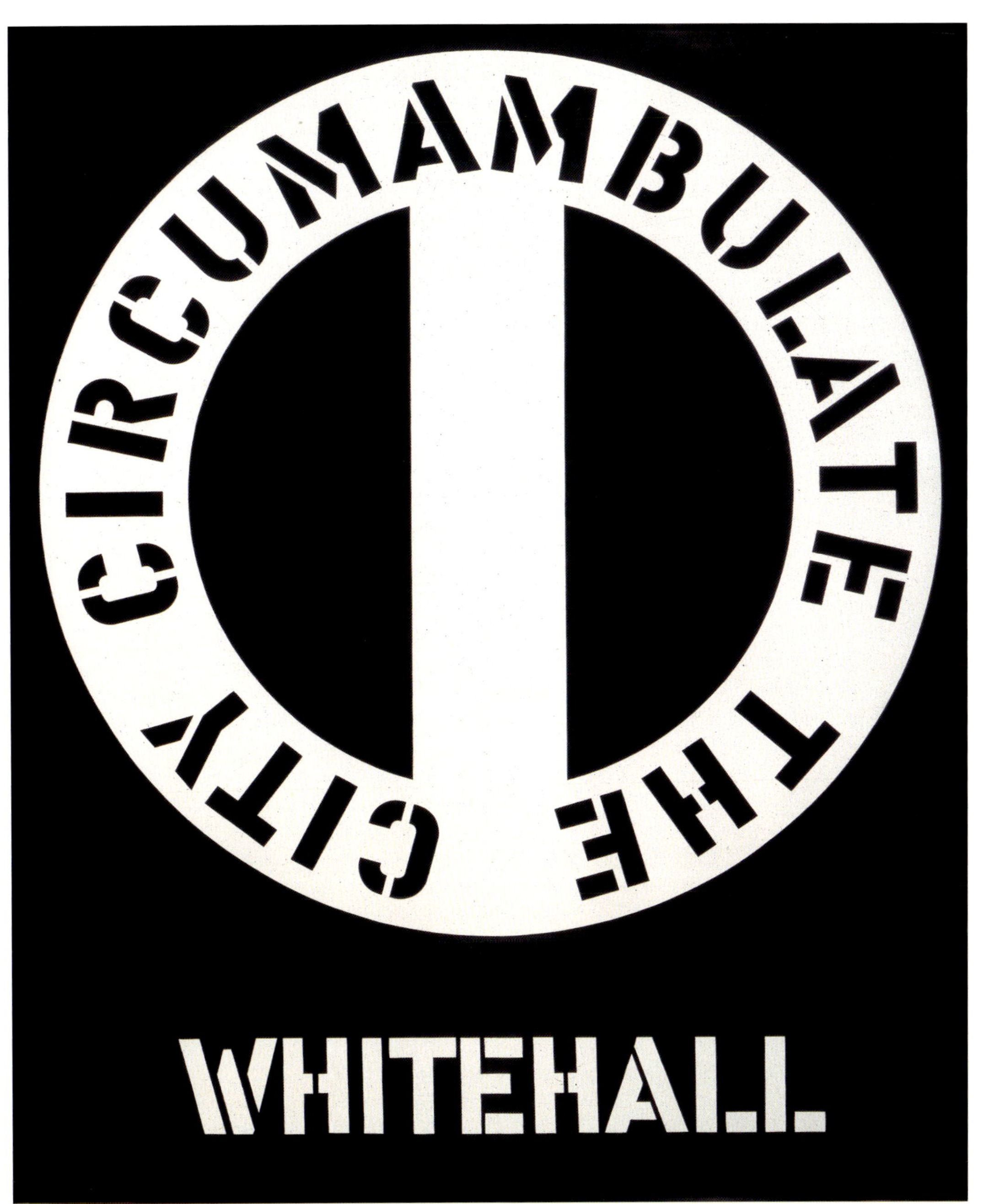
CIRCUMAMBULATE THE CITY
WHITEHALL

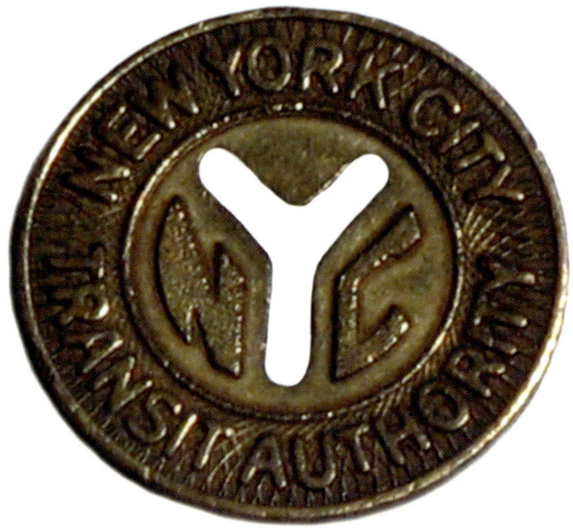

FIGURE 4

Transportation token: New York City Transit Authority, large Y-cut

Courtesy of New York Transit Museum

> There is now your insular city of the Manhattoes, belted round by wharves as Indian isles by coral reefs—commerce surrounds it with her surf. . . . Circumambulate the city of a dreamy Sabbath afternoon. Go to Corlears Hook to Coenties Slip, and from thence, by Whitehall, northward. What do you see?—Posted like silent sentinels all around the town, stand thousands upon thousands of mortal men fixed in ocean reveries. . . . Tell me, does the magnetic virtue of the needles of the compasses of all those ships attract them thither?[8]

On one level, Indiana alludes to the repeated circular entities Melville describes: "insular city," "belted round," "Indian isles," "commerce surrounds," "circumambulate," and "compasses." And within the painter's circles are lines that may refer to the people who have gone to stand "like silent sentinels," sit upon the pier heads or aloft in ships' rigging, or be pulled by the "needles of the compasses." In addition, Indiana links his circles to transportation on the river—the flywheels of vessels, paddle wheels of steamers—and, by suggestion, to Ishmael's grand journey, both literal and imaginative, out to the Atlantic and then the Pacific, in a partial circumnavigation of the globe itself. On a second level, the painter calls attention to train cars on barges in the river and modern traffic passing on the East River Drive. We may also recognize in the configuration of the middle circle the design of the old New York City subway token (FIGURE 4), and note that the popular Circle Line cruises provide tours around Manhattan by water today. Indiana played with the imagery again in *The Slips*, 1962, with its eight circles containing the names of Coenties and other familiar local piers.

● In his *Confederacy* series of four paintings that depict the states of Mississippi, Alabama, Georgia, and Florida, from the mid-1960s, Indiana introduced concentric circles that work in somewhat different ways. As in the Whitman and Longfellow compositions, the inner circles provide room for a longer narrative. There is perhaps an implication of travel, of the student activists and civil rights marchers who went

8. Herman Melville, *Moby Dick: or, The Whale* (New York: Modern Library, 1992), 2.

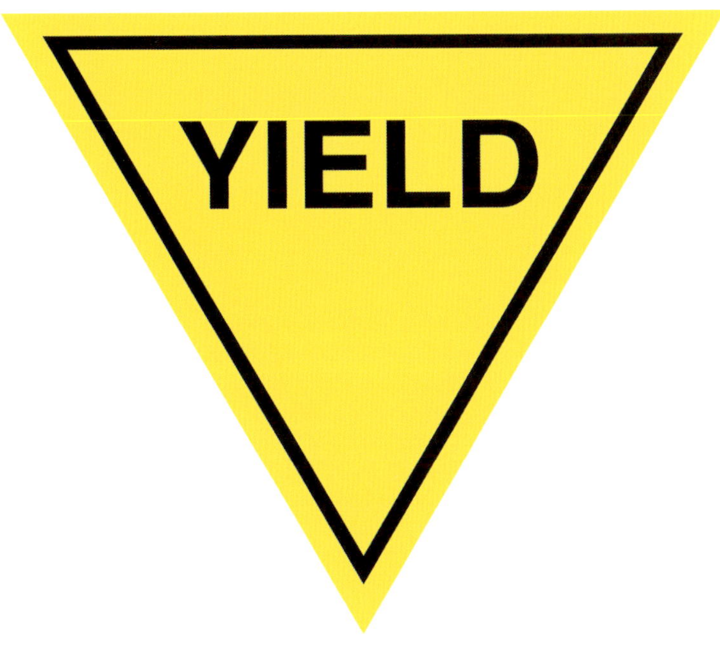

FIGURE 5

Standard American YIELD sign, 1954–71

to protest racism and segregation in Southern states, where violent confrontations were rampant. But the phrasing in each image—JUST AS IN THE ANATOMY OF MAN, EVERY NATION MUST HAVE ITS HIND PART—also moves us like a target from the outer circle to the center, where each respective "hind part" is rendered appropriately in a flesh pink. From the *Confederacy* canvases, Indiana made the print *1965 MISSISSIPPI* in 1971 for a series called *Decade*, which included a representative work from each year of the 1960s, a virtual cross-section of his first ten years of production (PLATES 3–12). He would return to this exact composition four decades later, when he painted a map of Afghanistan with Kabul at the center, another political protest marking a later generation's armed conflict. ● Partly because the circle seems such a pure and universal form, Indiana has been able to use it to explore, as we have seen, a flexible array of associations, from the specific to the cosmic. In fact, the wheels of transportation became an ongoing theme in his work, as seen in a print such as *AMERICAN DREAM #5*, 1980, one of his tributes to Charles Demuth's early modernist masterpiece *I Saw the Figure 5 in Gold*, 1928, which celebrated a fire engine moving through the dark streets of New York. Another print, *HIGH BALL on the REDBALL MANIFEST*, 1997, whose title comes from an old railroad expression meaning "all clear for a fast express," was an homage to Indiana's paternal grandfather, who had worked for the Pennsylvania Railroad. A syncopation of circular rhythms dominates both compositions, as it does as well in *1966 USA 666*, 1971, a print that references both the automobile and the train in its X-shaped emulation of a railroad crossing sign. Its yellow-and-black color scheme is that found on highway warning signs (FIGURE 5). In *1969 TERRE HAUTE NO. 2*, 1971, the stenciled name of the storied Midwestern railroad line WABASH contains funneled lines receding to the horizon below, suggesting the headlamp of an engine in the distance. ● Within the overall diamond of *1964 The Brooklyn Bridge*, 1971, four circles are filled with a straight-on view of the towers of John Roebling's famous span as seen from the roadway, reminding us of the wheeled vehicles crossing the river. Different aspects of the highway appear in other related images

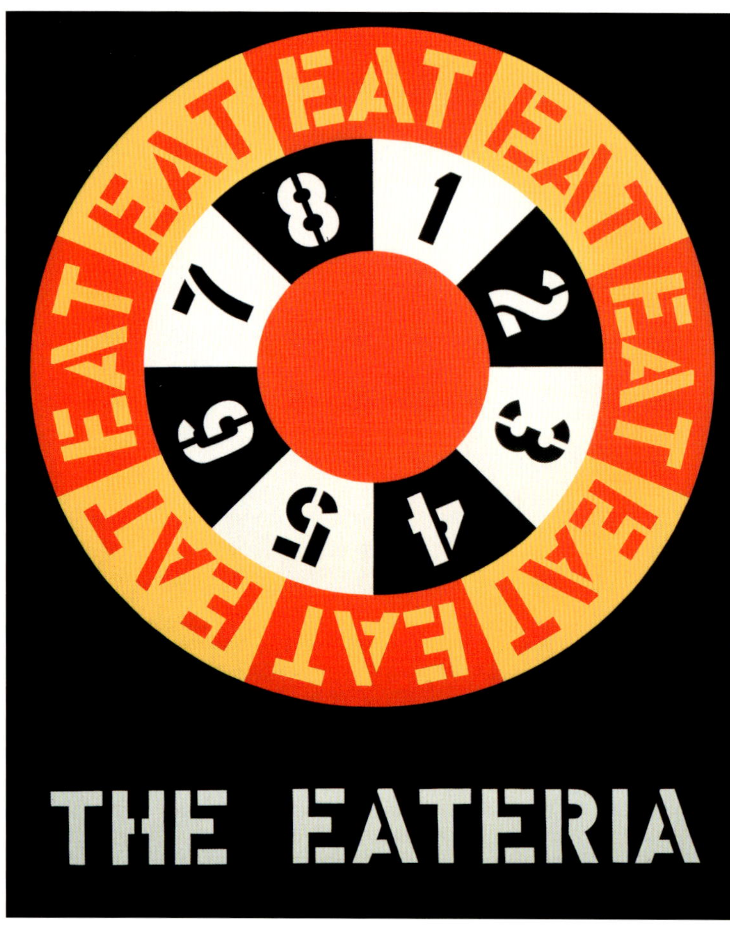

FIGURE 6

Robert Indiana, *The Eateria*, 1962

oil on canvas

60 ¼ × 47 ⅞ in. (153 × 121.6 cm)

Hirshhorn Museum and Sculpture Garden, Smithsonian Institution, Washington, DC, Gift of Joseph H. Hirshhorn, 1966

Photo by Lee Stalsworth

dealing with fast food, car accidents, and cheap entertainment. Both *THE AMERICAN DREAM #2*, 1982, incorporating the words EAT, JACK, and JUKE, and *EAT/DIE*, 1990, for example, offer allusions to playing cards, roulette wheels, music boxes, and pinball machines. "Die" is both a verb signaling death and the singular form of the noun "dice." These prints had counterparts in early paintings such as *THE AMERICAN GAS WORKS* and *The Eateria* (FIGURE 6), both 1962; the former has the look of a gas meter and the latter evokes a wheel at some gaming table. Indiana's painting *The American Dream, I* placed four circles enclosing words such as TAKE ALL and TILT on a slight incline to imitate the rolling ball of a pinball game, while *Beware—Danger American Dream #4*, 1963, revisited the motif with the words JUKE, TILT, and JILT. Chance and coincidence have long provided a preoccupying undercurrent for the artist. ● Early in his career, as noted, Indiana undertook a series of wood assemblages made mostly from scrap materials he salvaged from the old shipping warehouses near where he lived. The works owed their inspiration in part to the wood pieces made by his friend and neighbor Louise Nevelson and to the more recent combines of Rauschenberg. Indiana called his assemblages "herms," after Hermes, the messenger of the gods in ancient Greek culture.[9] They allude to early stone roadside markers dedicated to Hermes, some with human features, but also to archaic marble *kouroi*, which are among the earliest carved figures in Greek art. In a play on the history of sculpture, Indiana updated these forms into modern totems of the machine age and commercial civilization. *FOUR*, 1962, is a linguistic juggling of the verbal, the numerical, and the visual, incorporating a quartet of painted circles, the number 4 both as a numeral and written out, and an actual metal wheel with four spokes. Similarly, another juxtaposed the word TWO with the number 2, flanked by a pair of iron wheels below; and the freestanding *MOON*, 1960 (FIGURE 7), combined two sets each of four vertically disposed wheels and four painted orbs, as if that satellite were rising or descending in the sky. ● Probably the artist's most ambitious undertaking to center on the automobile was the pair of canvases he titled *Mother and Father*, 1963–67 (FIGURE 8).

9. For a discussion of the herms, see Allison Unruh, ed., *Robert Indiana: New Perspectives* (Ostfildern, Germany: Hatje Cantz, 2012), 175.

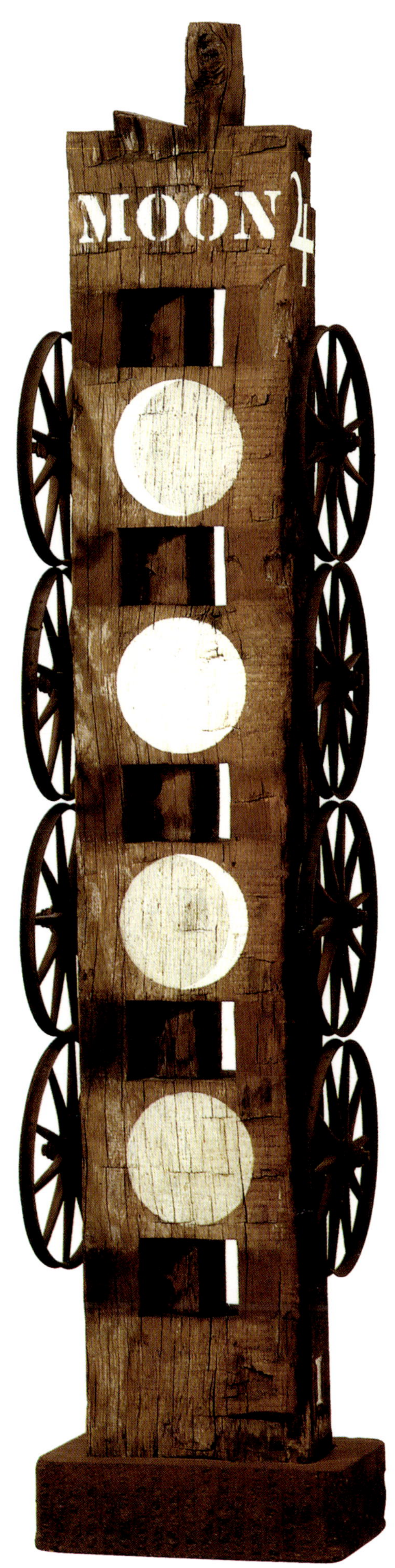

FIGURE 7

Robert Indiana, *MOON*, 1960

wood beam with iron-rimmed wheels, white paint, and concrete

78 × 17 ⅛ × 10 ¼ in. (198.1 × 43.5 × 26 cm) including base

The Museum of Modern Art, New York, Philip Johnson Fund

Photo: Courtesy of Morgan Art Foundation

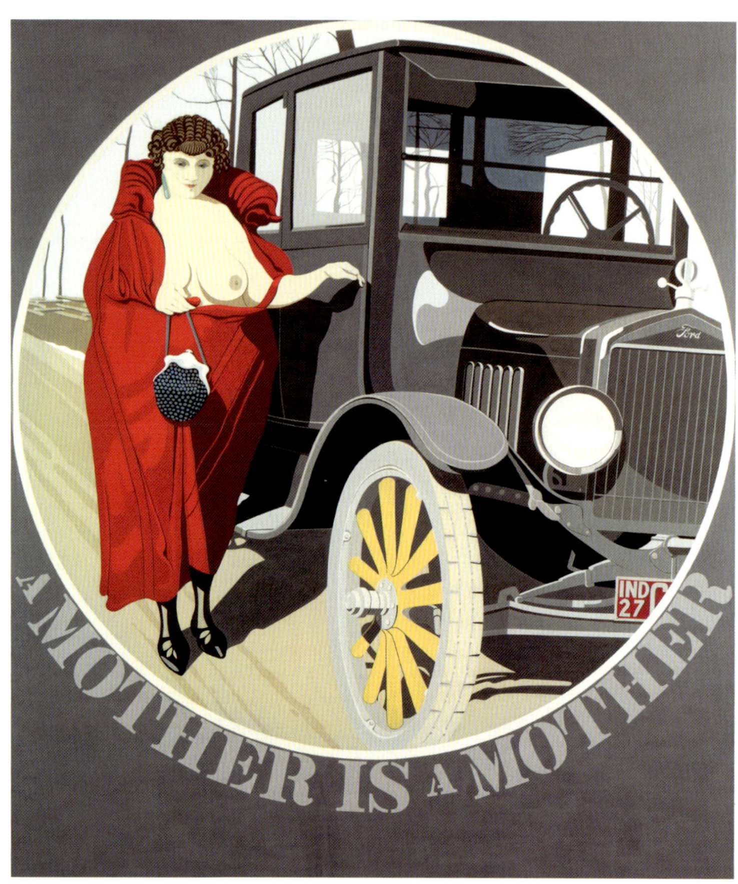

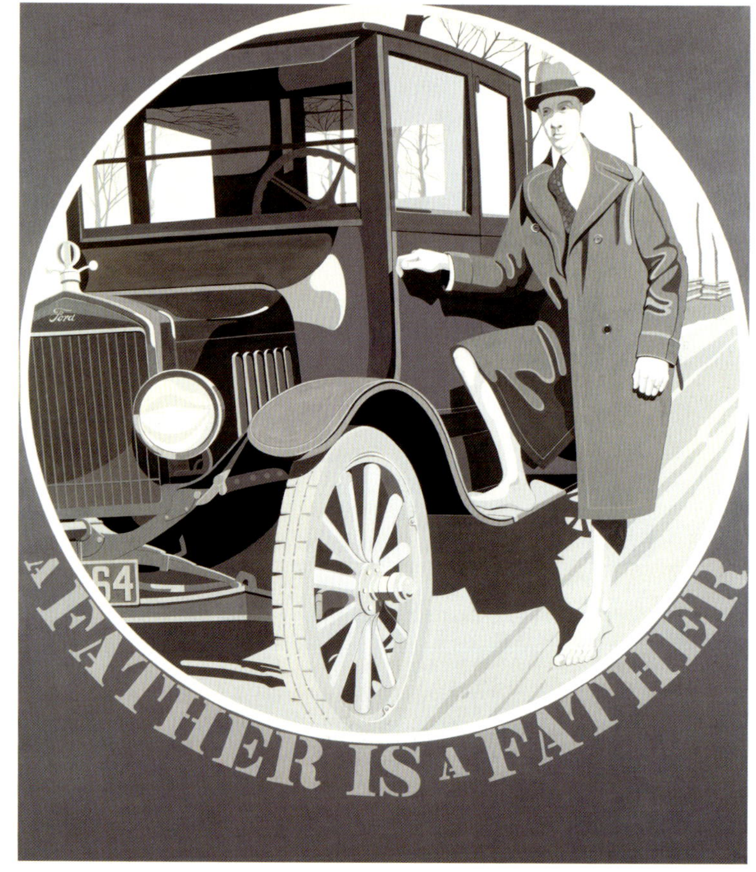

FIGURE 8

Robert Indiana, *Mother and Father*, 1963–67

oil on canvas (diptych)

72 × 60 in. (182.9 × 152.4 cm) each

Collection of the artist

Photo: Courtesy of Morgan Art Foundation

(These images have no counterparts as prints, though Indiana has recently said he might attempt to make prints from them.) The subjects go to the heart of his autobiographical impulses, which include, among other things, his reflection on the way his family moved repeatedly to different residences throughout his childhood and teenage years. In *Mother and Father* circles express the movement from place to place as well as the passage of time. The predominance of grays works well to convey memories of the past and the deaths of both parents, as if we were looking at faded snapshots in a family photo album. The artist's father, Earl, stands to the right of the couple's favorite Tin Lizzie, "as colorless as his name." By contrast, his mother, Carmen, is "warm and vibrant," expressed in the details of red and yellow, "a burst of warm sunshine." Her exposed breasts convey emotional comfort and nurturing, but they also suggest readily available sex. She was the second of three wives for Earl, in effect a disposable partner. As Indiana recounted, one day his father "took off with a new-found auto-mate." Carmen had become "fat and middle-aged and he ditched her for a new model; obsolescence Yankee-style." And in a poetic summary of his image, the painter stated, "Sealed in time here they stand fixed on this lonely dirt road frozen hard in midwinter."[10] Indiana has explained that the license plate visible in the left panel bearing the date 1927 was meant to allude to his conception, presumably in the back seat of the Ford (he was born the next year), while 1964 on the right was the year the unfinished paintings were first shown, on Mother's Day, at the Stable Gallery. The steering wheel, front tires, and headlights are echoing circles that speak to a sense of transience and mobility. ● Time's passage is a critical theme of the artist's numbers series, which he explored in paintings, prints, and sculpture. In the mid-1960s he painted the numbers one through four in expanding squares called *Exploding Numbers*. A related group of *Cardinal Numbers* occupied rectangular frames with the written words below. Indiana made prints of these for inclusion in a book with corresponding poems by Robert Creeley, published in 1968 (FIGURE 9).[11] Here, the numbers were enclosed within circles. The combination of numerical sequencing and repeated circles turned the images into a calendar of days or years, a metaphor for our voyage of life from birth to old age. The concluding zero in gray and white is omega, an expression of mortality and progression to the infinite. In other versions Indiana set the numerals within outer circles and inner geometries matching each number, thus a triangle for three, a square for four, a pentagon for five, and so on, up to a nonagon for nine. Circularity served the cycles of time as well as the visual play of noun and number. ● During the 1970s, the artist executed a set of ten numerical paintings in which he used the numbers zero to nine to correspond to each year in the previous decade and incorporated the names of places, words, or titles of works associated with that particular year. In each, an outer circle surrounds a denser and more fragmented interior, in which the large numeral intersects with a star and several stenciled references pertinent to Indiana's life. He made a corresponding series of screenprints called *Decade: Autoportraits* between 2001 and 2009. ● Concentric circles and a central star are used to different effect in Indiana's 1967 painting *The Metamorphosis of Norma Jean Mortenson*, a commemoration of Marilyn Monroe that he would translate more than twenty years later into a print. The outer circle bears her full original name, the inner her assumed identity as a celebrity. The letters of both are contained within smaller circles, reminding us of the rotary telephone that the actress had in hand at the time of her death. But these rings also serve as a zoom lens on the pin-up figure at the center, the target of so much popular fantasy and critical attention. Unlike most of the circular compositions discussed above, contained within vertical frames, this one sits within a diamond. Indiana had first used the diamond format for his 1964 painting *The Brooklyn Bridge*, which he converted to a print in the *Decade* suite of 1971. There we might argue that the vertical orientation of its angles adds a suitable dynamism to complement the pointed arches and soaring cables of the bridge. In the image of Marilyn, it conjures up her one-time marriage to Joe DiMaggio and the baseball diamond. To this we may add the slang understanding that reaching "home base" means "going all the way," just what we might associate with a sex goddess. ● Indiana

10. Ryan, *Robert Indiana: Figures of Speech*, 264–66.

11. Robert Indiana and Robert Creeley, *Numbers* (Stuttgart: Edition Domberger; Dusseldorf: Galerie Schmela, 1968).

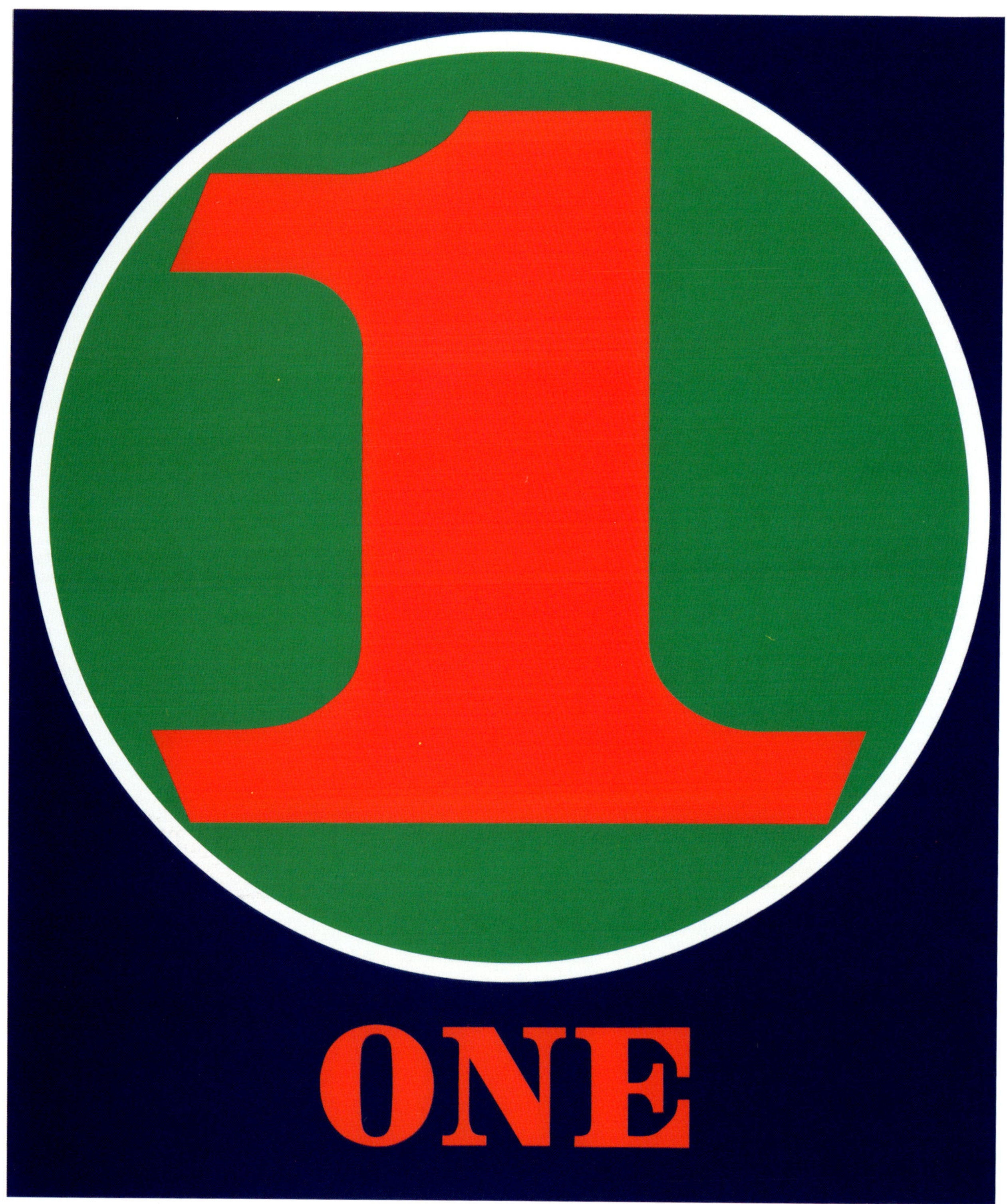

FIGURE 9

Robert Indiana, *1* from *NUMBERS*, 1968

screenprint

image: 23 ½ × 19 ⅝ in. (59.7 × 49.8 cm);
sheet: 25 ½ × 19 ⅝ in. (64.8 × 49.8 cm)

printed by K G Domberger; published by
Edition Domberger Stuttgart

Indianapolis Museum of Art, Gift of Robert Indiana

returned to the form in the early 2000s for a series of *Peace* paintings. The internal angles of the peace sign from the sixties, now brought to new life by the recently declared wars in Iraq and Afghanistan, worked well visually in the sharp diagonal format. He also completed his final *American Dream* paintings in 2000 with this composition, enclosing small circles bearing place names and painting titles from across his career that together form a sort of retrospective. *The Eighth American Dream* (FIGURE 10) is especially poignant, for it and smaller painted variants include phrases such as "August is bittersweet" and "August is Memory/Carmen." Here the number 8 sits within an octagon. As the artist has recounted many times, when he returned from the army to see his dying mother, her last words to him were, "Do you want something to eat?" Ever since, he has toyed with the notion of "eight" equaling "ate," the past tense of "eat." Not only that, his mother, Carmen, died in August, the eighth month of the year, hence, a bittersweet memory. In turn, *The Ninth American Dream* bears the phrase "Remember November," marking the controversy surrounding the Bush-Gore presidential race that year. ● Even as Indiana integrates circles with squares, rectangles, diamonds, and secondary geometric shapes, they remain dominant in his designs. The circle is the prominent motif in his *Hartley Elegies*, a symbol of the unifying friendship between the artist Marsden Hartley, his presumed lover Karl von Freyburg, and their chess companion Arnold Rönnebeck at the outset of World War I in Berlin. The American modernist painter had gone to Germany in 1913 in search of subject matter and became enamored of the rising militarism and cult of masculinity he encountered. It led to a series of strong, colorful portraits of German officers constructed of abstracted forms and signs, such as *Portrait of a German Officer*, 1914 (FIGURE 11), derived partially from recent cubist precedents and examples of German expressionism. When Indiana settled in Maine in the 1970s, he discovered that Hartley had spent part of the summer of 1938 on Vinalhaven Island, in a nearby house on Main Street. Inspired by that coincidence and by an empathy for the anguish the earlier Maine artist might have felt because of his sexuality, Indiana constructed a series of paintings and prints based on Hartley's *Portrait of a German Officer*. Aside from alluding to the universality of love, the circles that recur throughout Indiana's suite also suggest medals, targets, gun barrels, and other emblems in uniforms and flags. ● Another perfect geometric form recurs throughout Indiana's *Hartley Elegies*: the equilateral triangle. Indiana had occasionally used it before as a visualization of the number three—for example, in the herm *ORB*, 1960. On the front of that wood plank are three painted circles, one containing a numeral 3 and another a triangle. In 1962, in a now unlocated painting titled *YIELD BROTHER*, he integrated the upside-down triangle of the "Yield" road sign with the peace sign. In the Hartley tributes, the triangle became a reinforcing symbol of reciprocal artistic friendship among three companions. ● Among some other favorite configurations employed by Indiana is the five-pointed star, a motif that appears in very early works such as the wood herm *STAR*, 1962, in which the stenciled word appears with the painted image, one of the artist's typical verbal/visual combinations. It was then a ubiquitous and everyday emblem, found on truck signage, billboards, posters, and supermarket packaging. About this time, it also played a serendipitous role in the creation of Indiana's most famous image. He had designed a painting with four stars arranged in a square and the word LOVE stenciled below. A couple of years later, the Museum of Modern Art asked him to produce a Christmas card, which prompted him to replace the stars with LOVE, configured in the now familiar block of four letters with the O tilted to the right. The star is also, appropriately, the backdrop for the central pin-up figure in *The Metamorphosis of Norma Jean Mortenson*, signifying her celebrity status once she became Marilyn. It is furthermore central to all the later *Autoportraits* screenprints that Indiana made from the 1980s to the 2000s. In these works packed with a density of personal references and associations, the star has a direct link to the name of the artist's dwelling on Vinalhaven, the Star of Hope Lodge—a fortuitous coincidence that made Indiana feel almost as though his moving into the property had been ordained. ● The star also played a powerful role in Indiana's

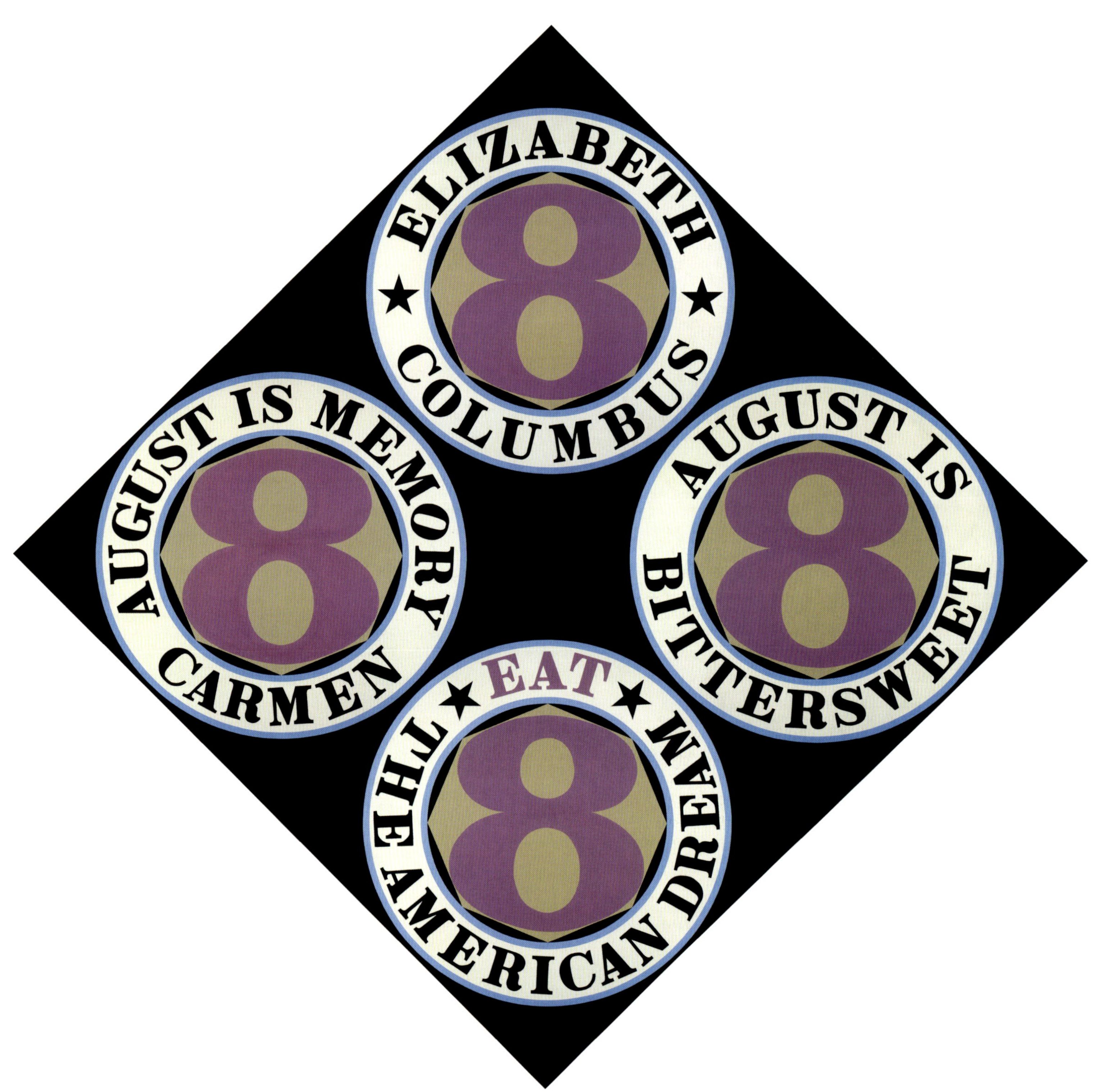

FIGURE 10

Robert Indiana, *The Eighth American Dream*, 2000

oil on canvas

170 × 170 in. (431.8 × 431.8 cm)

Courtesy of Paul Kasmin Gallery

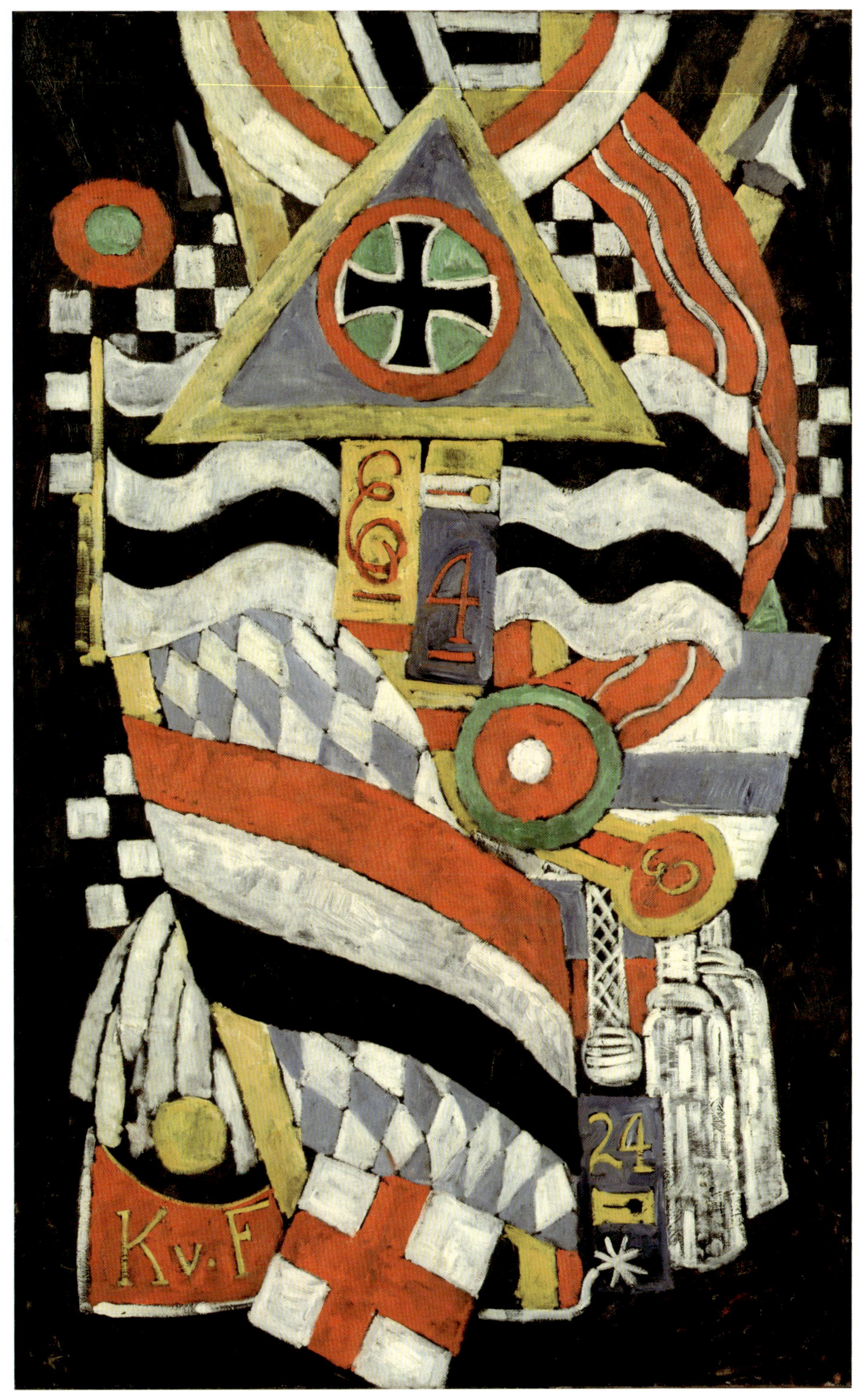

FIGURE 11

Marsden Hartley, *Portrait of a German Officer*, 1914

oil on canvas

68 ¼ × 41 ⅜ in. (173.4 × 105.1 cm)

The Metropolitan Museum of Art, New York,
Alfred Stieglitz Collection, 1949

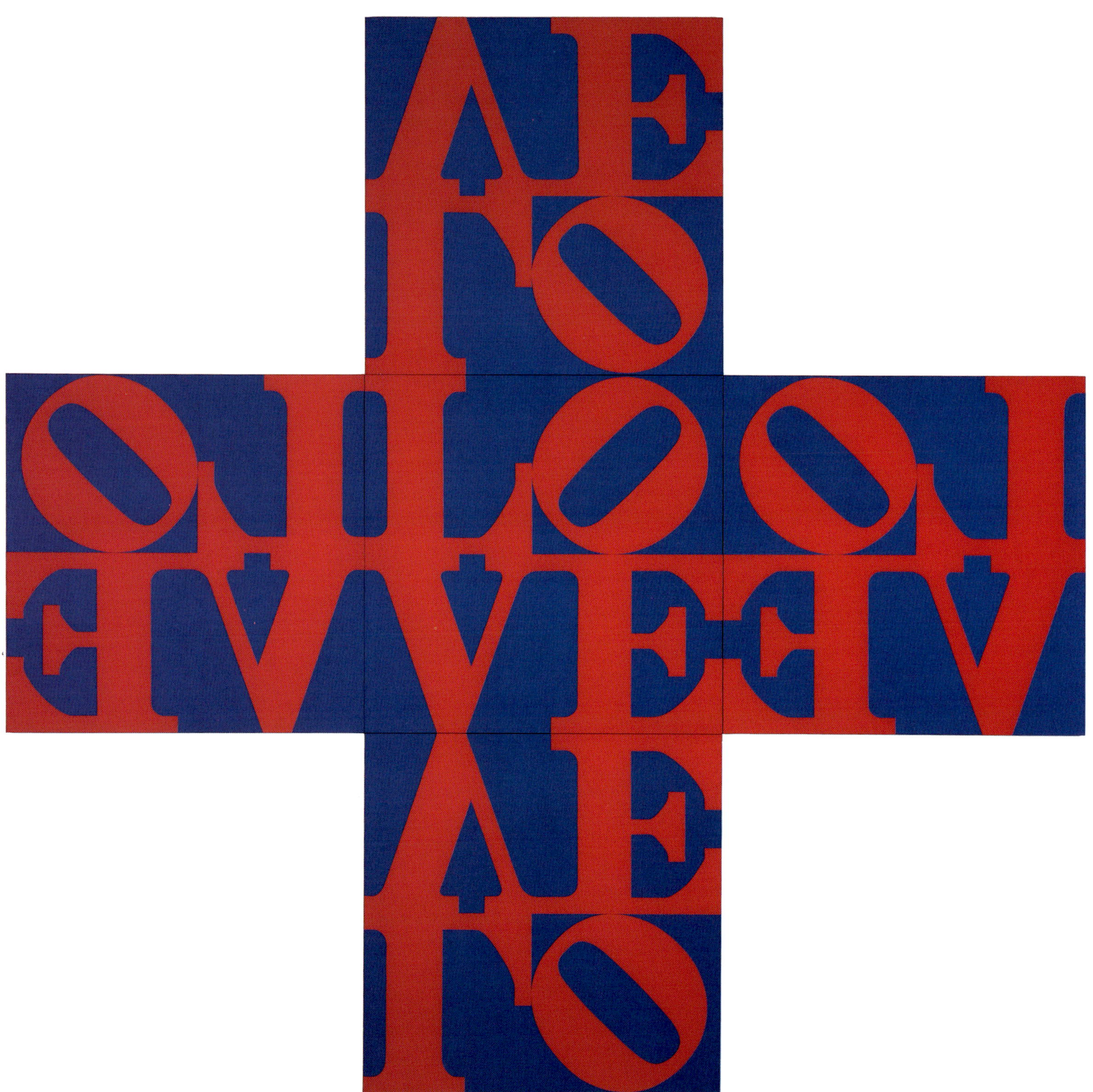

FIGURE 12

Robert Indiana, *Love Cross*, 1968

oil on canvas, 5 panels, overall 15 ft. (4.6 m), each panel 60 × 60 in. (152.4 × 152.4 cm)

The Menil Collection, Houston

Photo by George Hixson

various tributes to Demuth's masterwork *I Saw the Figure 5 in Gold* (on view, coincidentally, at the Metropolitan Museum of Art, New York, like Hartley's *Portrait of a German Officer*). The red five-pointed star does not appear in Demuth's painting, but for Indiana it was a natural addition as a visual counterpart to the gold number 5, thus subtly overlaying the original rendering of a fire engine with a modern hard-edged commercial look, as in the 1963 painting *The Demuth American Dream No. 5*. That work also makes use of the cruciform shape, a variation on Indiana's X design in *USA 666*. Both formats consist of five square (or diamond) canvases hung together. Correspondingly, he produced the Demuth *Dream* as five separate screenprints in *AMERICAN DREAM #5*. ● The cruciform, of course, carries religious connotations. Even though Indiana has never seemed very interested in religion personally or artistically, one of the first and largest paintings he did after his arrival in New York was *Stavrosis*, 1958, whose title means crucifixion. This was a mural-scale work executed in printer's ink on old paper that Indiana found in his Coenties Slip loft; its generalized abstract forms aimed to depict three figures on crosses. To support himself, Indiana had taken part-time work typing correspondence for Bishop James Pike, then Dean of the Cathedral of St. John the Divine in upper Manhattan. Recently published religious literature in Pike's possession proved to have a strong impact on the concept for Indiana's painting.[12] In *Stavrosis*, it is possible to discern the vague elevation of a Gothic cathedral interior; we also find several of Indiana's earliest abstract forms, such as the ginkgo leaf and avocado pit, which became the basis for some of his first canvases that recall the work of Ellsworth Kelly. ● A year after he began his first variations of the Demuth tributes in 1963, Indiana painted *LOVE IS GOD* in a diamond format, with gray and white rays fanning out from the center. It is no accident, then, that besides the Demuth *Dream*, Indiana arranged one other major artistic image in a cross design, the *Love Cross* (FIGURE 12), an appropriately sacramental form. His treatment of the Demuth imagery has a similar devotional character. Indiana explained the many biographical coincidences he shared with the earlier artist, which inspired admiration, sympathy, even a spiritual bond. But there was an additional association. As Indiana described: "For the major painting of this 'Dream' I chose the cruciform, a polyptych of unusual form in the history of painting if not sculpture—the obvious exception of this of course being Cimabue's *Crucifix*, so recently nearly destroyed."[13] He was referring to the devastating floods that rose through Florence in the early 1960s and damaged many religious Renaissance masterpieces on the ground floor of the Uffizi Gallery. The Demuth original led Indiana to configure several different variants on canvas and in prints, which together are among the strongest works in his career, as much for their sheer visual power as for the many-layered content.

12. For fuller elaboration of this work and its background, see Joachim Pissarro, *Robert Indiana: Rare Works from 1959 on Coenties Slip* (Zurich: Galerie Gmurzynska, 2011), 13–17.

13. "The Demuth American Dream No. 5," in *Robert Indiana* (Philadelphia: Institute of Contemporary Art of the University of Pennsylvania, in association with the Falcon Press, 1968), 27.

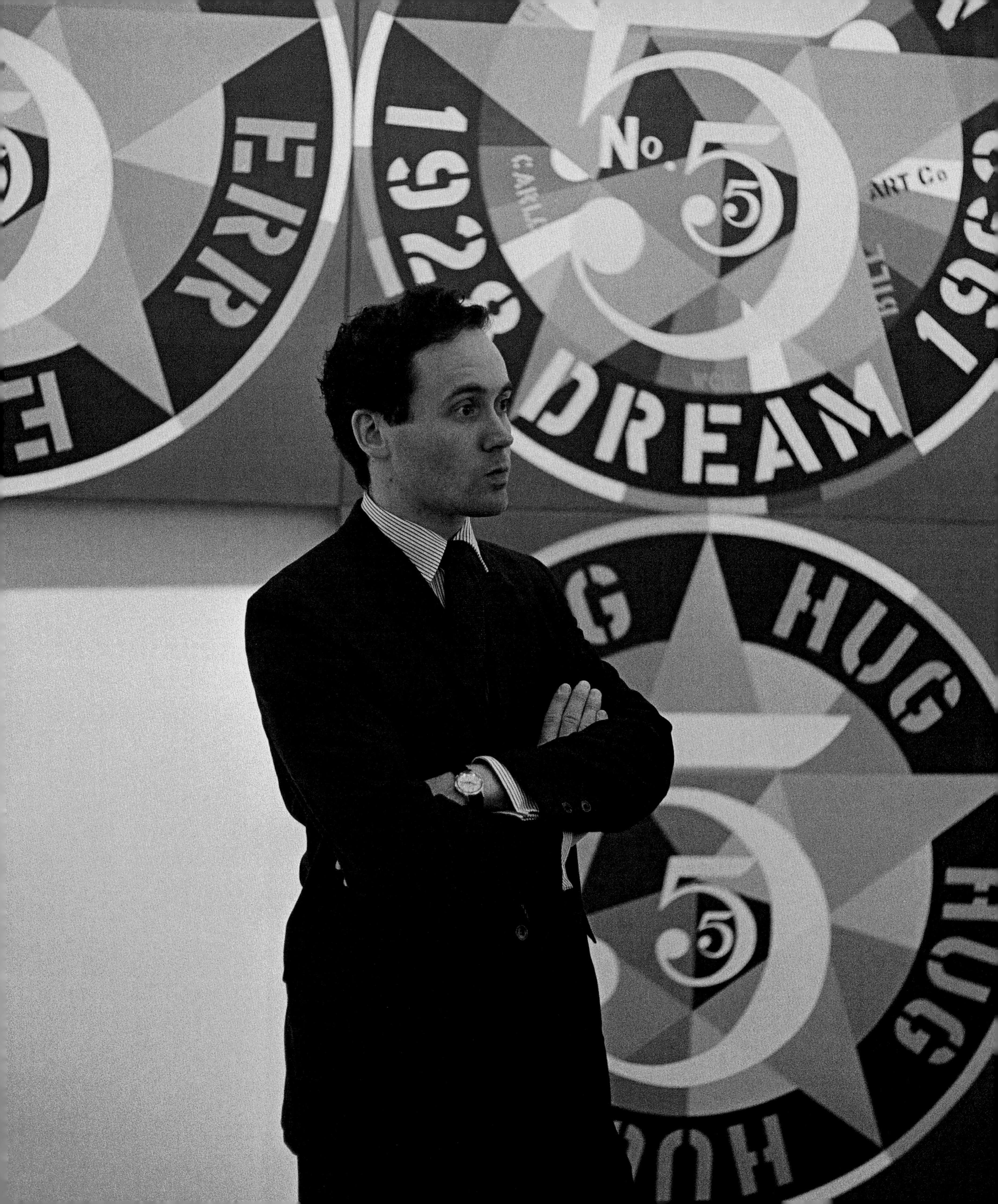
No 5
ART Co
DREAM
HUG
HUG

PLATES

AUTHORS' NOTE
In accordance with this volume's emphasis on the autobiographical nature of Robert Indiana's work, the following entries appear in the chronological order of the images' first appearance (usually as paintings), rather than by their date of publication as prints, which could be decades later. The integrity of multiprint portfolios, however, has been maintained, even though the images therein may span a decade.

PLATE 1

EAT/DIE, 1990

screenprint on two sheets

edition of 50

image: 11 × 9 3⁄16 in. (27.9 × 23.3 cm) each;
sheet: 17 7⁄8 × 13 3⁄4 in. (45.4 × 35 cm) each

printed by Alexander Heinrici, New York;
published by Indianakatz, New York

Collection of the artist

This diptych was published with considerable irony in conjunction with a dinner at Chanterelle in New York, given in Indiana's honor by his longtime companion and collaborator William Katz. Eight proofs of *EAT* were used as the menu for the event, with the bill of fare handwritten on the reverse.[1] ● While the artist paired these two words several times in the 1960s, this screenprint is a distillation of the *EAT/DIE* diptych of 1962 (Private collection) painted in the same red and black palette. Although the word EAT alone might conjure up memories of roadside diners, the pairing had a different meaning for the artist:

> Key words in my early paintings, before I even approached *LOVE* of course, were the word "Eat" and the word "Die" and it just so happened that in my childhood during the Depression my mother used to work in restaurants and have her own restaurants. So they came from a direct personal experience, not just an influence of the landscape. The most personal aspect of the matter was that the word "Eat" was the last word my mother said before she died, which accounts for the diptych *EAT/DIE*. This doesn't have too much to do with American road signs. This is a very personal jump across a very peculiar gap and there's no doubt there was that influence.[2]

By Indiana's report, his estranged father died much the same way in Florida: "He was eating breakfast one morning and dropped dead (EAT/DIE)."[3]

1. Susan Sheehan, *Robert Indiana Prints: A Catalogue Raisonné, 1951–1991* (New York: Susan Sheehan Gallery, 1991), 79.
2. "Conversations with Robert Indiana," in *Robert Indiana* (Austin: University Art Museum, University of Texas, 1977), 33.
3. "A MOTHER IS A MOTHER AND A FATHER IS A FATHER," in *Robert Indiana* (Philadelphia: Institute of Contemporary Art of the University of Pennsylvania, in association with the Falcon Press, 1968), 36.

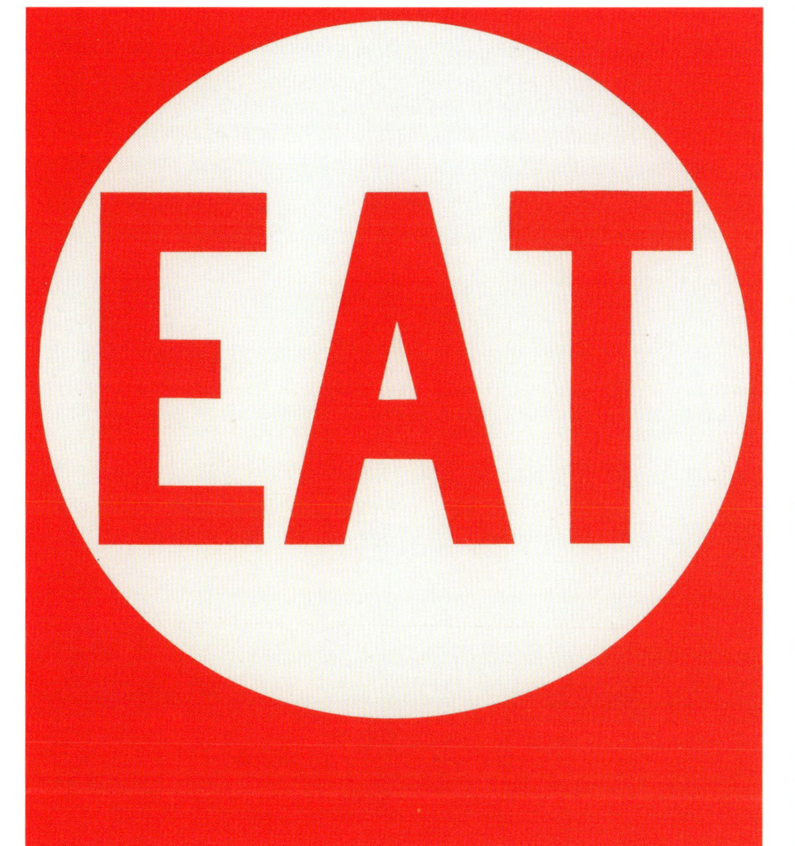
EAT
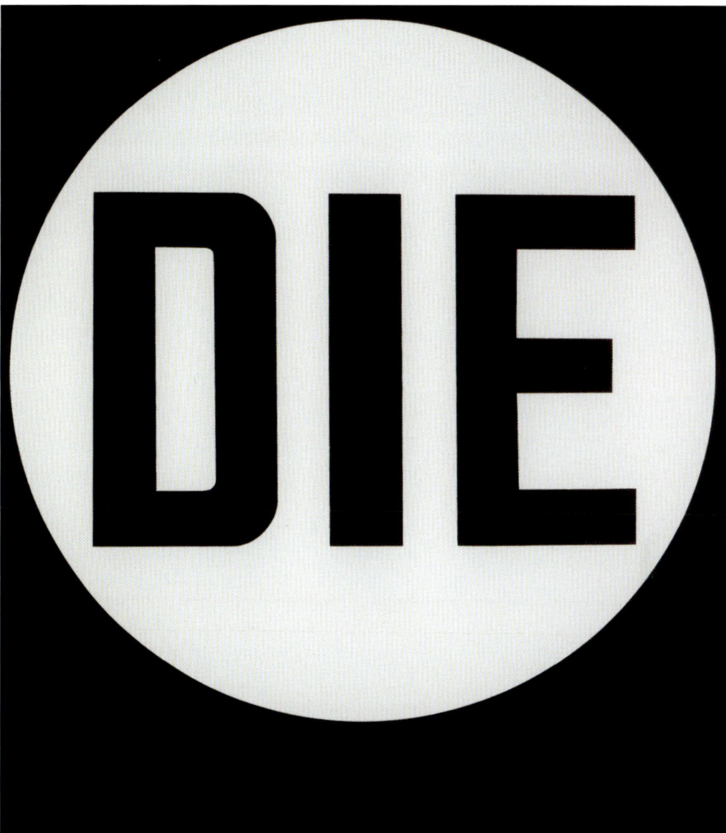
DIE

PLATE 2

LOVE, 1967

screenprint

edition of 250

image: 34 × 34 in. (86.4 × 86.4 cm); sheet: 36 × 36 in. (91.4 × 91.4 cm)

printed by Sirocco Screenprinters, New Haven, Connecticut; published by Multiples, Inc., New York

Collection of the artist

What began as a Christmas card design morphed into the most recognizable of Indiana's glyphs and became one of the most bastardized and bowdlerized icons in the history of American art. Indiana prepared a series of small square maquettes in oil featuring the now-familiar four-letter stack in a variety of color combinations for the Museum of Modern Art, New York, to choose for its 1965 card. The museum opted for the most vibrant (and Christmassy) combination: red, green, and blue. The same color combination was used for the keynote *LOVE* painting of 1966 (Indianapolis Museum of Art) and for the poster for Indiana's *LOVE* show at the Stable Gallery, New York, in May 1966, which featured a number of *LOVE* paintings in various configurations and combinations of these three colors. Although Indiana subsequently presented this image in other colors, he always considered red, green, and blue the prime *LOVE* colors for reasons that were unknown to the critics in 1966 and revealed only years later in an interview given to Barbaralee Diamonstein:

> Most of my work is very autobiographical in one way or another. In the thirties, my father worked for Phillips 66, when all Phillips 66 gasoline stations were red and green: the pumps, the uniforms, the oil cans. . . . When I was a kid, my mother used to drive my father to work in Indianapolis and I would see, practically every day of my young life, a huge Phillips 66 sign. So it is the red and green of that sign against the blue Hoosier sky. The blue in the *LOVE* is cerulean. Therefore my *LOVE* is a homage to my father.[4]

As early as 1963, Indiana said that this sign was the most fascinating visual object in his youth.[5] ● Earl Clark died in December 1965, and the *LOVE* paintings in this three-color combination then underway became a memorial to him, but the inclusion of the red-green-blue variant in the MoMA samples in the first months of 1965 was probably due rather to Indiana's sense that this combination contained "the most charged colors of my palette, bringing an optical, near-electric quality to my work."[6]

4. Barbaralee Diamonstein, *Inside New York's Art World* (New York: Rizzoli, 1979), 153.
5. Oral history interview with Robert Indiana by Richard Brown Baker, September 12–November 7, 1963, Archives of American Art, Smithsonian Institution, Washington, DC, online at http://www.aaa.si.edu/collections/interviews/oral-history-interview-robert-indiana-12936.
6. "Introduction," *Robert Indiana* (1968), 29.

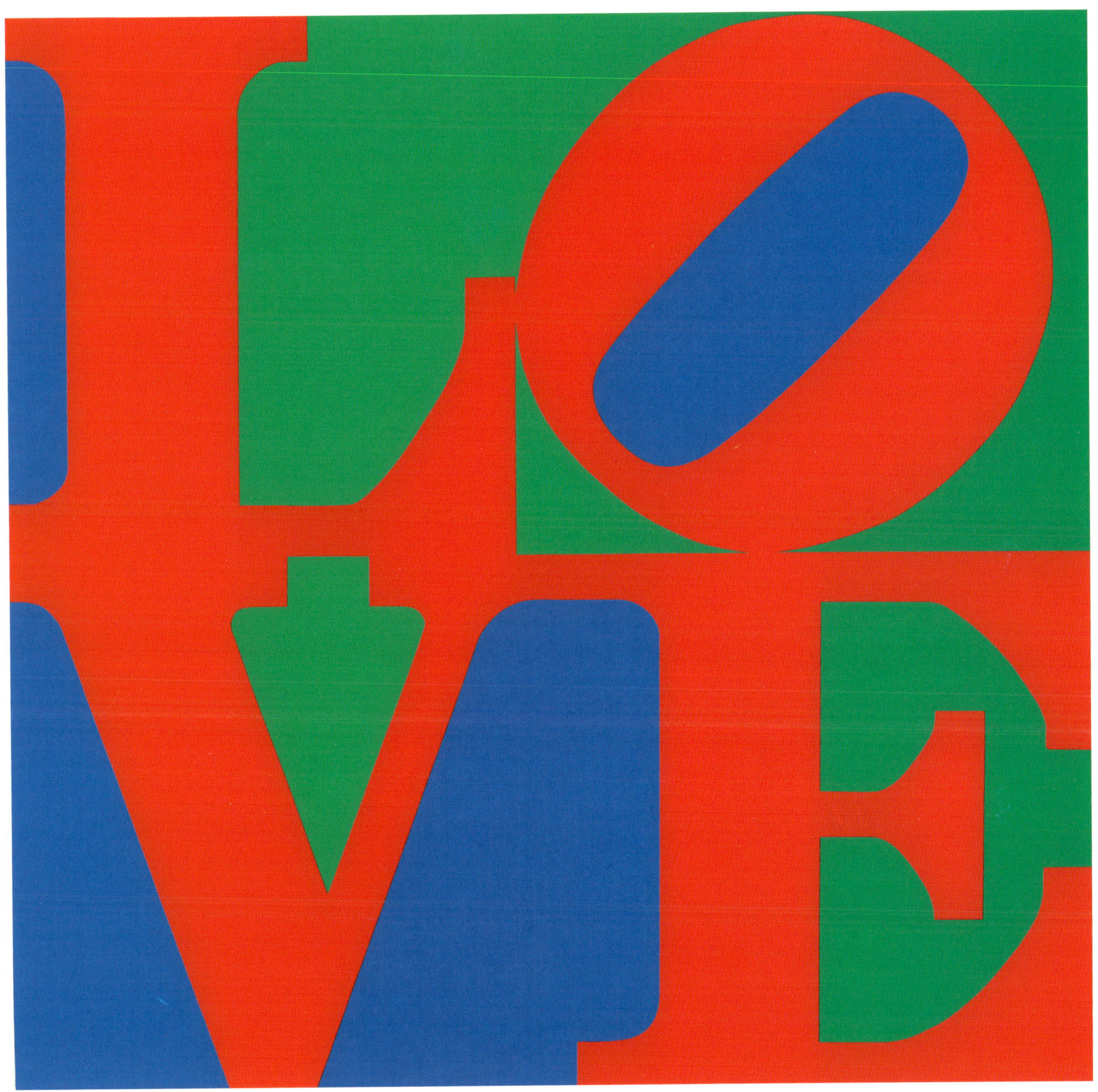

LOVE

In 1971, Indiana took a retrospective look at his previous decade and refashioned verbatim a significant painting from each year as a screenprint. Although Indiana had no experience in screenprinting before 1963, virtually all of his prints since then have been in that medium. He explained in 1991 that the choice was made "because it is so related to the nature of my paintings. It was by far the medium that best translated my painting ideally."[7] ● *The American Dream, I,* begun in 1960 and completed in 1961, was a pivotal painting for Indiana. Not only did it inaugurate a long series of *American Dream* paintings, it was acquired by the Museum of Modern Art, New York, soon after it was first exhibited in 1961. In an artist's questionnaire completed for MoMA in December 1961, Indiana explained that the painting was:

> loaded with "personal," "topical," and "symbolic" significance, namely all those dear and much-traveled US Routes #40, #29, #37 (on which I have lived) and #66 of US Air Force days; those awful five bases [*sic*] of The American Game; the TILT of all those millions of Pin Ball machines and Juke Boxes in all those hundreds of thousands of grubby bars and roadside cafes, alternate spiritual Homes of the American; and star-studded Take All, well-established American ethic in all realms—spiritual, economic, political, social, sexual, and cultural. Full-stop.[8]

When referring to the painting in 1968, he adjusted the self-referential symbolism to his father: "He was the American Dreamer (The American Dream: the No.'s 37, 29, 40, and 66 inscribed therein are highways he rode in his quest) high in the seat of his ambitions, a Lindbergh of the Plains, who never quite got there."[9]

PLATE 3

1960 THE AMERICAN DREAM

from *Decade*, 1971

screenprint

edition of 200

image: 35 ⅝ × 30 in. (90.5 × 76.2 cm);
sheet: 39 × 32 in. (99.1 × 81.3 cm)

printed by Domberger KG, Stuttgart;
published by Multiples, Inc., New York

Collection of the Indianapolis Museum of Art, Museum Purchase through Multiples, Inc., 71.88.1A

7. Robert Indiana interviewed by Poppy Gandler Orchier in Sheehan, *Robert Indiana Prints*, 12.
8. Susan Elizabeth Ryan, *Robert Indiana: Figures of Speech* (New Haven: Yale University Press, 2000), 91. Indiana never lived on US Routes 37 and 29; State Routes 37 and 29 pass through Indianapolis, however.
9. "A MOTHER IS A MOTHER AND A FATHER IS A FATHER," in *Robert Indiana* (1968), 36.

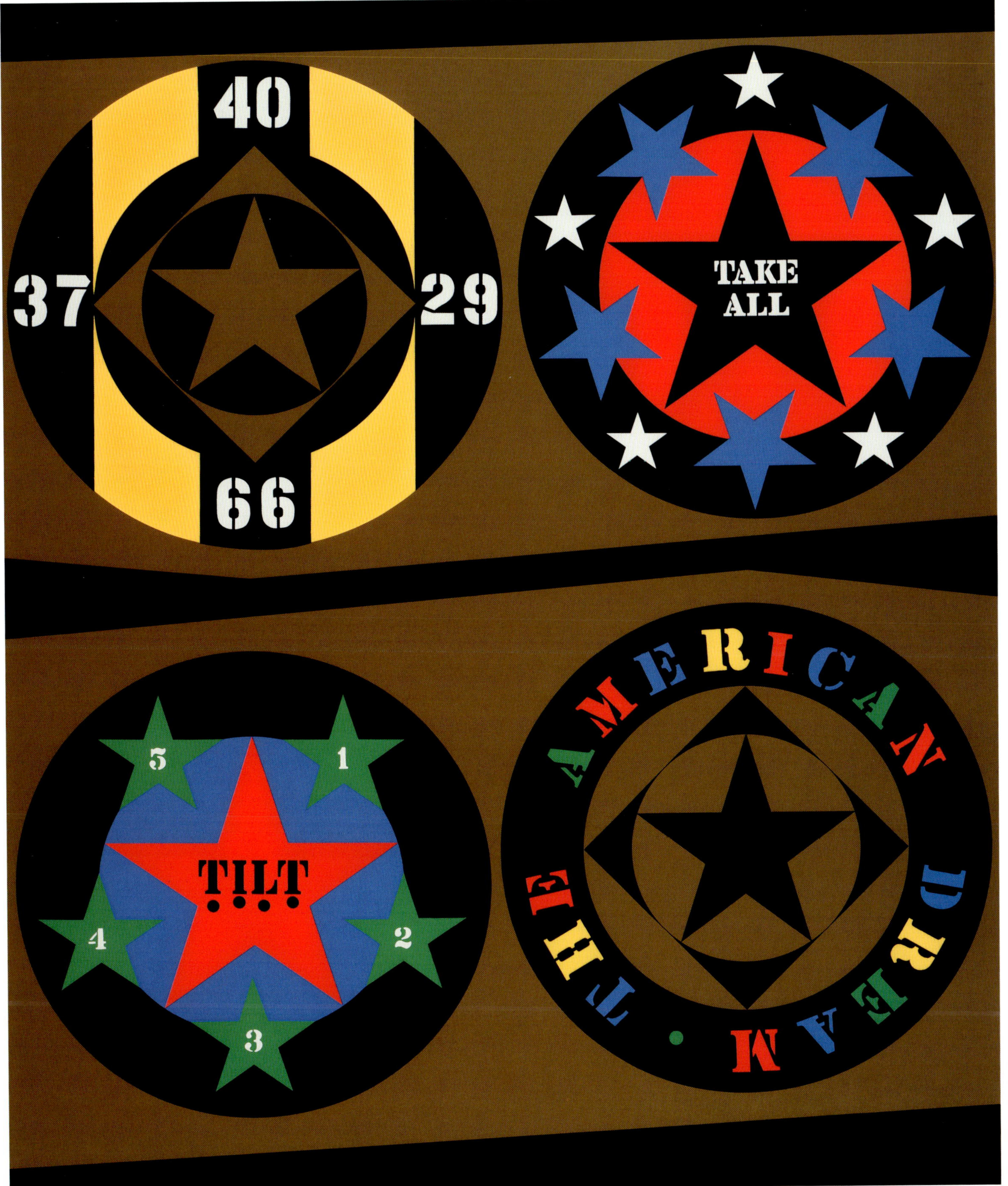
40
37
29
66
TAKE ALL
5
1
TILT
4
2
3
THE AMERICAN DREAM

PLATE 4

1961 THE CALUMET

from *Decade*, 1971

screenprint

edition of 200

image: 31 ¾ × 29 ¾ in. (80.6 × 75.6 cm);
sheet: 39 × 32 in. (99.1 × 81.3 cm)

printed by Domberger KG, Stuttgart;
published by Multiples, Inc., New York

Collection of the Indianapolis Museum of Art,
Museum Purchase through Multiples, Inc., 71.88.2A

THE CALUMET, 1961 (Rose Art Museum, Brandeis University, Waltham, Massachusetts), was inspired by the first lines of the first chapter of Henry Wadsworth Longfellow's 1855 epic poem *The Song of Hiawatha*:

> "Gitche Manito, the mighty,
> Calls the tribes of men together,
> Calls the warriors to his council!"
> Down the rivers, o'er the prairies,
> Came the warriors of the nations,
> Came the Delawares and Mohawks,
> Came the Choctaws and Camanches,
> Came the Shoshonies and Blackfeet,
> Came the Pawnees and Omahas,
> Came the Mandans and Dacotahs,
> Came the Hurons and Ojibways,
> All the warriors drawn together
> By the signal of the Peace-Pipe.[10]

Indiana reportedly liked the cadence of the litany of Indian names,[11] and his work in 1961 was dominated by subjects inspired by mid-nineteenth-century literature, particularly the works of Walt Whitman and Herman Melville. It was in this year that Indiana declared, echoing Whitman: "I am an American painter of signs charting the course."[12] ● The predominating red of the image is also the dominant color in the first chapter of the poem, from "the great Red Pipe-stone Quarry" where the tribes gathered, to waters "soiled and stained with streaks of crimson" and warriors "painted like the leaves of Autumn." The circle, which is the principal shape in this image and in almost every Indiana work, was an enduring symbol from the artist's childhood exposure to Christian Science, where it exemplified eternal life.[13] Here, it is equally an icon of inclusion and of the unity of the tribes gathering around the smoke (PUKWANA) of the peace pipe (CALUMET), which had summoned them.

10. Henry Wadsworth Longfellow, *The Poetical Works of Henry Wadsworth Longfellow in Four Volumes*, vol. 2, *The Song of Hiawatha: 1. The Peace-Pipe* (Boston: Houghton, Mifflin, 1882), 17, online at http://books.google.com/books?id=2jtaAAAAYAAJ.
11. "Introduction," in *Robert Indiana* (1968), 17.
12. Ibid., 9.
13. Diamonstein, *Inside New York's Art World*, 161.

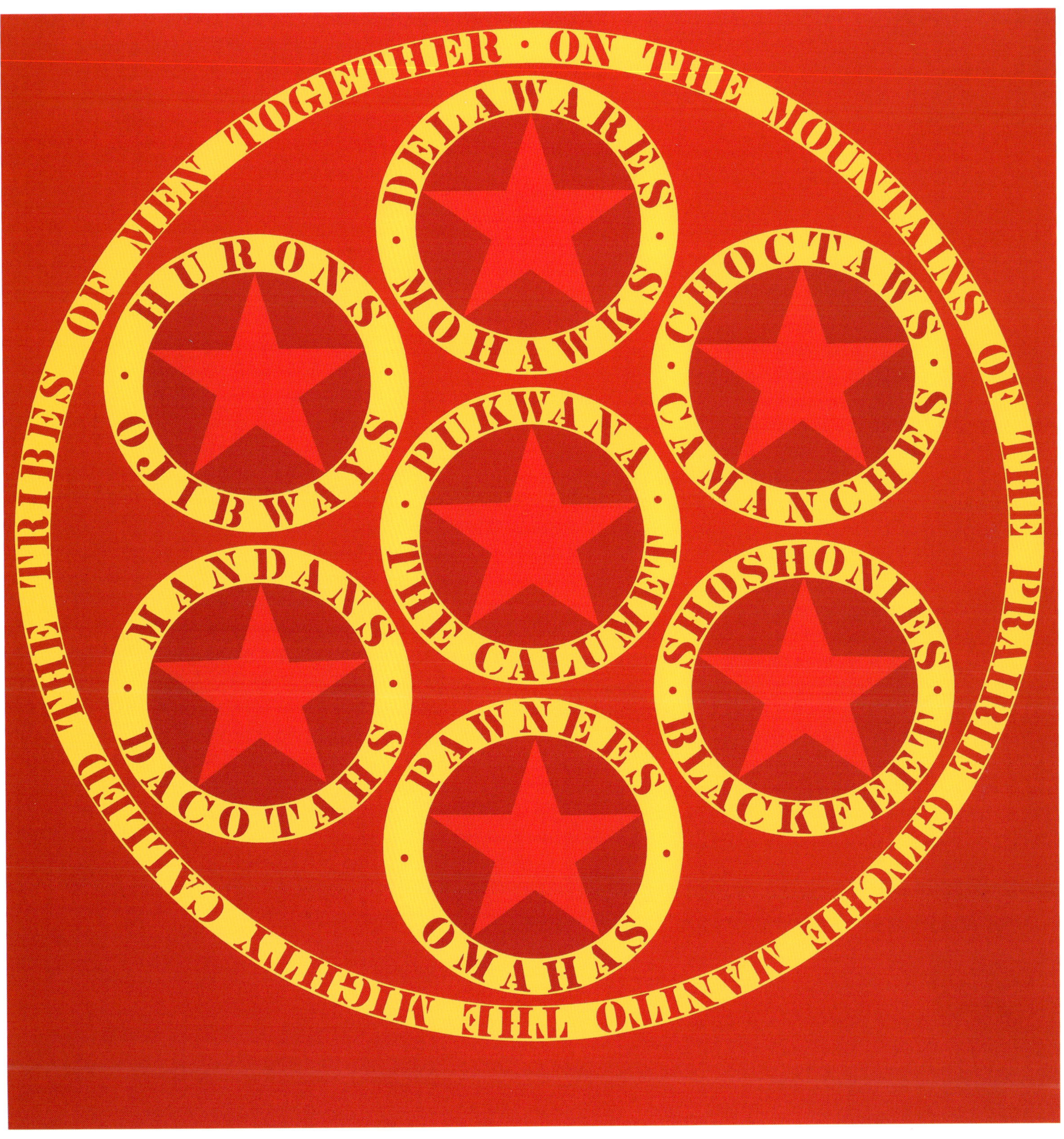

GITCHE MANITO THE MIGHTY CALLED THE TRIBES OF MEN TOGETHER · ON THE MOUNTAINS OF THE PRAIRIE
DELAWARES · MOHAWKS ·
HURONS · OJIBWAYS ·
CHOCTAWS · CAMANCHES ·
PUKWANA · THE CALUMET ·
MANDANS · DACOTAHS ·
SHOSHONIES · BLACKFEET ·
PAWNEES · OMAHAS ·

PLATE 5

1962 YIELD BROTHER

from *Decade*, 1971

screenprint

edition of 200

image: 35 ¾ × 29 ¾ in. (90.8 × 75.6 cm);
sheet: 39 × 32 in. (99.1 × 81.3 cm)

printed by Domberger KG, Stuttgart;
published by Multiples, Inc., New York

Collection of the Indianapolis Museum of Art,
Museum Purchase through Multiples, Inc., 71.88.3A

The 1962 painting (whereabouts unknown) from which this screenprint was made was hanging on the wall of Indiana's studio on Coenties Slip in Lower Manhattan when the artist was interviewed by Richard Brown Baker on September 12, 1963. During the interview, Indiana explained:

> This painting, *YIELD BROTHER,* actually has been painted expressly for the [Bertrand Russell Peace] Foundation, and in it I have incorporated a symbol which the "Ban the Bomb" people use . . . which is actually an old medieval symbol, and "death to man" is the significance of it. And, of course, that's what the bomb stands for.[14]

He went on to explain that this was preceded by a previous *YIELD BROTHER*, which had no political connotations, but was a biblically inspired message on social tolerance built around the familiar yellow-and-black "Yield" and other cautionary road signs. This connection emerged in Indiana's next expository statement, in 1968, on *YIELD BROTHER*:

> Yield: Arrogant admonition of the American highway, by far the most provocative of all road signs, emblazoned too on that unexpected shape: the descending triangle. Wildly indecorous for a humorless Highway Department that never follows "Soft Shoulders" with "Supple Hips." However, *Yield*—as humble injunction—[is] appropriate and pressing for the whole troubled world.[15]

The recurrent Y-shape of the "Ban the Bomb" symbol also had precedent in Indiana's painting, having appeared in the centerpiece of his *Melville Triptych* of 1961 (pages 22–23) as a cartographic representation of Coenties Slip, the historic East River wharf in lower Manhattan where Indiana had his studio.

14. Oral history interview with Robert Indiana by Richard Brown Baker.
15. "YIELD," in *Robert Indiana* (1968), 20.

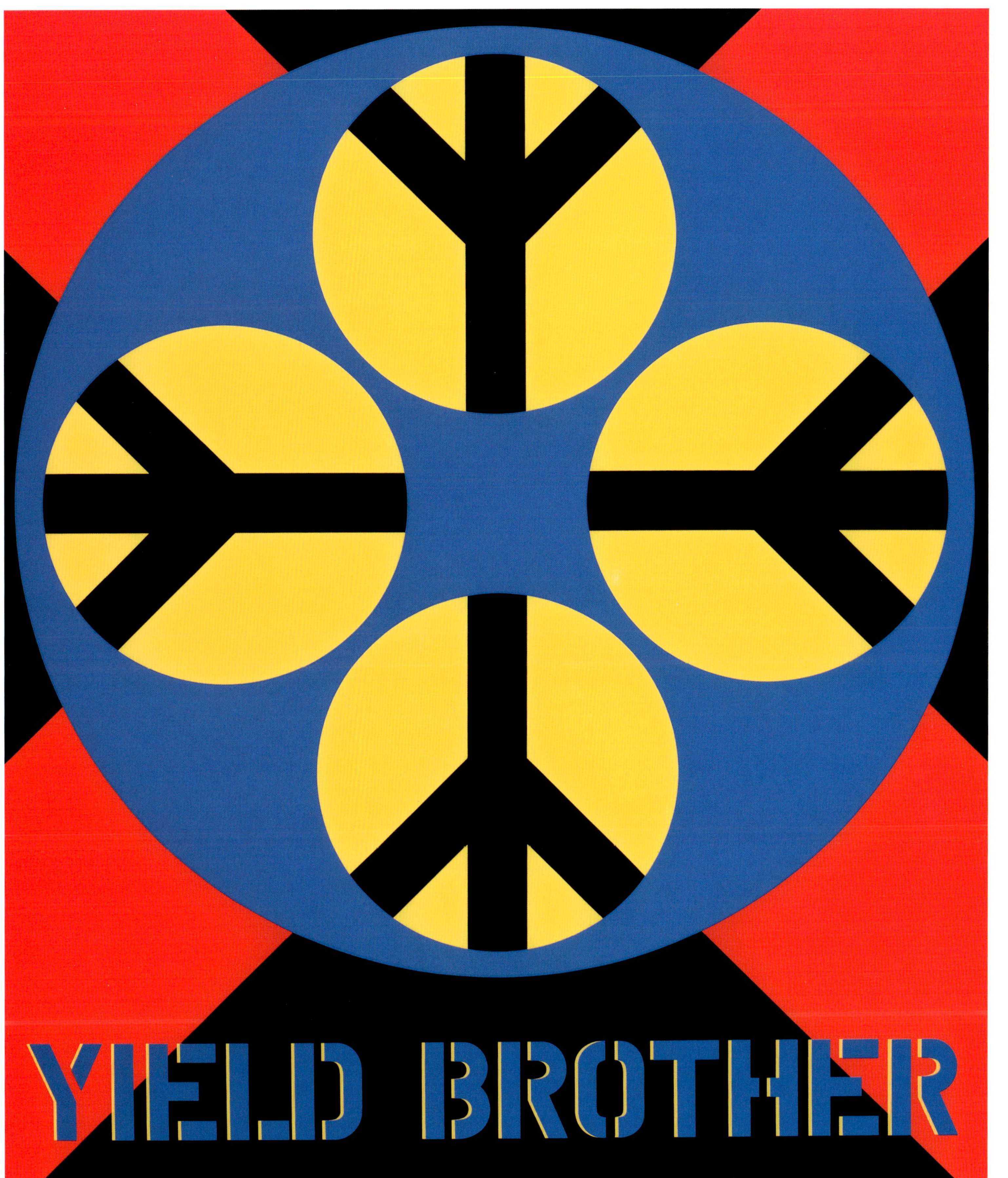
YIELD BROTHER

PLATE 6

1963 THE FIGURE FIVE

from *Decade*, 1971

screenprint

edition of 200

image: 35 ¾ × 29 ¾ in. (90.8 × 75.6 cm);
sheet: 39 × 32 in. (99.1 × 81.3 cm)

printed by Domberger KG, Stuttgart;
published by Multiples, Inc., New York

Collection of the Indianapolis Museum of Art,
Museum Purchase through Multiples, Inc., 71.88.4A

THE FIGURE FIVE was directly inspired by Charles Demuth's 1928 painting *I Saw the Figure 5 in Gold*, Indiana's favorite American painting in the Metropolitan Museum of Art, New York, the genesis of which was related by Indiana:

> For in 1928, the year of my birth, Demuth painted his "picture" inspired by his friend's poem "The Great Figure." It was on a hot summer day in New York early in this century that William Carlos Williams, on his way to visit the studio of another American artist of the time, Marsden Hartley, on Fifteenth Street, . . . heard "a great clatter of bells and the roar of a fire engine passing the end of the street down Ninth Avenue." He turned in time to see a golden figure 5 on a red background flash by. He was so impressed he took out a piece of paper from his pocket and wrote the following poem on the spot: Among the rain / and lights / I saw the figure 5 / in gold / on a red / fire truck / moving / tense / unheeded / to gong clangs / siren howls / and wheels rumbling / through the dark city.[16]

Indiana quoted the three approaching, enlarging golden fives in Demuth's lyrical font rather than his own typically Roman type. He divorced the numeral from Demuth's cubist cityscape and replaced it with four of his recurrent three-letter verbs—EAT, HUG, ERR, DIE—encompassing for him the cycle of the human condition. These are inscribed in a hexagon created by the five points of a star, to Indiana "the American symbol," and, as if to emphasize this fact, he completed the hexagon with USA.[17] ● The painting on which this print was based, *THE FIGURE FIVE* (Smithsonian American Art Museum, Washington, DC), was but one of six variants painted in 1963 that sprang from the Demuth painting and flowed from Indiana's feeling of kinship with the earlier American artist, who was, like Indiana, a formal painter and a symbolic portraitist. Indiana's Demuth paintings, as construed by art historian Susan Elizabeth Ryan, "portray himself (a poet/painter) via a painter (Demuth), in terms of that painter's portrait of a poet (Williams), via the poet's poem that is a portrait of a fire truck."[18]

16. "The Demuth American Dream No. 5," in *Robert Indiana* (1968), 27.
17. Diamonstein, *Inside New York's Art World*, 161.
18. Ryan, *Robert Indiana*, 139.

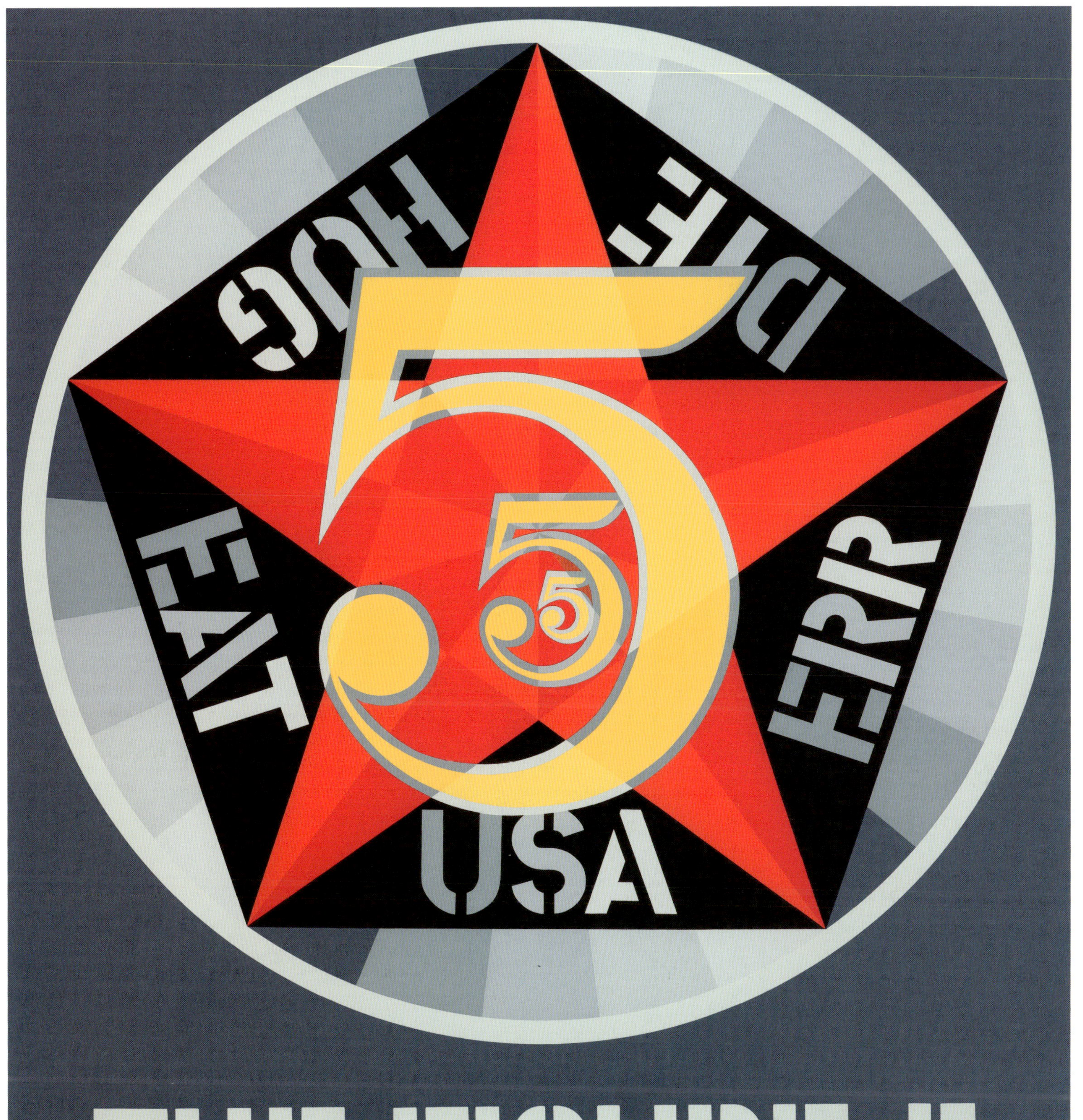
HUG
DIE
5
EAT
ERR
USA
THE FIGURE 5

PLATE 7

1964 The Brooklyn Bridge

from *Decade*, 1971

screenprint

edition of 200

image: 22 ½ × 22 ½ in. (57.2 × 57.2 cm);
sheet: 39 × 32 in. (99.1 × 81.3 cm)

printed by Domberger KG, Stuttgart;
published by Multiples, Inc., New York

Collection of the Indianapolis Museum of Art,
Museum Purchase through Multiples, Inc., 71.88.5A

This image takes as its point of departure Joseph Stella's 1919 paintings of the Brooklyn Bridge, in which the landmark became a cathedral of cubistic modernism colored like fragmented shards of stained glass. As critic Gene Swenson remarked in a 1964 review:

> Stella recognized the inherent multicolors of those fractions, which, unlike those of Classical Cubism, clarify a stable image; Indiana, with sure instinct and intellectual grasp of the style, reduces instead of multiplies the facets and sets what still remains of their multicolors in a monochrome pattern of greys. These pictures are flawless.[19]

In line with his own literary paintings, which were coming to their end around this time, and with William Carlos Williams's word portrait of fire engine number 5, noted in the previous entry, Indiana quotes here from Hart Crane's 1930 book-length poem *The Bridge*. The four lines he incorporates—one surrounding each variant image, which in the original 1964 painting (Detroit Institute of Arts) were painted on four separate canvases butted together to form the whole—describe the bridge in four distinct modes:

> And we have seen night lifted in thy arms
>
> Silver-paced as though the sun took step of thee
>
> Thy cables breathe the North Atlantic still
>
> How could mere toil align thy choiring strings

Crane knew these moods well; living in Columbia Heights, he had the Brooklyn Bridge in constant view. So too did Indiana, from Coenties Slip on the Manhattan side, where he lived from 1956 to 1965 and from whence, he wrote, he could see the far side of the bridge "through whose antique cables the sun rises each morning."[20]

19. G. R. S. [Gene Swenson], "Robert Indiana (Stable)," *Art News* 63, no. 4 (Summer 1964): 13.
20. "Coenties Slip," in Ryan, *Robert Indiana*, 257.

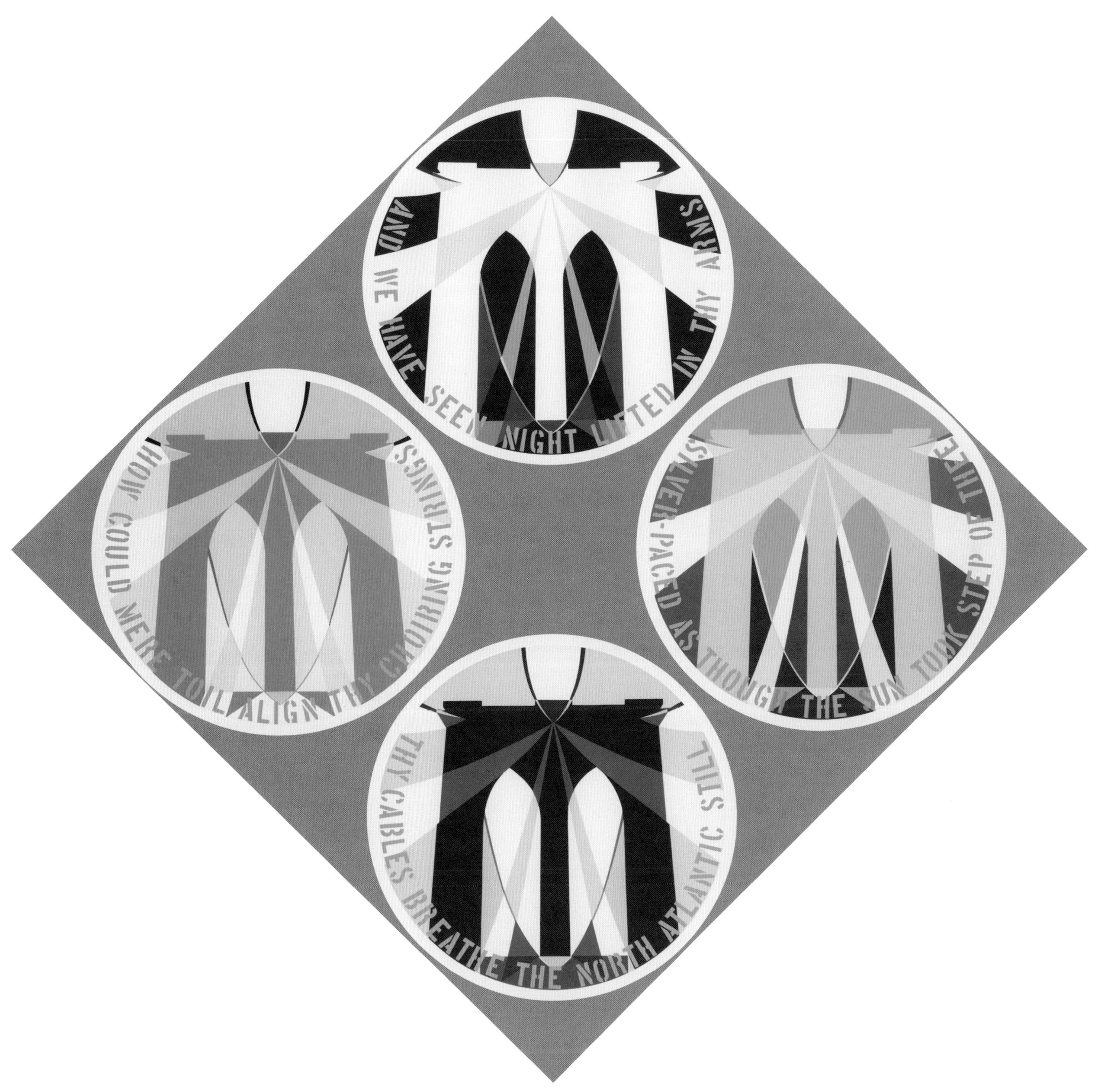
AND WE HAVE SEEN NIGHT LIFTED IN THY ARMS
HOW COULD MERE TOIL ALIGN THY CHOIRING STRINGS
SILVER-PACED AS THOUGH THE SUN TOOK STEP OF THEE
THY CABLES BREATHE THE NORTH ATLANTIC STILL

PLATE 8

1965 MISSISSIPPI

from *Decade*, 1971

screenprint

edition of 200

image: 34 ⅞ × 29 ⅞ in. (88.6 × 75.9 cm);
sheet: 39 × 32 in. (99.1 × 81.3 cm)

printed by Domberger KG, Stuttgart;
published by Multiples, Inc., New York

Collection of the Indianapolis Museum of Art,
Museum Purchase through Multiples, Inc., 71.88.6A

In the early 1960s, Indiana felt great sympathy for the civil rights movement that was taking hold in the United States. In 1965, he began his *Confederacy* series, of which he wrote three years later:

> That the countryside is peppered with "Yield" signs hasn't affected the national conscience much—particularly in our least yielding region entrenched as it is in the doctrine of White Supremacy. Against the recalcitrance of the South, I have aimed the salt of the Confederacy Series, *Florida* in this exhibition, but *Mississippi* too, and *Alabama* and *Louisiana* and eventually I mean to encompass all 13 of the Secessionist States whose citizens were willing to die for the perpetuation of human slavery, indicated here with "JUST AS IN THE ANATOMY OF MAN EVERY NATION MUST HAVE ITS HIND PART."[21]

In *MISSISSIPPI* (Robert B. Mayer Family Collection, Chicago), as in the other three works completed in the series, a map of the offending state, rendered in fleshy pink, appears in the center, surrounded by Indiana's admonition in a double band of stenciled letters interrupted by a circlet of stars, creating a quasi–State Seal. ● Within the map, the town of Philadelphia, Mississippi, is indicated (as were Bogalosa, Louisiana, and Selma, Alabama, in those respective paintings), and it was in Philadelphia on June 21, 1964, that three civil rights activists—one black and two white—were lynched. The three were organizers for the Congress on Racial Equality (CORE). Not coincidentally, *MISSISSIPPI* was painted to support CORE and shown in its 1965 benefit exhibition.[22]

21. "YIELD," in *Robert Indiana* (1968), 20.
22. "Autochronology," in *Robert Indiana* (1968), 57.

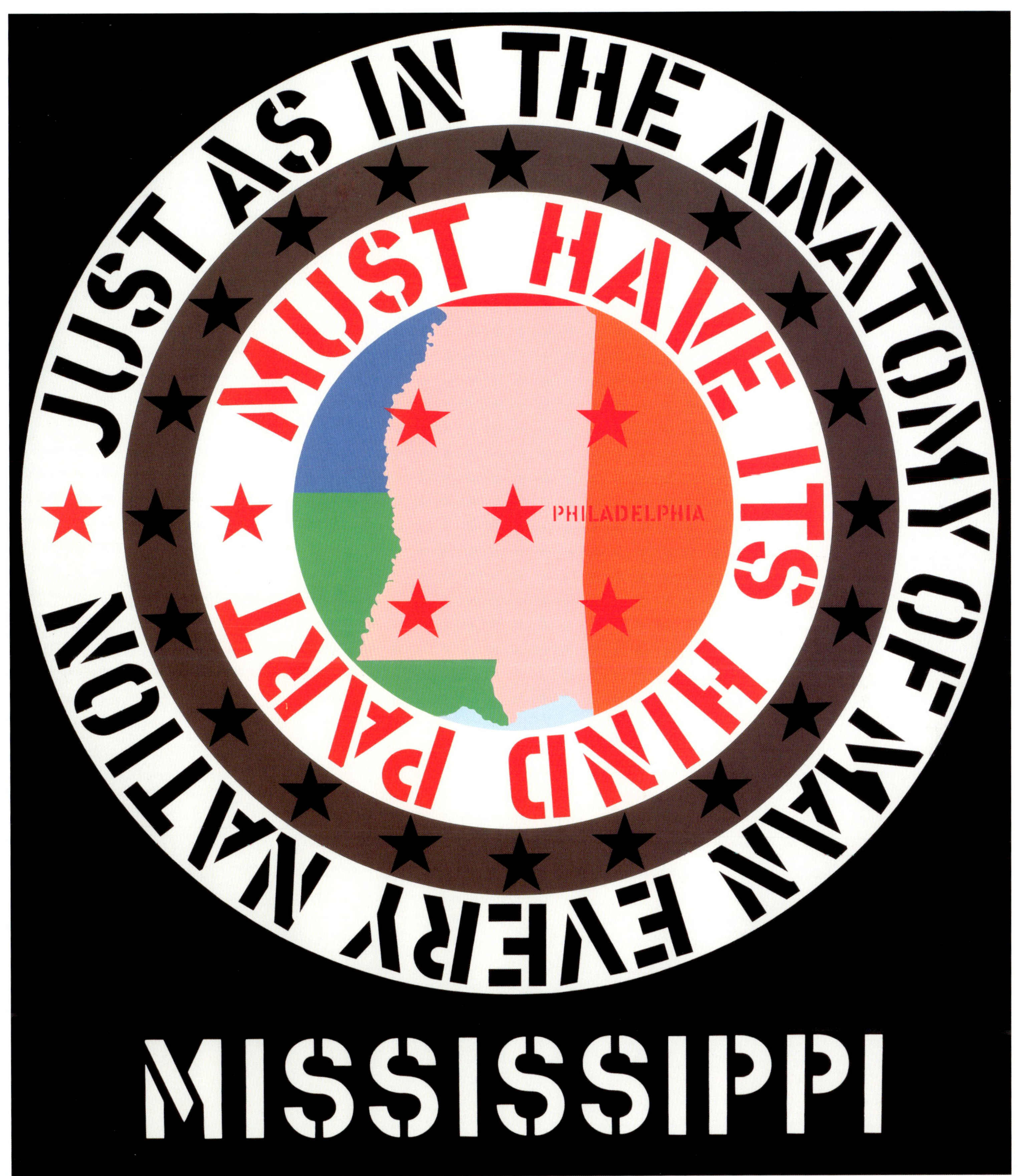
JUST AS IN THE ANATOMY OF MAN EVERY NATION
MUST HAVE ITS HIND PART
PHILADELPHIA
MISSISSIPPI

PLATE 9

1966 USA 666

from *Decade*, 1971

screenprint

edition of 200

image: 28 ¼ × 28 ¼ in. (71.8 × 71.8 cm);
sheet: 39 × 32 in. (99.1 × 81.3 cm)

printed by Domberger KG, Stuttgart;
published by Multiples, Inc., New York

Collection of the Indianapolis Museum of Art,
Museum Purchase through Multiples, Inc., 71.88.7A

Rendered in the yellow-and-black color scheme of cautionary highway signage and arranged like the cross arms of a railroad crossing warning sign, *USA 666* is a memento of the American highway. It is also self-referential: "Yellow is my color," Indiana wrote, "especially in its darker form. Expansive and ardent, yellow is a male color, at the edge of blackness in its relation to sulfur."[23] Simultaneously, *USA 666* became an homage to his father, who had died in December 1965 while this painting was in process. The conjunction was explained by the artist in the catalogue for *Environment U.S.A., 1957–1967*, an exhibition of recent American paintings, including *USA 666*, that opened in September 1967 in São Paulo, Brazil:

> [The image] actually comes from multiple sources: the single six of my father's birth month, June; the Phillips 66 sign of the gasoline company he worked for. . . . It also conjures up Route 66, the highway west for Kerouac and other Americans for whom "Go West" is a common imperative, whereas for a common cold it is "Use 666," the patent medicine that is the final referent and which on small metal plates affixed to farmers' fences—black and yellow—dotted the pastures and fields like black-eyed susans in perennial bloom. . . . In perhaps lesser profusion over the countryside bloomed the EAT signs that signaled the roadside diners. . . . In similar cheap cafes my Mother supported herself and son by offering "home-cooked" meals for 25 cents when Father disappeared behind the big 66 sign in a westerly direction out Route 66.[24]

EAT and DIE were always paired in Indiana's mind as representing the boundary between life and death, a demarcation related specifically to the deaths of both his parents (see Plate 1).

23. Quoted without citation, Christie's, New York, sale catalogue, May 13, 2008, 194. *USA 666* was offered at this sale.
24. Reprinted in "Introduction," in *Robert Indiana* (1968), 29.

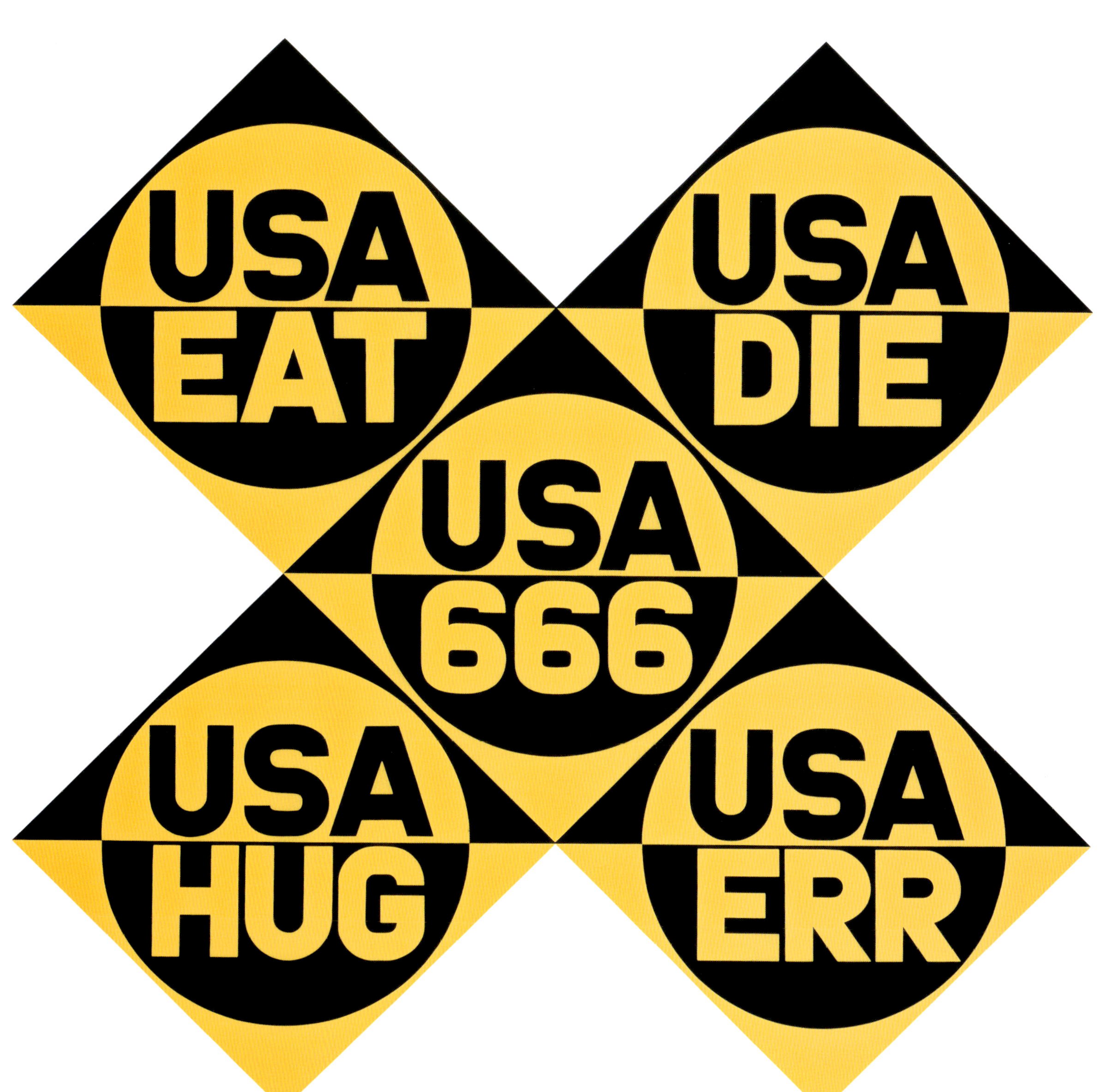
USA
EAT
USA
DIE
USA
666
USA
HUG
USA
ERR

PARROT is one of Indiana's few (and one of his last) figurative images. It represents another of his childhood memories. While most of Indiana's extended clan came from his father's side, his uncle George Potts lived with Indiana's maternal grandmother, and Uncle George had a pet parrot that perched on his shoulder. The bird squawked "Eureka," which Indiana, a keen classical scholar, would have known to mean "I have found it," famously uttered by the Greek inventor Archimedes. Therefore, Indiana renders the word in "rough and perhaps enigmatic Greek," as he described it on the contents page of the *Decade* portfolio. ● Indiana was a four-year Latin student at Arsenal Technical High School in Indianapolis and won the silver medal for Latin as a senior. His first combination of words and imagery occurred at that time at the urging of his Latin teacher, Irene McLean, and his art teacher, Sara Bard, whom Indiana remembered as "a tyrant," but from whom he "learned more . . . than any other teacher."[25] Indiana took five passages from the Gospel of St. Luke, wrote them out in medieval Latin script, and illuminated them with gouache. He gave the five panels to the school upon his graduation in 1946.

PLATE 10

1967 PARROT

from *Decade*, 1971

screenprint

edition of 200

image: 35 ½ × 30 ½ in. (90.2 × 77.5 cm);
sheet: 39 × 32 in. (99.1 × 81.3 cm)

printed by Domberger KG, Stuttgart;
published by Multiples, Inc., New York

Collection of the Indianapolis Museum of Art,
Museum Purchase through Multiples, Inc., 71.88.8A

25. "Artist Robert Indiana Recalls Tech Years," *Indianapolis Star*, September 21, 1968.

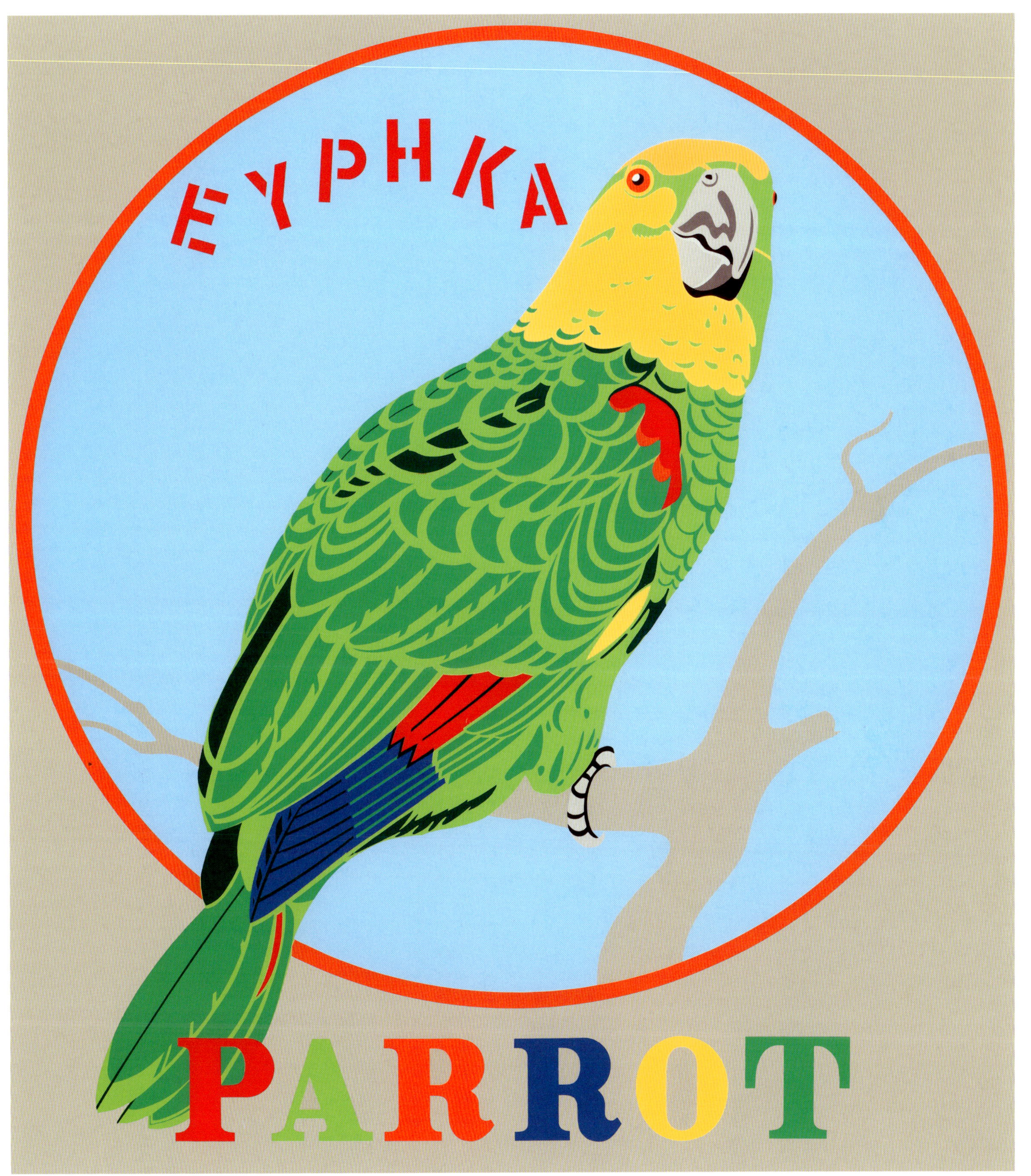
ΕΥΡΗΚΑ
PARROT

PLATE 11

1968 Black and White LOVE

from *Decade*, 1971

screenprint

edition of 200

image: 29 ¾ × 29 ¾ in. (75.6 × 75.6 cm);
sheet: 39 × 32 in. (99.1 × 81.3 cm)

printed by Domberger KG, Stuttgart;
published by Multiples, Inc., New York

Collection of the Indianapolis Museum of Art,
Museum Purchase through Multiples, Inc., 71.88.9A

Black and White LOVE is an example of Indiana's *LOVE* "walls," which first appeared in his *LOVE* show at the Stable Gallery, New York, in 1966. The *LOVE* walls were painted on four identically sized square canvases that were stacked to make a larger square, which, if rotated, would always present one LOVE correctly oriented; likewise, if each individual panel were rotated ninety degrees, one of the four letters would always be mirroring itself in the center of the composite image. In this way, the composition becomes quite abstract, as critics noted at the time. Lucy Lippard, for example, described them as "exuberant, exquisitely rendered works, decorative in a good sense and the products of a sophisticated innocence."[26] This accords with a direction Indiana had hoped his art was taking in 1963, as he informed interviewer Richard Brown Baker:

> I am very much impressed and I have always been impressed how with a little concentration and a little mental exercise, if one concentrates long enough on a word or figure, it's very easy to lose the conscious grasp of what that is, and one can look at a word, and after concentrating on it for a little while, one has almost forgotten what that word is. And I should like in a way [for] this to be a part of my work, too.[27]

The painting *Black and White LOVE*, 1968, differs from the earlier prototypes in its grand scale—measuring six feet per side—and its change from the red, green, and blue palette to black and white, a basic scheme that, surprisingly, given the usual chromatic éclat of his work, the artist admits to liking very much.[28] While this painting was underway, the Rev. Dr. Martin Luther King Jr. was assassinated in Memphis on April 4, 1968, and Indiana dedicated this work to him. It was donated to CORE, then bought and donated to Spellman College in Atlanta.[29] It is now in the Ludwig Collection in the Museum Moderner Kunst, Vienna.

26. Lucy Lippard, "New York Letter," *Art International* 10, no. 6 (Summer 1966): 115.
27. Oral history interview with Robert Indiana by Richard Brown Baker.
28. Sheehan, *Robert Indiana Prints*, 14.
29. "Autochronology," *Robert Indiana* (1968), 58.

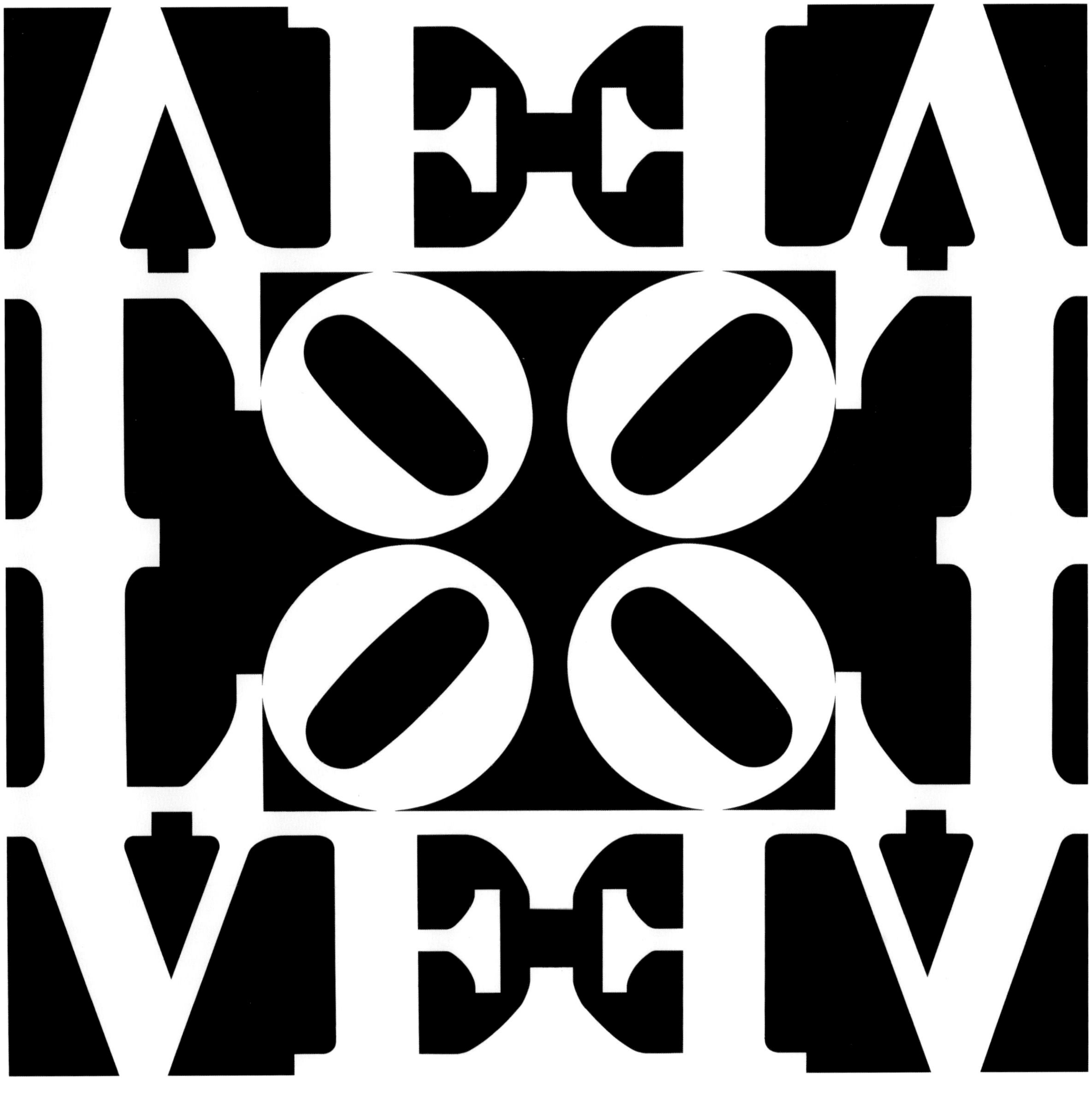

PLATE 12

1969 TERRE HAUTE No. 2

from *Decade*, 1971

screenprint

edition of 200

image: 35 ¾ × 29 ¾ in. (90.8 × 75.6 cm);
sheet: 39 × 32 in. (99.1 × 81.3 cm)

printed by Domberger KG, Stuttgart;
published by Multiples, Inc., New York

Collection of the Indianapolis Museum of Art, Museum Purchase through Multiples, Inc., 71.88.10A

On the contents page of the *Decade* portfolio, Indiana cast this screenprint in mythical garb:

> Here on the highest point in the state of Indiana, where the white-columned grave of the Hoosier poet laureate James Whitcomb Riley crowns the hill, the artist looks due west toward the farthest town on the border, Terre Haute, which lies astride the National Road (Route #40) at its crossing with the Wabash River.

Even from the site of Riley's tomb, located at the highest point of Crown Hill Cemetery in Indianapolis (although this is no longer held to be the highest point in the state), it is not possible to see across the seventy-seven westward miles to Terre Haute, near the Illinois border. But it was an image that grew from a youthful fascination, as the artist explained in a 1976 interview with Donald Goodall:

> *Terre Haute* is really what I would consider, for me, a landscape. *Terre Haute* is about geography. *Terre Haute* is probably one of my less autobiographical works. I've never lived in Terre Haute and never really had any particular Terre Haute experiences. The fascination there was simply the eccentricity of the fact that a little Indiana town would bear such a fancy name, which, of course, is badly pronounced in Indiana; it becomes something entirely different. With the Hoosier farmers, it's "Terry Hut," which is a long way from "Terre Haute."[30]

TERRE HAUTE (Indiana State Museum, Indianapolis) appeared in 1960 as one of Indiana's first word paintings, followed nine years later by *TERRE HAUTE No. 2* (Private collection). They share the same elements: a stenciled title, two stars, the word WABASH, and the number 40. But in the second version, TERRE HAUTE looms on the far horizon, suggesting Indiana's perspective from Indianapolis, the two cities joined together by US 40, the Old National Road built in the 1830s to provide a way west from the Cumberland Gap to the Mississippi. WABASH, the name of the quintessential Indiana river, springs from the horizon, its onrush evoking the mythical train called the Wabash Cannonball.

30. "Conversations with Robert Indiana," in *Robert Indiana* (1977), 30.

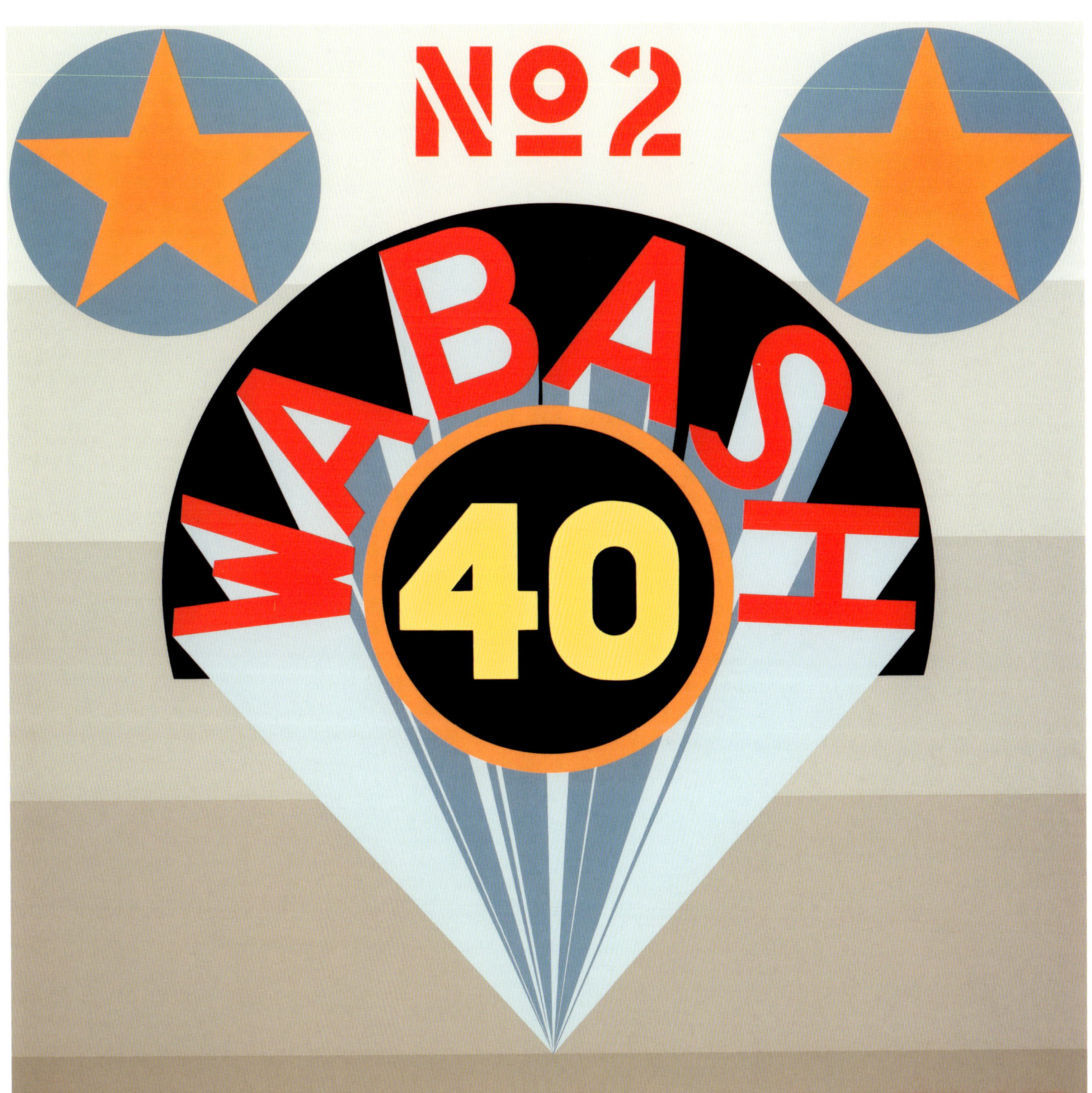
No 2
WABASH
40
TERRE HAUTE

PLATE 13

THE AMERICAN DREAM #2, 1982

screenprint on four sheets

edition of 100

image: 24 × 24 in. (61 × 61 cm) each;
sheet: 26 ¾ × 26 ¾ in. (68 × 68 cm) each

printed by Domberger KG, Filderstadt;
published by Prestige Art Ltd., Mamaroneck, New York

Collection of Morgan Art Foundation, courtesy Marc Salama-Caro

The Black Diamond American Dream #2 (Sintra Museum of Modern Art, Lisbon, Portugal), painted in 1962 and published as a screenprint twenty years later, is the lineal descendant of *The American Dream, I* of 1961. While adopting a diamond format as the title suggests (on a single canvas rather than on the four sheets of the screenprint), it carries forward the allusions Indiana made in the first painting: "of Pin Ball machines and Juke Boxes in all those hundreds of grubby bars and roadside cafes, alternate spiritual homes of the American."[31] Certainly these were Indiana's surrogate homes, frequented as they were by his vagabonding parents during the Great Depression. This verbal/visual evocation of the road is even more explicit here with the introduction of JUKE, mating it with JACK (slang for money) and EAT. And the palette is more amped up, with dominating reds and blacks, an indication, according to Indiana, of a work's emotional effect: "If it's a subject I'm feeling intensely about, it's apt to be black and red."[32] Elsewhere he associates black with his father and red with his mother.[33] His father, he said, "was the American Dreamer," and Indiana associated the word EAT with signage on the diners in which his mother worked during the Depression.[34] The acrostic configuration of EAT here was modified two years later into an X-shaped, twenty-foot-tall electrified sign commissioned for the exterior of the Circarama at the New York World's Fair in 1964. *EAT* remained unlit after its first day on display because, ironically, it was mistaken by the tourists for a restaurant sign.[35] ● The emotional thrust of the first four of his *American Dream* series was, Indiana admitted, "caustic" and derived from the irony that "instead of being an idealistic thing, the 'Dream' had been perverted into a very cheap, tawdry experience. And the whole Depression period was, from my standpoint as a child, bleak, cheap, and tawdry."[36]

31. "Introduction," in *Robert Indiana* (1968), 23.
32. Ryan, *Robert Indiana*, 128.
33. "A MOTHER IS A MOTHER AND A FATHER IS A FATHER," in *Robert Indiana* (1968), 36.
34. "Conversations with Robert Indiana," in *Robert Indiana* (1977), 33.
35. "Autochronology," *Robert Indiana* (1968), 56.
36. "Conversations with Robert Indiana," in *Robert Indiana* (1977), 29.

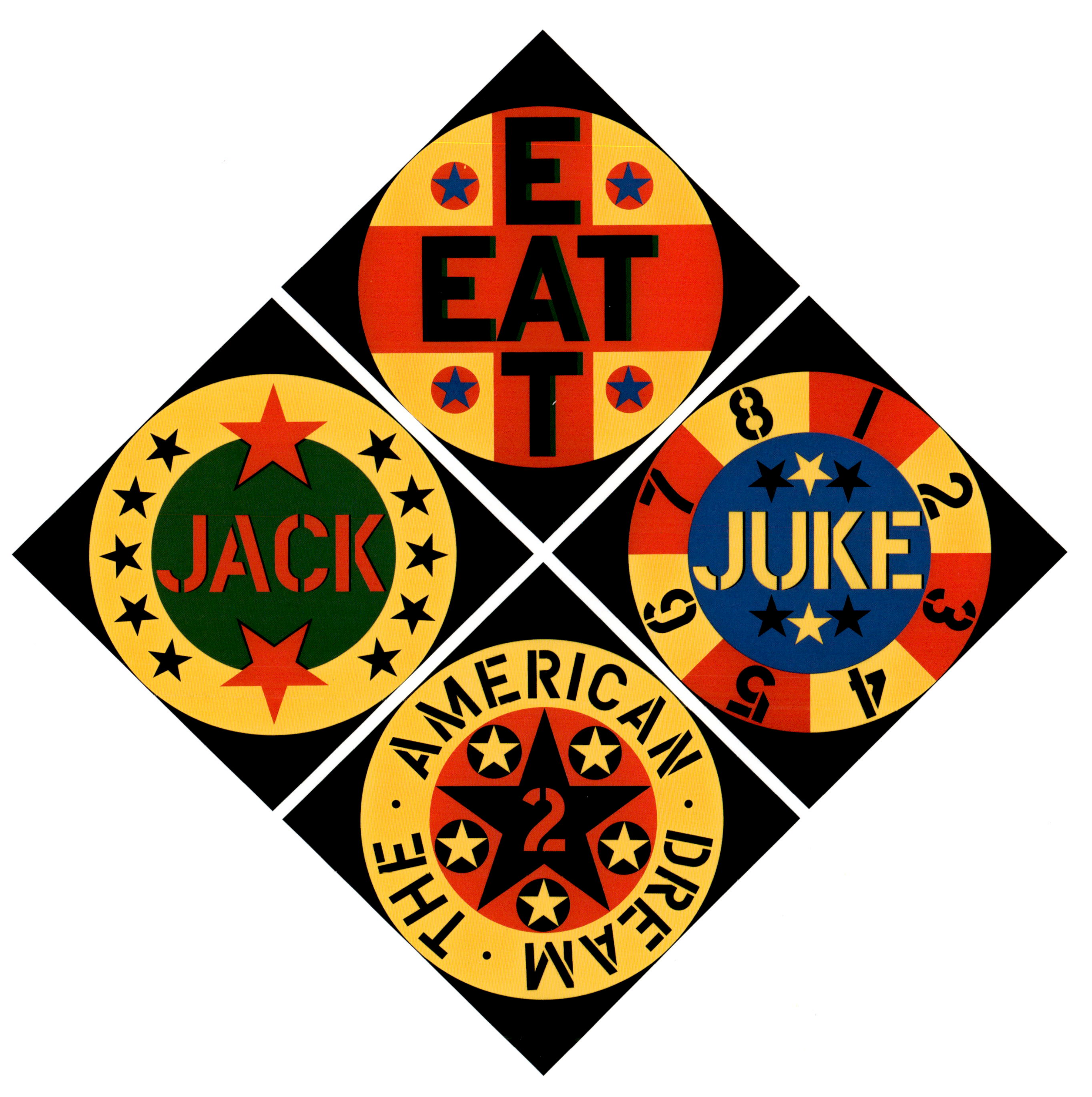
EAT
JACK
JUKE
1 2 3 4 5 6 7 8
THE AMERICAN DREAM
2

With *AMERICAN DREAM #5*, 1963 (Art Gallery of Ontario, Toronto), Indiana moved from the caustic, ironic tenor of earlier manifestations of the series to a celebratory one that continued into his *Autoportraits*, which the artist considered an extension of the series.[37] This work—a symbolic portrait of an artist (Charles Demuth) portraying a poet (William Carlos Williams) picturing an object (fire engine) quoted for other purposes (Indiana's)—is an elaboration of *THE FIGURE FIVE* (see Plate 6). In the *Dream* variant, Indiana's familiar cycle of life tropes—EAT, HUG, ERR, DIE—are spun off onto their own panels arranged in a cross, about which Indiana remarked:

> I did my painting in 1963, which when subtracted by 1928 leaves 35—a number suggested by the succession of three fives (5 5 5) describing the sudden progression of the firetruck in the poet's experience. In 1935 Demuth died, either from an overdose or an underdose of insulin (he suffered for years from diabetes) according to Dr. Williams, the pediatrician-poet who birthed thousands of babies as well as hundreds of poems, and then in 1963 the venerable doctor died, completing the unpremeditated circle of numerical coincidence woven within the "Fifth Dream."

Appearing on the central panel are 1928 and 1963: the dates, respectively, of Demuth's *I Saw the Figure 5 in Gold* and of Williams's death, but also the birth date of Indiana and the date of his painting, thus making the polyptych his own. Indiana continued:

> For the major painting of this "Dream" I chose the cruciform . . . by the use of which I meant to set this particular painting most apart from all others given that its theme and internal form is in direct dialogue with the original inspiration. The head, the arms, the foot, or less particularly the surrounding members echo and reinforce Demuth's composition though somewhat simplified to fit the nature of my own work, stripped as it is of the allusions to a cubist cityscape.[38]

Not all of Demuth's allusions are stripped away, however. Within the central circle of the central panel appear the following: CD, CARLO, WCW, BILL, and ART Co. Quoted from Demuth's painting, these are the initials, nicknames, and mutual interest of the artist and the poet that transformed a cubist abstraction into a vivid, if abstracted, portrait.

PLATE 14

AMERICAN DREAM #5, 1980

screenprint on five sheets

edition of 100

image: 24 × 24 in. (61 × 61 cm) each;
sheet: 26 ¾ × 26 ¾ in. (68 × 68 cm) each

printed by Domberger KG, Filderstadt;
published by Prestige Art Ltd., Mamaroneck, New York

Collection of Morgan Art Foundation, courtesy Marc Salama-Caro

37. Ibid., 27.
38. "The Demuth American Dream No. 5," in *Robert Indiana* (1968), 27.

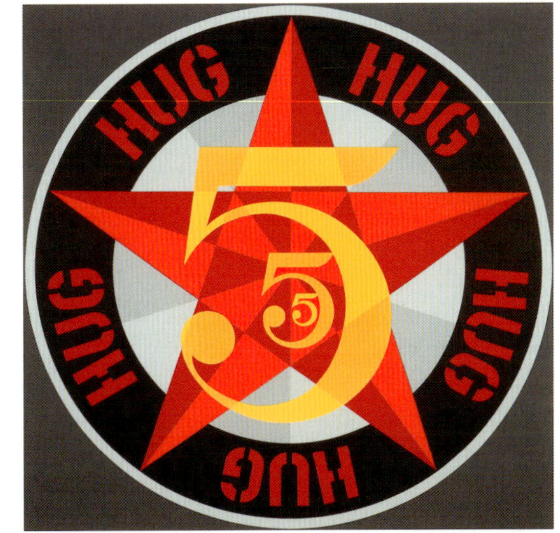
HUG HUG HUG HUG HUG
5

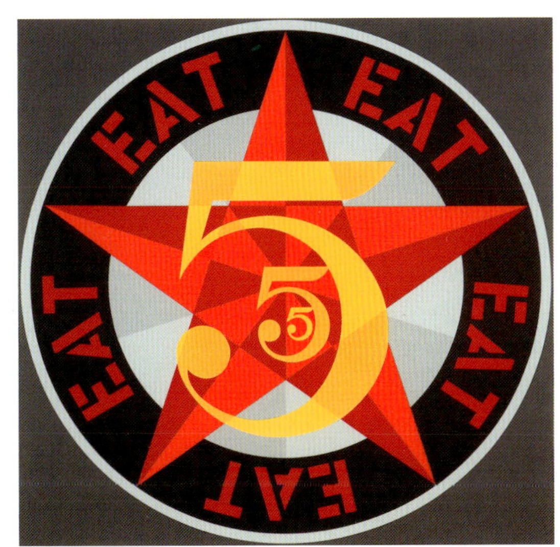
EAT EAT EAT EAT EAT
5

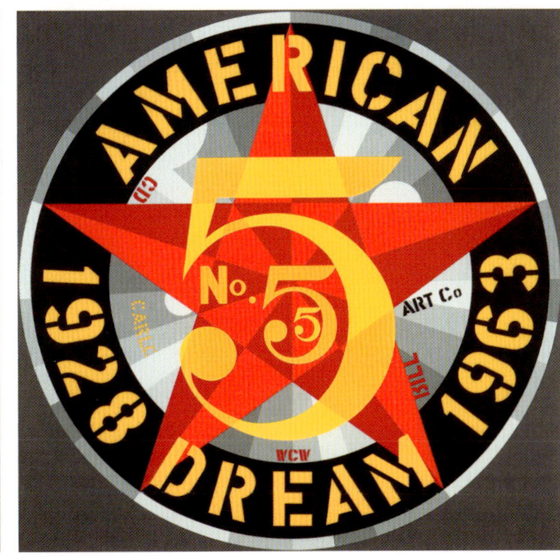
AMERICAN
1928
No. 5
ART Co
1963
DREAM

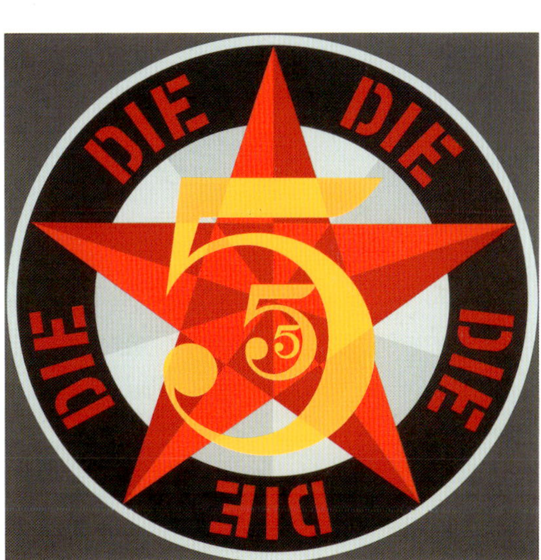
DIE DIE DIE DIE DIE
5

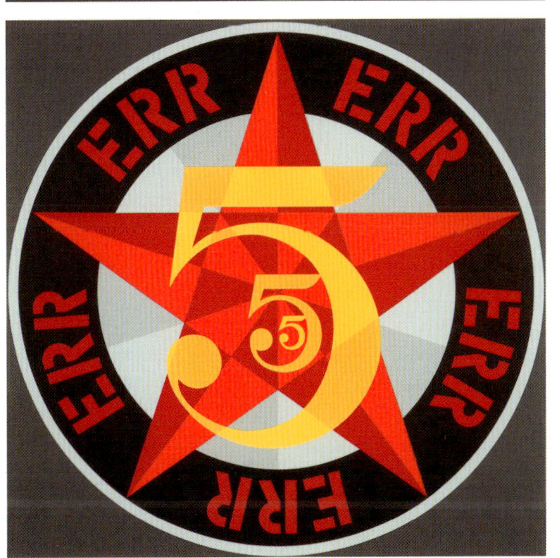
ERR ERR ERR ERR ERR
5

This screenprint, based on a 1963 painting (Michener Collection, Blanton Museum of Art, University of Texas, Austin), is more representational than almost any other of Indiana's works. It is a schematized but recognizable head-on view of a steam locomotive. Two circular steam chests flank the cowcatcher. The border of the circular smokebox bears the title, and in its center, where the engine number often appeared, is 25, the street number of Indiana's address on Coenties Slip at the time of the painting's creation. ● Like the similarly representational *PARROT* (Plate 10), *HIGH BALL on the REDBALL MANIFEST* had a familial connection. REDBALL MANIFEST was an old railroad term for priority freight such as perishable goods, and HIGH BALL came from the railway signal for "fast ahead." Indiana associated this painting with both of his grandfathers: his maternal grandfather, a traveling insurance salesman, who criss-crossed the country by rail, and his paternal grandfather, who was an engineer for the Pennsylvania Railroad.[39]

PLATE 15

HIGH BALL on the REDBALL MANIFEST

from *The American Dream*, 1997

screenprint

edition of 395

image: 16 ½ × 14 in. (41.9 × 35.6 cm);
sheet: 22 ½ × 17 ½ in. (57.2 × 44.5 cm)

printed and published by Marco Fine Arts Contemporary Atelier, El Segundo, California

Courtesy of Taglialatella Galleries, New York

39. Ryan, *Robert Indiana*, 264; Oral history interview with Robert Indiana by Richard Brown Baker.

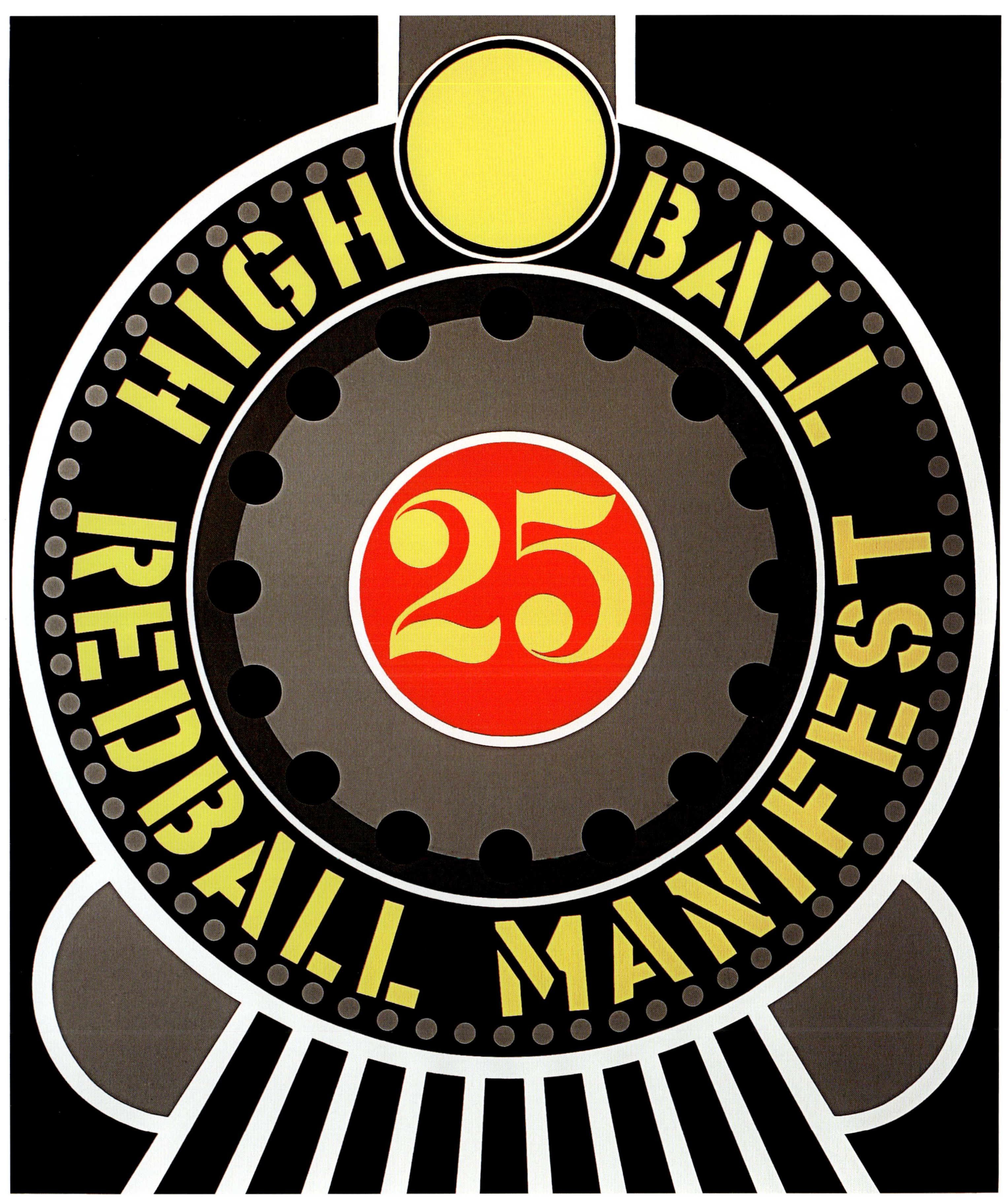
HIGH BALL
25
REDBALL MANIFEST

PLATE 16

The Metamorphosis of Norma Jean Mortenson, 1998

screenprint

edition of 90

image: 30 × 30 in. (76.2 × 76.2 cm); sheet: 35 × 35 in. (88.9 × 88.9 cm)

Collection of the artist

Marilyn Monroe's death in 1962 inspired a slew of Marilyn paintings in the Pop idiom. As for Indiana, he waited, he said, a "respectable time before jumping on the hearse."[40] Though not immune to Monroe's iconic cult stature, he picked her as a subject in 1967 because of certain mysterious coincidences that he found in her chronology, her given name, and her stage name. ● Indiana had been fascinated by numbers since childhood, stemming from the family's multitude of ever-changing street addresses. His research into Monroe's life revealed that the numbers 2 and 6 had mystical meaning: she had been born in 1926 and died in 1962. She had died on the 6th day of August, the eighth month (6 + 2). In '52 (26 + 26), at the age of 26, she had her first starring dramatic role, which brought in $26,000.00 in its first week's run in Manhattan.[41] ● Mirroring, in Indiana's estimation, her transformation from orphaned waif to celluloid goddess, the actress's given name, Norma Jean Mortenson, seemingly metamorphosed into Marilyn Monroe, her stage name. Six letters repeat in the two names, as Indiana indicated in the picture by rendering each instance of the letter in the same color scheme: M (lilac), A (red), R (green), O (orange), N (blue), and E (yellow). Indiana used a uniform gray for the three letters in each name that do not repeat: J S T and I L Y. He described this and other correspondences in 1968:

> From the letters of her original name someone drew—almost anagrammatically—those of her fame. Three were added; three were subtracted. Six again. In gray. Encircled by the telephone dial–like ring of her destiny and death (it was this instrument she was clutching) Marilyn is posed—in the cosmetic colors of her much-vaunted femininity—against the golden star of her dreams though its tips, however, point to the letters I MOON. Her stylized image comes, of course, from the famous nude calendar "Golden Dreams," which, upon finding by chance in a Greenwich Village shop called "The Tunnel of Love," I turned over and discovered that our last Goddess of Love had been printed in Indiana.[42]

40. "Autochronology," in *Robert Indiana* (1968), 54.
41. "THE METAMORPHOSIS OF NORMA JEAN MORTENSON," in *Robert Indiana* (1968), 45.
42. Ibid.

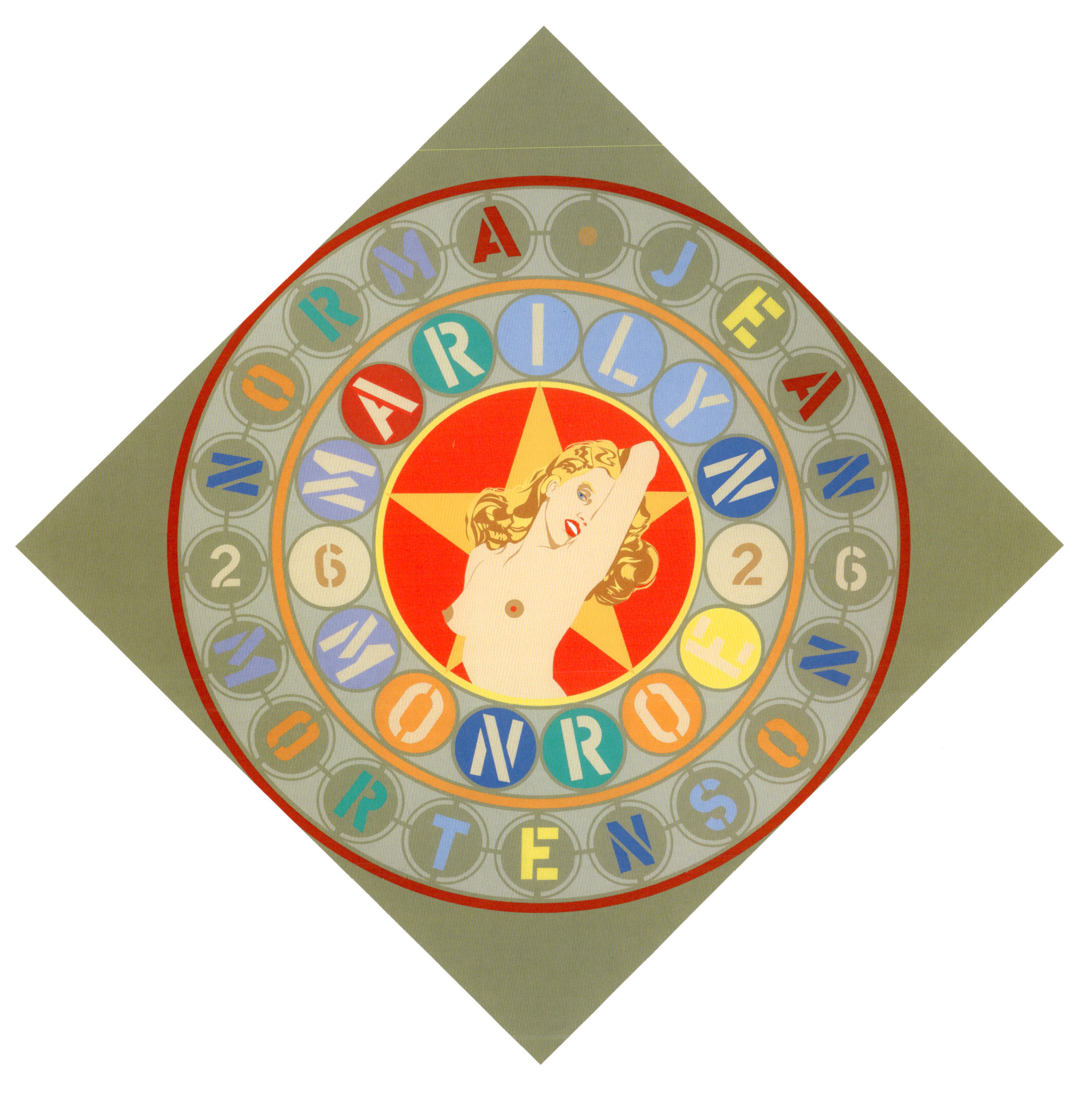
NORMA • JEAN
MORTENSON
MARILYN
MONROE
26
26

By 1972 Indiana had completed his first set of painted *Autoportraits*, one for each year from 1960 to 1969. Between 1972 and 1977, he completed a second set, with each canvas measuring six by six feet. It is from this second set that these screenprints derive. These symbolic self-portraits have more in common than their format, as Indiana explained in 1977:

> In a sense this series is an extension of my *American Dream*, and my *American Dreams* are, after all, *my* American dreams and how I relate to that whole business. . . . Everything begins with the circle . . . the symbolization of eternal life. So we start with eternal life, because we all just know it goes on and on forever, and of course, cast in the circle is a decagon and I'm very fond of geometry. I hated arithmetic and algebra, but I loved geometry. The decagon says decade. Within the decagon, hitting every other point, is the five-pointed star, which, I assume, is the American symbol. If one is going to be an American and talk about things American, one has to have a star someplace. . . . Then, cast on top of those is the number one. . . . Number one is there because after all it's a self-portrait, and that is what one is all about.[43]

PLATE 17

Decade: Autoportrait 1960, 2009

screenprint

edition of 50

image: 30 ⅛ × 30 ⅛ in. (76.5 × 76.5 cm);
sheet: 37 ¼ × 36 ¼ in. (94.6 × 92.1 cm)

printed by Brand X Editions, Ltd., New York;
published by G & S Editions, New York

Collection of Morgan Art Foundation, courtesy Marc Salama-Caro

Within this common template, Indiana floated directional arrows, place names, proper names, and other words that were pertinent to each year, as well as his own last name and the year he began the series, 1972. ● In this work, devoted to 1960, BROOKLYN and HARBOUR are geographical references. From 1956 to 1965 Indiana lived and worked in warehouse lofts on Coenties Slip, an abandoned wharf near the southern tip of Manhattan and New York Harbor, across the East River from Brooklyn Heights and near the Brooklyn Bridge. ELL is the abbreviation for Ellsworth Kelly, who was the first artist to befriend Indiana in New York in 1955, and who took a studio on the Slip in 1956. He introduced Indiana to hard-edged painting, and he was, Indiana admitted long after their personal falling-out around 1959, the artist who exerted the greatest influence on him personally.[44]

43. Diamonstein, *Inside New York's Art World*, 160–61.
44. Ibid., 162; Ryan, *Robert Indiana*, 78.

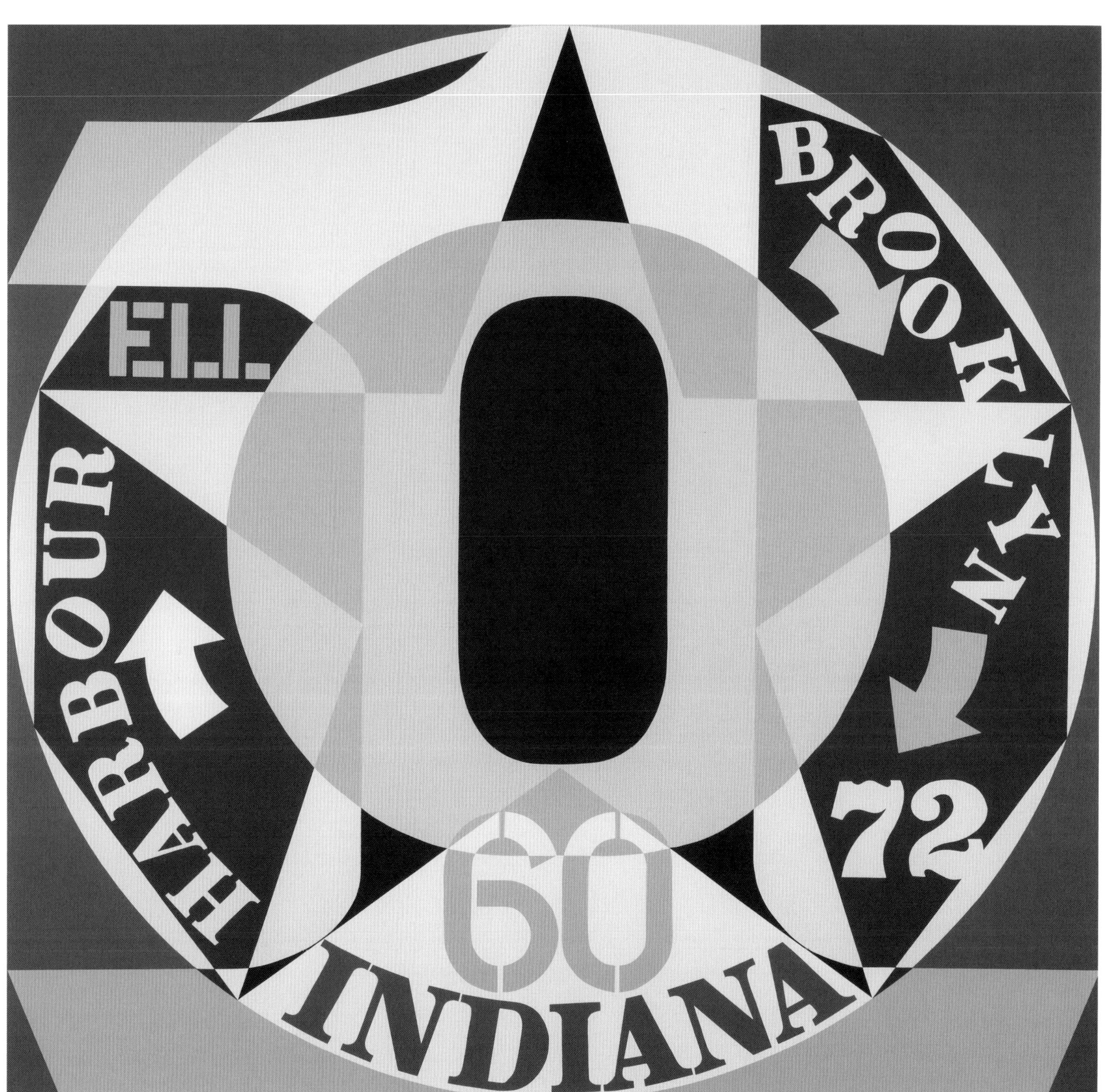

BROOKLYN
E.I.
HARBOUR
72
60
INDIANA

The year referenced in this work, 1961, was, for Indiana, "when it all really started to happen."[45] He first exhibited a work at the Museum of Modern Art, New York, when his herm *MOON* was included in the 1961 *Art of Assemblage* exhibition, and later that year MoMA acquired Indiana's *The American Dream, I.* There are three allusions to that painting in this *Autoportrait*: the initials USA; the overall palette and the sequence of green-red-blue-yellow-red-blue in INDIANA, which mirrors the painted title of the MoMA work; and the word BAR at the upper left. BAR was the title stenciled on one of Indiana's anthropomorphic herms, assemblages constructed of discarded wood beams he found in his loft that preceded his word paintings. But as he revealed in 1990, it is also short for Alfred H. Barr Jr., the director of MoMA who had purchased *The American Dream, I.*[46] Barr's reaction to the painting was always cited by Indiana in his published "Autochronologies": "Because I do not understand why I like it so much, Robert Indiana's *The American Dream* is for me one of the two most spell-binding paintings in the show [of recent acquisitions]."[47] ● The final two references are again geographical. The SOUTH FERRY connecting Manhattan to Staten Island was three blocks from Indiana's place on Coenties Slip. The reference to CHICAGO, however, is obscure, as the artist seemingly returned to that city for the first time since art school in the spring of 1963, not in 1961.[48]

PLATE 18

Decade: Autoportrait 1961, 2001

screenprint

edition of 50

image: 30 ⅛ × 30 ⅛ in. (76.5 × 76.5 cm);
sheet: 37 ¼ × 36 ¼ in. (94.6 × 92.1 cm)

printed by Brand X Editions, Ltd., New York;
published by G & S Editions, New York

Collection of Morgan Art Foundation, courtesy Marc Salama-Caro

45. Diamonstein, *Inside New York's Art World*, 161.
46. Ryan, *Robert Indiana*, 276n84.
47. "Autochronology," *Robert Indiana* (1968), 53.
48. Oral history interview with Robert Indiana by Richard Brown Baker.

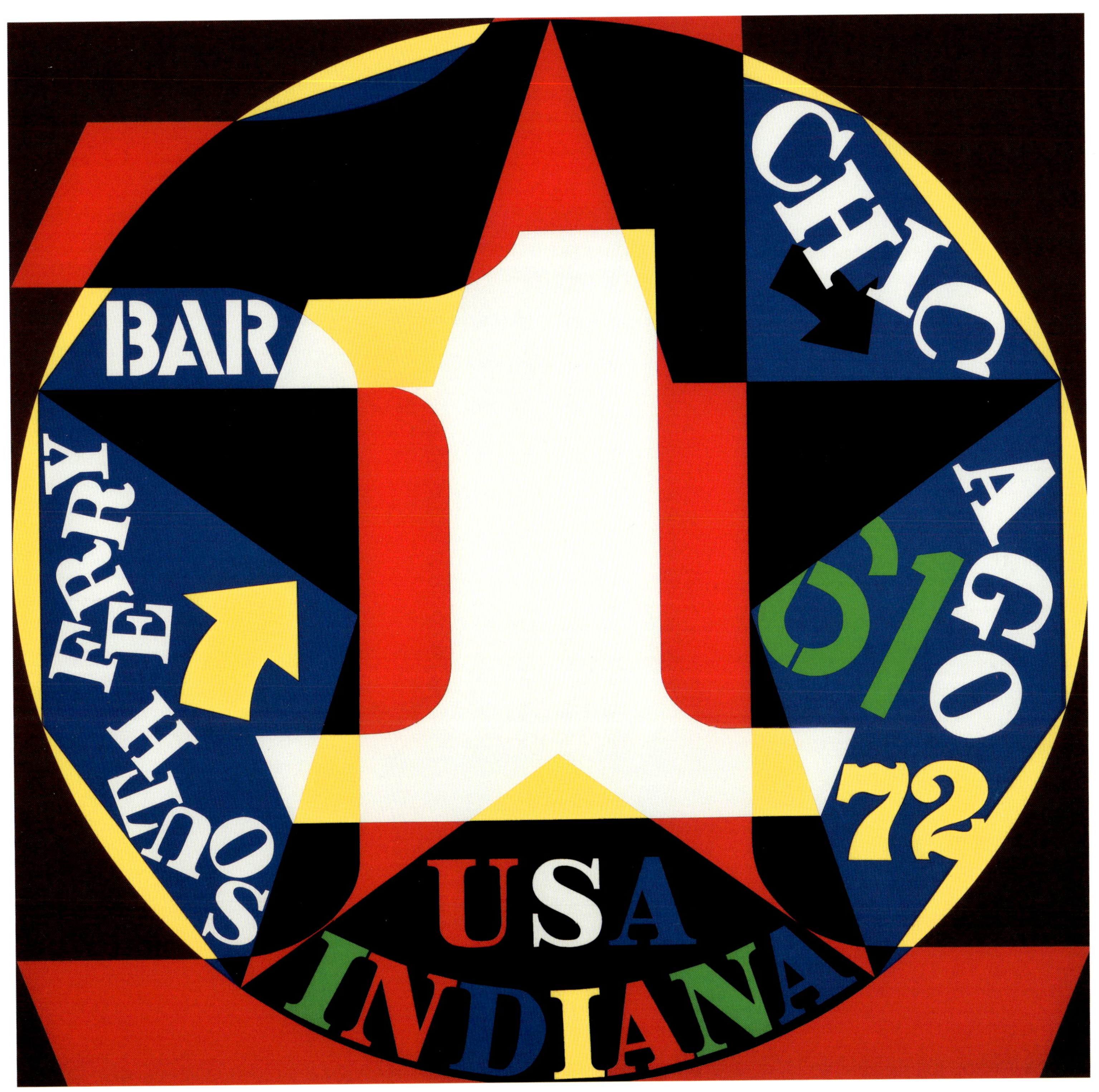

BAR
CHIC
AGO
72
SOUTH
FERRY
USA
INDIANA

Indiana remained on Coenties Slip near THE BATTERY in 1962, a year that saw his first solo show at the Stable Gallery in New York and the appearance of his major painting *The Black Diamond American Dream #2*, which was soon acquired for the private collection of the president of the Museum of Modern Art. The palette of this *Autoportrait* approaches that of *The Black Diamond American Dream #2*. The word JACK appears in both paintings. In *The Black Diamond American Dream #2*, with its pinball imagery, when JACK was paired with JUKE, it represented a slang term for money, as in "Jackpot." It has been posited that it could also refer to John F. (Jack) Kennedy, who was still in the White House in 1962 and who was highly regarded by Indiana.[49] In this *Autoportrait*, however, the reference back to *The Black Diamond American Dream #2*, though reasonable, is apparently nonpertinent. When asked, Indiana simply replied that Jack was "a friend." That is likely to be either Jack Curtis, a former classmate at the School of the Art Institute of Chicago and close friend or, more likely, the fashion designer John "Jack" Kloss, who shared Indiana's studio and with whom he was having a relationship at the time.[50]

PLATE 19

Decade: Autoportrait 1962, 2009

screenprint

edition of 50

image: 30 1/8 × 30 1/8 in. (76.5 × 76.5 cm);
sheet: 37 1/4 × 36 1/4 in. (94.6 × 92.1 cm)

printed by Brand X Editions, Ltd., New York;
published by G & S Editions, New York

Collection of Morgan Art Foundation, courtesy Marc Salama-Caro

49. A postcard sent by Indiana to the directors of the Stable Gallery from Washington in 1962 bears a photograph of the president on which Indiana wrote: "Glorious in Jack's town." Alison Unruh, ed., *Robert Indiana: New Perspectives* (Ostfildern, Germany: Hatje Cantz, 2012), 124, reprod.

50. Oral history interview with Robert Indiana by Richard Brown Baker; Ryan, *Robert Indiana*, 132.

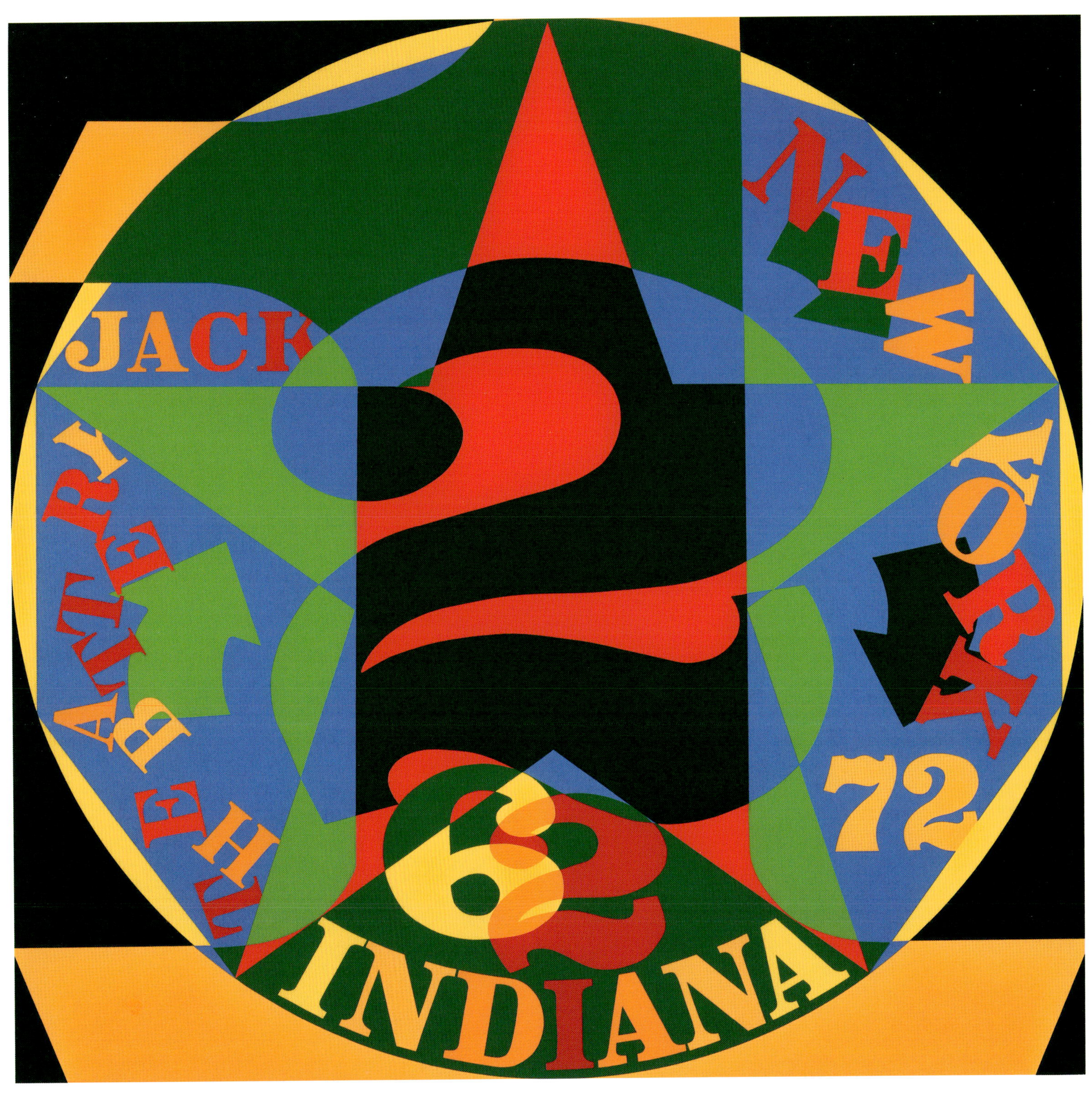

JACK
NEW
YORK
THE BATTERY
72
2
INDIANA

THE SLIP (Coenties Slip) remained Indiana's address through 1963. PARIS, which the artist had visited ten years earlier on a travel fellowship from the Art Institute of Chicago and to which he felt no inducement to return, is referenced here to mark the destination not for the artist but for his paintings, namely, some of his early *Numbers*, which, according to Indiana, the American Cultural Center was showing to "reluctant Paris."[51] As usual with Indiana, DIE has a multilayered meaning. It had been paired with EAT in paintings since 1962. He singled out those two words as favorites at the time, and they became integral components of his *American Dream* cycle as well as stand-alone diptychs. He always associated these two words with a vivid memory of his mother, as mentioned, but in the consumerist world of Pop art, they also described American overindulgence. Indiana acknowledged that the combination of EAT and DIE was a commentary on "the consumers of America" (an interesting turn of phrase) and also had something to say perhaps about "the destiny of all organisms."[52] The more personal nature of the *Autoportraits* would suggest that the inclusion of DIE in 1963 might have yet another connotation, and Indiana admitted to that: "For instance, the word Die does appear frequently, and it appears in a year, say, like 1963, when there was a major assassination."[53] President John F. Kennedy was shot in Dallas on November 22, 1963.

PLATE 20

Decade: Autoportrait 1963, 2009

screenprint

edition of 50

image: 30 1/8 × 30 1/8 in. (76.5 × 76.5 cm);
sheet: 37 1/4 × 36 1/4 in. (94.6 × 92.1 cm)

printed by Brand X Editions, Ltd., New York;
published by G & S Editions, New York

Collection of Morgan Art Foundation, courtesy Marc Salama-Caro

51. Oral history interview with Robert Indiana by Richard Brown Baker; "Autochronology," in *Robert Indiana* (1968), 55.
52. Diamonstein, *Inside New York's Art World*, 158.
53. Ibid., 162.

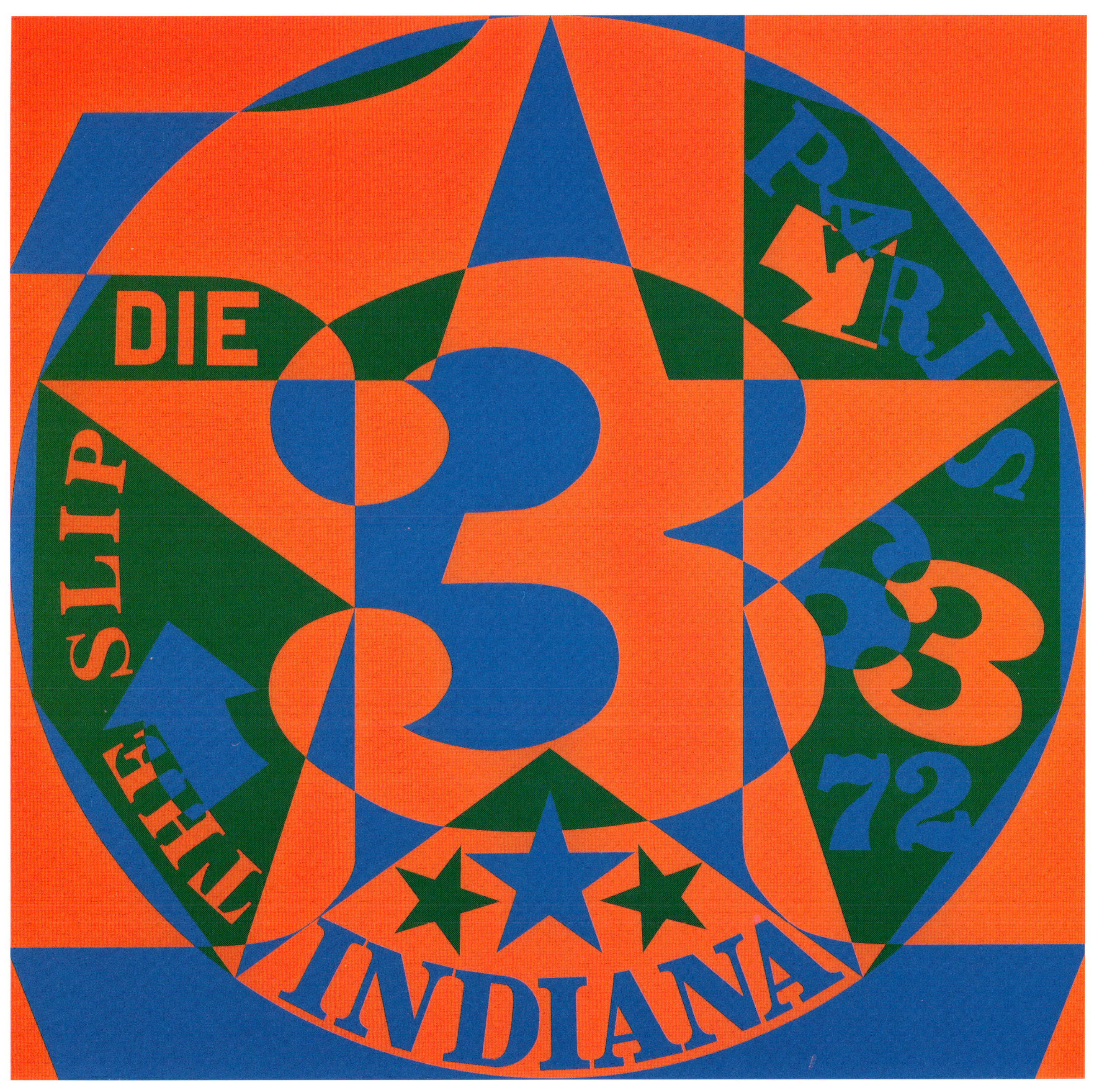

DIE
SLIP
THE
PARIS
3
72
INDIANA

With DIE appearing in the 1963 *Autoportrait*, it is little surprise that EAT, its habitual partner in Indiana's work, followed in 1964. The three-letter verb, which the artist appropriated from common roadside signage and which had particular associations with his mother's employment in diners, loomed large in the artist's work this year. It served to fulfill Indiana's first public commission, from the architect Philip Johnson, in the form of a twenty-foot electrified sign to adorn the exterior of the New York State Pavilion at the New York World's Fair, in the company of works by his friends Andy Warhol, James Rosenquist, Robert Rauschenberg, and Ellsworth Kelly. EAT was also the title of one of Warhol's early film projects, which was shot, according to Indiana, in 1964.[54] The film was a twenty-minute portrait of Indiana doing nothing more than slowly eating a mushroom, which Warhol slowed down even further to a forty-minute running time. It was shot in Indiana's third-floor studio at 25 Coenties Slip. This address, shortened to COENTIES, appears in the *Autoportrait* in the usual geographical position at the lower left. LONDON, which unlike Paris was a city that Indiana enjoyed, was referenced for the artist's inclusion in that year's Tate Gallery exhibition *Painting and Sculpture of a Decade '54–'64*.

PLATE 21

Decade: Autoportrait 1964, 2009

screenprint

edition of 50

image: 30 ⅛ × 30 ⅛ in. (76.5 × 76.5 cm);
sheet: 37 ¼ × 36 ¼ in. (94.6 × 92.1 cm)

printed by Brand X Editions, Ltd., New York;
published by G & S Editions, New York

Collection of Morgan Art Foundation, courtesy Marc Salama-Caro

54. "Autochronology," in *Robert Indiana* (1968), 55; Ryan, *Robert Indiana*, 126, says it was "shot late in 1963."

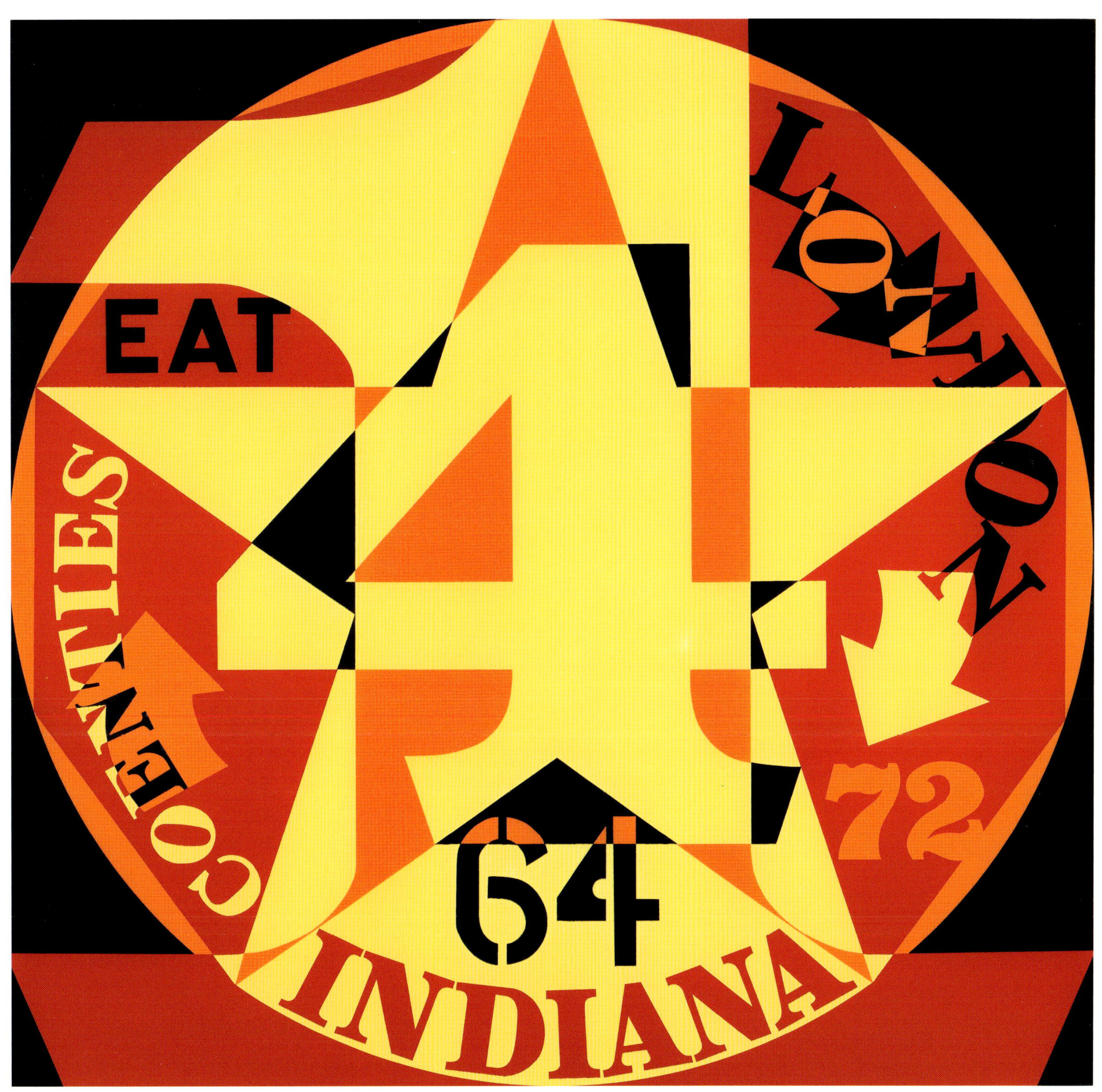
EAT
COENTIES
64
72
INDIANA

CHIEF, at five letters, was the longest word Indiana had inscribed on one of his anthropomorphic herms, made from a repurposed wood beam found in his dockside neighborhood between 1960 and 1962. This herm was inspired by Longfellow's 1855 epic poem *The Song of Hiawatha*, as was his 1961 painting *THE CALUMET* (see Plate 4), "mating" these two works in Indiana's mind.[55] The painting, owned by Brandeis University, was hanging in the White House in 1965 as part of the White House Festival of the Arts to which another "chief"—the commander-in-chief, Lyndon B. Johnson—invited the artists for a dinner on the East Lawn.[56] CHIEF, appearing in the Spencerian script made famous by Coca-Cola, anchored this patriotic red, white, and blue *Autoportrait*. ● WASHINGTON loomed large for Indiana in 1965. He was awarded an entire room at that year's *29th Biennial Exhibition of Contemporary American Painting* at the Corcoran Gallery of Art, and his 1963 painting *THE FIGURE FIVE* was displayed at the Senate Office Building at the invitation of Indiana Senator Birch Bayh, in anticipation of the state's sesquicentennial celebration in 1966. It then hung for two years in the White House at the invitation of the National Collection of the Fine Arts (now the Smithsonian American Art Museum).[57] SPRING, in the usual address location in the *Autoportraits*, announced Indiana's forced move from Coenties Slip to make way for urban renewal. He leased the upper two lofts in a five-story former sweatshop luggage factory at 2 Spring Street in lower Manhattan.

PLATE 22

Decade: Autoportrait 1965, 2001

screenprint

edition of 50

image: 30 ⅛ × 30 ⅛ in. (76.5 × 76.5 cm);
sheet: 37 ¼ × 36 ¼ in. (94.6 × 92.1 cm)

printed by Brand X Editions, Ltd., New York;
published by G & S Editions, New York

Collection of Morgan Art Foundation, courtesy Marc Salama-Caro

55. Ryan, *Robert Indiana*, 118.
56. "Autochronology," in *Robert Indiana* (1968), 57.
57. Ibid.

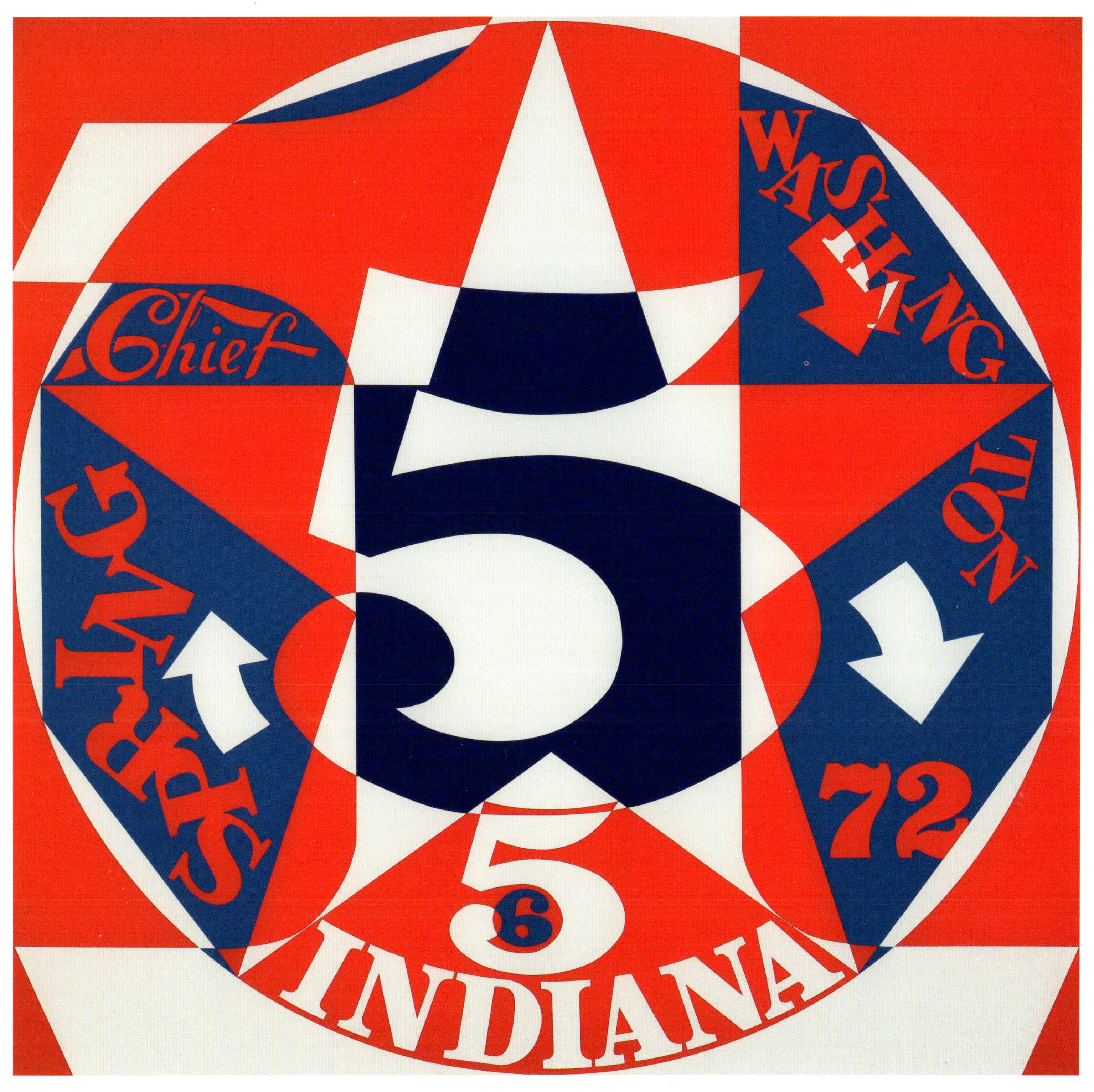
Chief
WASHINGTON
SPRING
5
72
5
6
INDIANA

With his new studio/home at the corner of Spring Street and the BOWERY, 1966 was the year of LOVE. Various configurations of the *LOVE* painting, with its vibrant red, green, and blue color scheme, dominated Indiana's third solo show at the Stable Gallery in New York to the extent that he referred to it as the "*LOVE* Show."[58] That palette, also used for this *Autoportrait,* was common to the Phillips 66 sign, which has personal connections for the artist (see Plate 2). The connection is deepened by the italicizing and skewing of the 66 of the painting's date and the 666 at the upper left, which follow the typographic style of the oil company's logo. The latter reference is to the painting *USA 666* (Christie's, New York, May 13, 2008), which was begun in 1964 but finished in 1966. It debuted in the first month of that year in the annual exhibition *Painting and Sculpture Today* at the John Herron Art Institute (now Indianapolis Museum of Art). On that occasion, Indiana delivered a lecture at the museum, which marked his first return in fourteen years to the state that had provided him with his "nom de brush" in 1958.[59]

PLATE 23

Decade: Autoportrait 1966, 2009

screenprint

edition of 50

image: 30 1/8 × 30 1/8 in. (76.5 × 76.5 cm);
sheet: 37 1/4 × 36 1/4 in. (94.6 × 92.1 cm)

printed by Brand X Editions, Ltd., New York;
published by G & S Editions, New York

Collection of Morgan Art Foundation, courtesy Marc Salama-Caro

58. Ibid., 58.
59. Oral history interview with Robert Indiana by Richard Brown Baker.

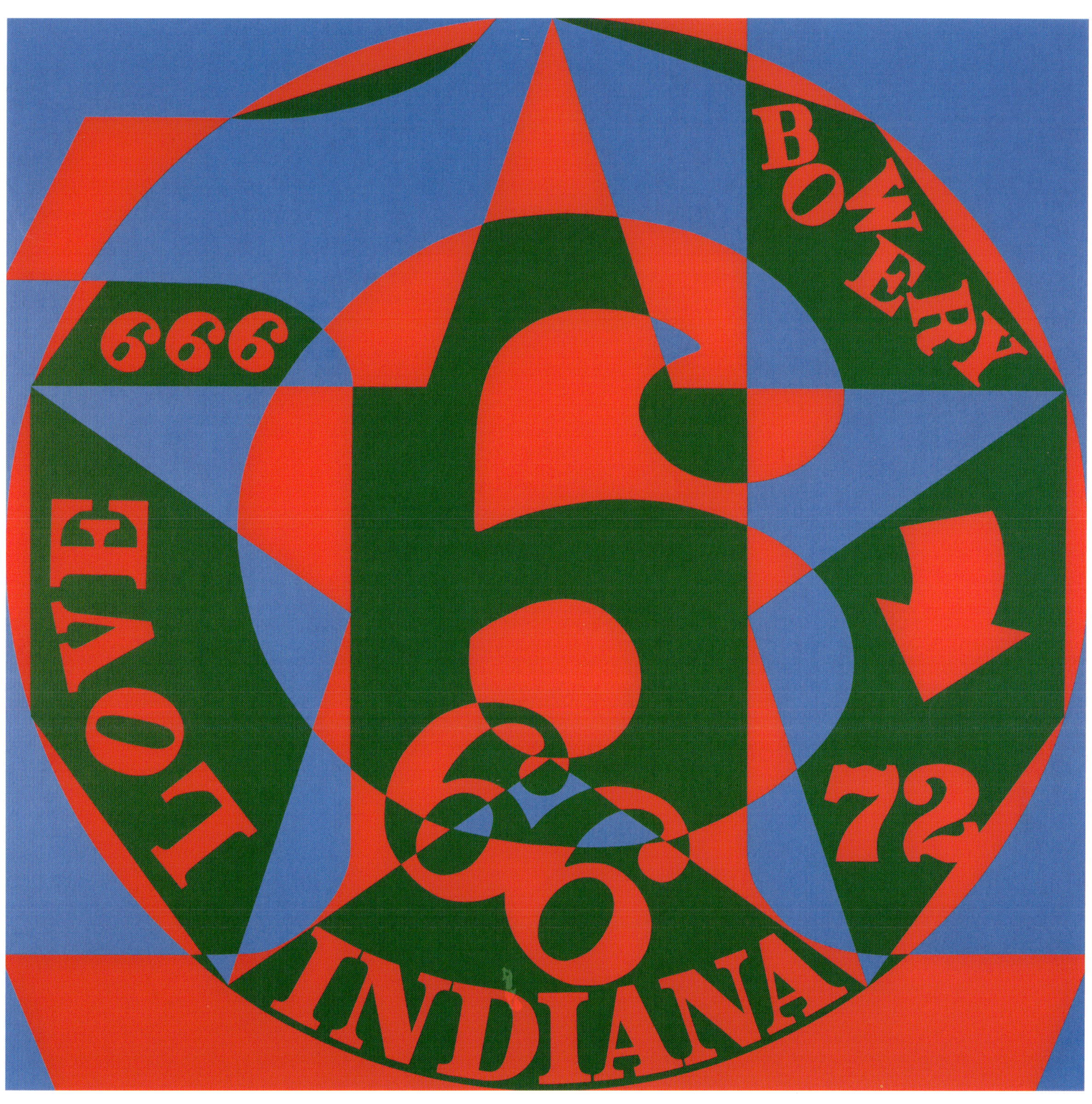
BOWERY
666
LOVE
72
INDIANA

If 1966 was the year of LOVE, 1967 was dominated by MOTHER. Having worked four years on his *Mother and Father* diptych (page 28), Indiana finally completed it to his satisfaction. The canvases were shown in January 1967 at the Walker Art Center in Minneapolis; the event coincided with the Walker's Center Opera Company production of *The Mother of Us All*, which featured set and costume designs by Indiana. The opera, written in 1946 by Virgil Thomson with a libretto by his friend Gertrude Stein, chronicles the life of the suffragette Susan B. Anthony. Indiana admired Stein for her writing and knew Thomson, with whom he exchanged works in 1966: his painting *YIELD, BROTHER VIRGIL* for the composer's piano portrait of Indiana, *Edges*.[60] When Thomson invited Indiana to make the designs, the artist felt he was "predestined" to do so, as he shared part of his name with one of the opera's characters—Indiana Elliot.[61] ● EIR was an abbreviation for Eire (Ireland). Indiana's *LOVE* wall was shown in *Rosc '67*, the first quadrennial exhibition of modern art held in November on the grounds of the Royal Dublin Society. The exhibition, whose title is an old Gaelic word meaning the poetry of vision, was organized by James Johnson Sweeney, a former curator at the Museum of Modern Art, New York, and until 1960 the director of the Solomon R. Guggenheim Museum.[62] BOWERY again referred to the location of Indiana's studio-residence.

PLATE 24

Decade: Autoportrait 1967, 2009

screenprint

edition of 50

image: 30 ⅛ × 30 ⅛ in. (76.5 × 76.5 cm);
sheet: 37 ¼ × 36 ¼ in. (94.6 × 92.1 cm)

printed by Brand X Editions, Ltd., New York;
published by G & S Editions, New York

Collection of Morgan Art Foundation, courtesy Marc Salama-Caro

60. Ryan, *Robert Indiana*, 103.
61. Carl J. Weinhardt Jr., *Robert Indiana* (New York: Harry N. Abrams, 1990), 126.
62. "Autochronology," in *Robert Indiana* (1968), 59.

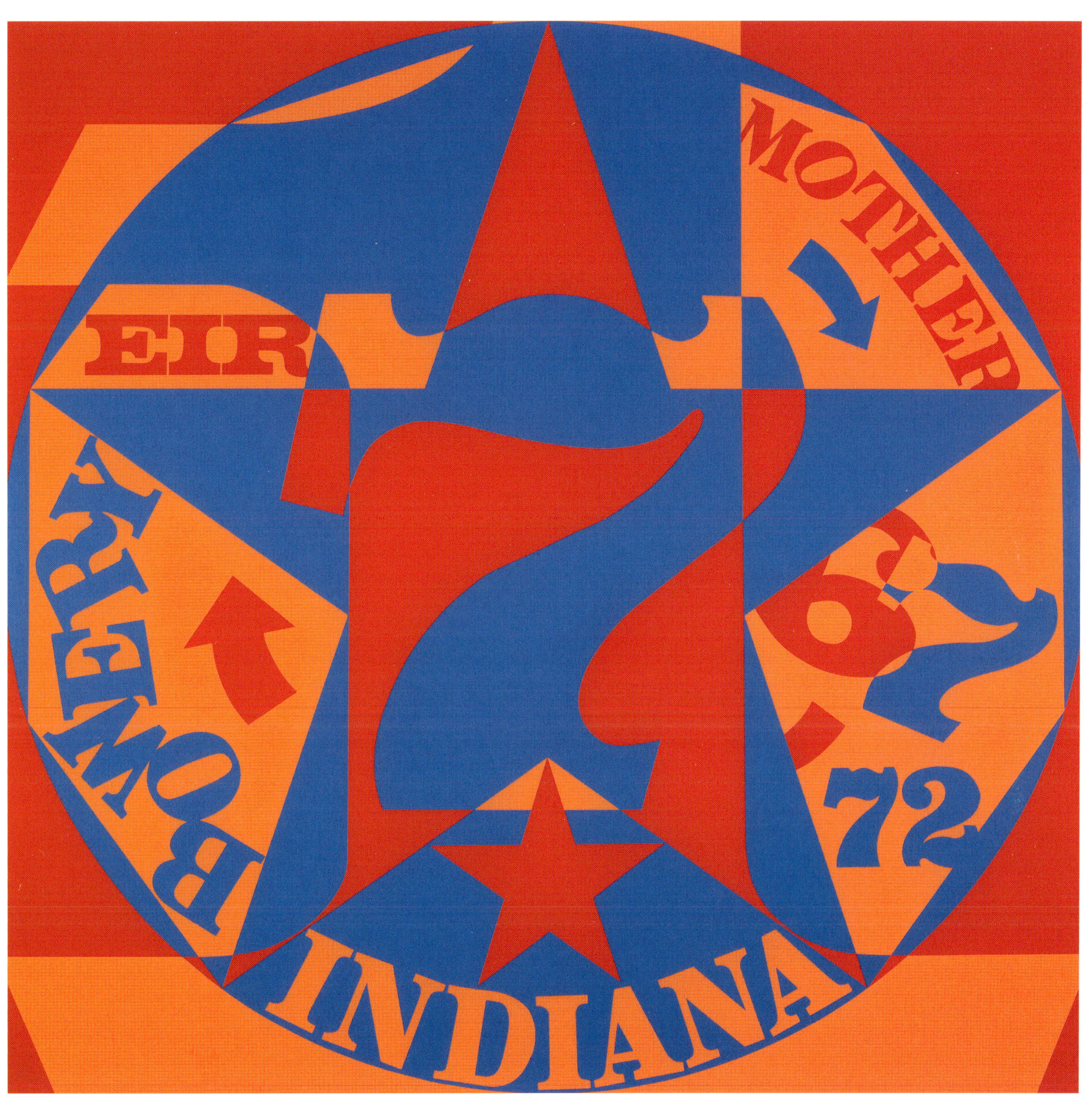
EIR
MOTHER
BOWERY
72
INDIANA

In this work, the Bowery becomes BOUWERIE in recognition of the street's origin in the seventeenth century as the road that ran north from New Amsterdam to Director-General Peter Stuyvesant's farm (*bouwerij*). The other two references, ASP and COLORADO, allude to Indiana's two-month stint in the summer of 1968 as an artist-in-residence at the Aspen Center for Contemporary Art, where he had a role, he said, in "spreading culture." As Indiana explained, the Center was "part of the Aspen Institute of Humanistic Studies and the goal is to make the American businessman a Renaissance man."[63]

PLATE 25

Decade: Autoportrait 1968, 2001

screenprint

edition of 50

image: 30 1/8 × 30 1/8 in. (76.5 × 76.5 cm);
sheet: 37 1/4 × 36 1/4 in. (94.6 × 92.1 cm)

printed by Brand X Editions, Ltd., New York;
published by G & S Editions, New York

Collection of Morgan Art Foundation, courtesy Marc Salama-Caro

63. "Robert Indiana, Signs of the Times," *Indianapolis Star Magazine*, September 8, 1968, 41.

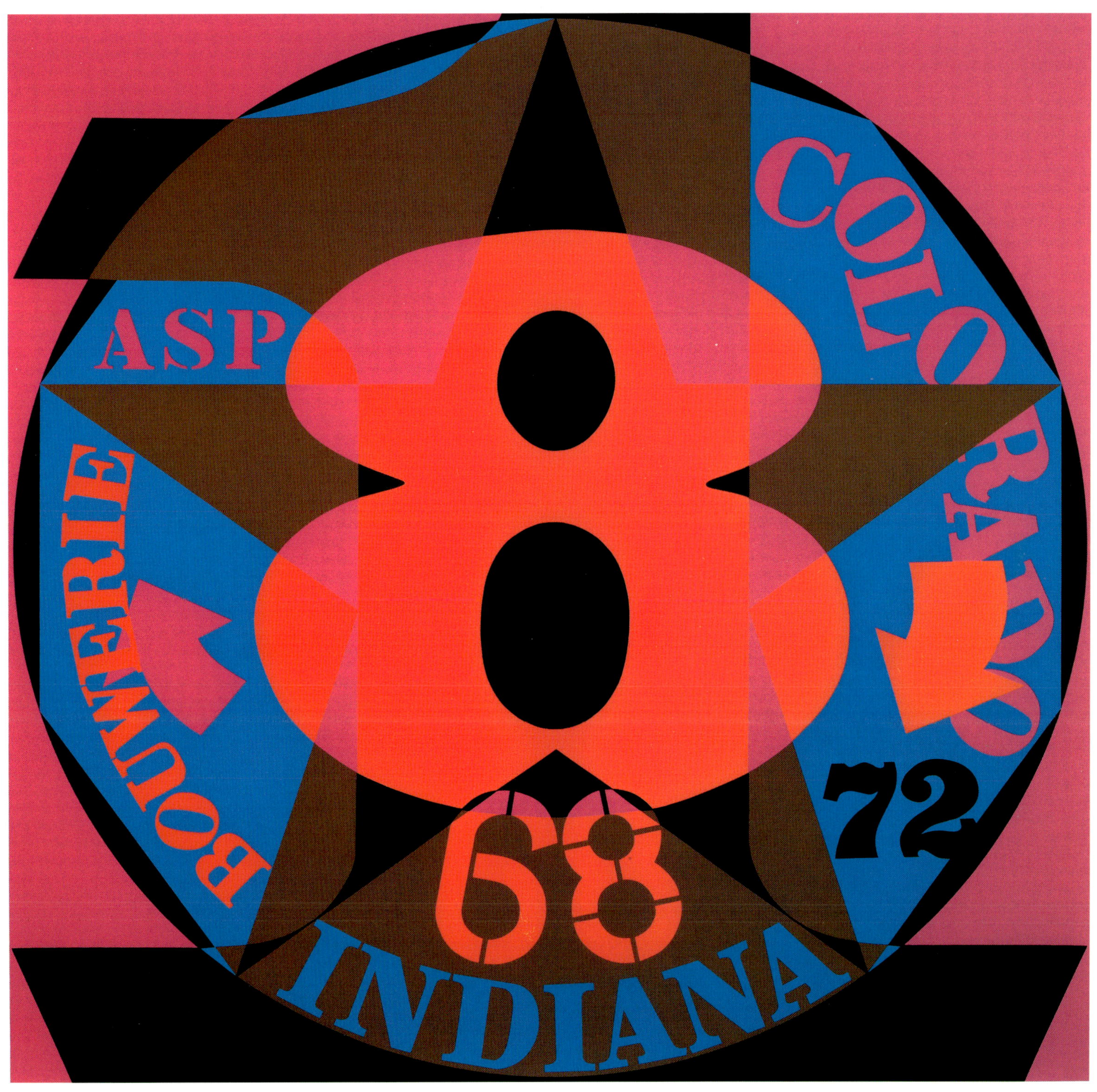
8
ASP
COLORADO
BOUWERIE
72
68
INDIANA

Even as the Bowery was becoming somewhat gentrified in the 1960s with the arrival of artists such as Indiana, Louise Nevelson, Mark Rothko, Roy Lichtenstein, and Adolph Gottlieb, it remained Manhattan's SKID ROW, as Indiana reelingly indicated in this work. ● The year of this *Autoportrait*, 1969, marked an event, seemingly unremarkable at the time, that would be of major import in his life. As he described in 1977 in his revised "Autochronology":

> **1969** - Indiana discovers Vinalhaven. . . . [While visiting the Skowhegan School of Painting and Sculpture in Maine, which Indiana had attended in 1953] meets Eliot Elisofon, formerly staff photographer for *Life* magazine, painter, collector of primitive art, world traveler, and writer, who invites Indiana and his assistant, William Katz, to visit his summer home on the island of Vinalhaven in Penobscot Bay. The ferry there leaves from Rockland, American hometown of Louise Nevelson, Indiana's neighbor on Spring Street. Staying over just one night, the next day upon leaving, he finds his future home and studio, hundred-year-old Odd Fellows lodge building, once named "The Star of Hope."[64]

At the time, he could not have foreseen this eventuality, but within two weeks of Indiana's visit, Elisofon purchased the abandoned derelict building in order that the artist might use it as a summer studio.[65] In 1977, four years after Elisofon's death, Indiana bought the building from his estate.[66] This first visit is memorialized in the *Autoportrait* painted eight years after the fact with the words PENOBSCOT and ELI (short for Eliot and Elisofon). The Star of Hope Lodge is indicated by the three oval links at the base of the image, which quote from a carved relief in the pediment above the building's second-story window, and which Indiana knew to be the symbol of the Odd Fellows' ideals: "the first ring is friendship and the third ring is truth and the middle ring is *love*."[67]

PLATE 26

Decade: Autoportrait 1969, 2009

screenprint

edition of 50

image: 30 ⅛ × 30 ⅛ in. (76.5 × 76.5 cm);
sheet: 37 ¼ × 36 ¼ in. (94.6 × 92.1 cm)

printed by Brand X Editions, Ltd., New York;
published by G & S Editions, New York

Collection of Morgan Art Foundation, courtesy Marc Salama-Caro

64. "Autochronology," in *Robert Indiana* (1977), 51.
65. Diamonstein, *Inside New York's Art World*, 164.
66. Michael Komanecky, *Robert Indiana and the Star of Hope* (Rockland, Maine: Farnsworth Art Museum, 2009), 51.
67. Diamonstein, *Inside New York's Art World*, 163.

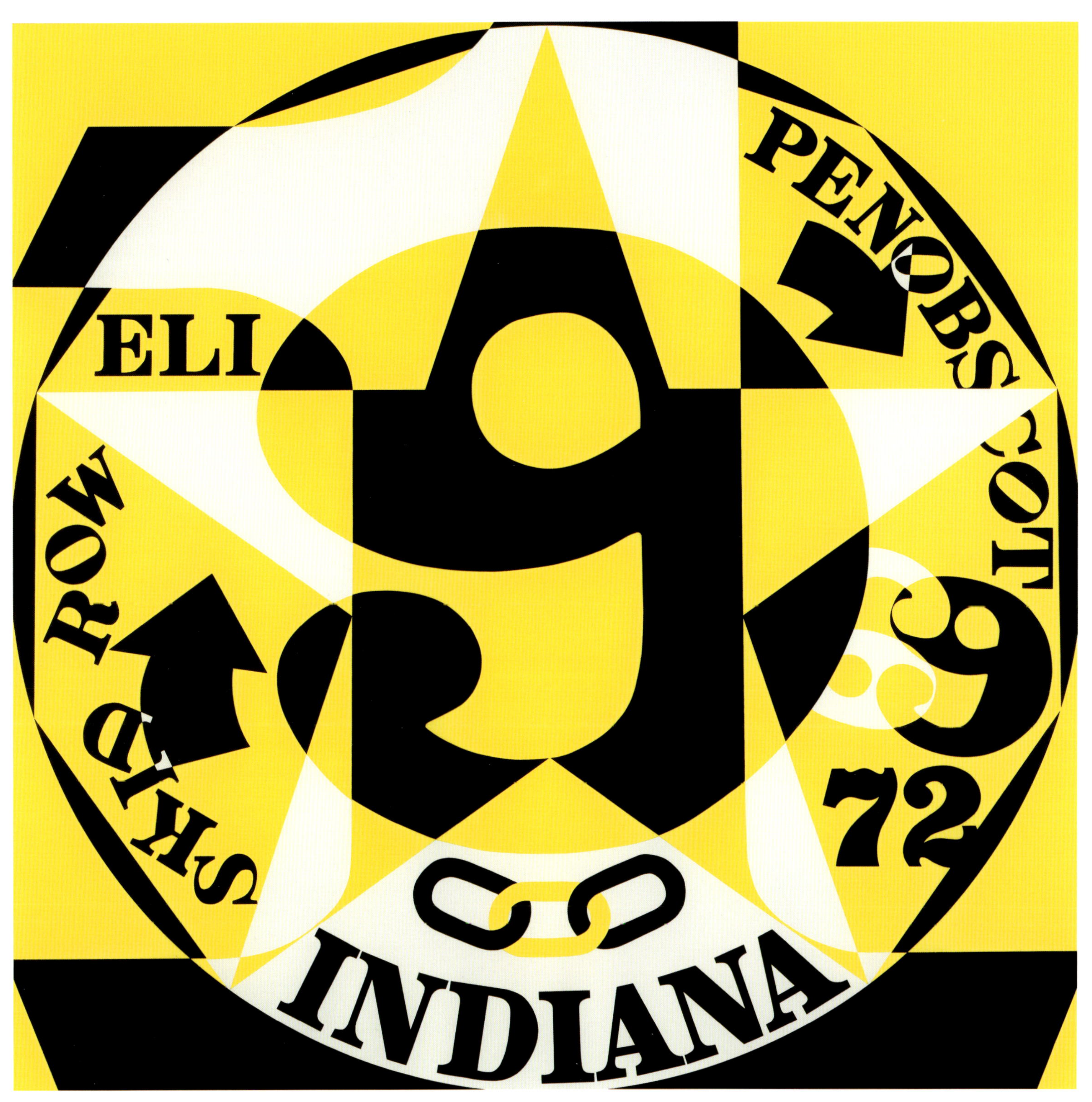
PENOBSCOT
ELI
SKID ROW
9
72
INDIANA

This *Autoportrait* does not derive from the second set of *Decade: Autoportraits* painted between 1972 and 1977 as do the previous ten screenprints (Plates 17–26), but from the first set of canvases finished in 1971 and exhibited at the Galerie Denise René in New York the following year. There are many similarities between the two sets, including the basic structure of personal emblems: the number 1 superimposed on a five-pointed star touching every other angle of a decagon (for decade) inscribed in the circle of the yearly cycle. Even the palette for the two 1969 *Autoportraits* is the same. Yellow, black, and white (along with red) were colors that Indiana associated with his "winter" paintings, thus forming an appropriate color scheme for the tenth and last painting of the cycle.[68] ● The visit to Vinalhaven did not yet have the import in 1971 that it would have in 1977, when the second set was completed and Indiana was at the point of permanently relocating to Maine. Here, VINALHAVEN and SKID ROW are joined by HALLELUJAH and TIGER. The former refers to a 1969 painting, *HALLELUJAH (JESUS SAVES)* (Collection of the artist), and the second to a current favorite among Indiana's various pet cats.[69]

PLATE 27

Decade: Autoportrait 1969, 1973

color lithograph

edition of 125

image: 10 11⁄16 × 10 9⁄16 in. (27.1 × 26.8 cm);
sheet: 22 1⁄8 × 14 1⁄8 in. (56.2 × 35.9 cm)

printed by Fernand Mourlot, Paris;
published by XXe Siècle, Paris and New York

Collection of the artist

68. Oral history interview with Robert Indiana by Richard Brown Baker.
69. "Cat-Lady of Manhattan," *New York Magazine*, July 22, 1968, 62.

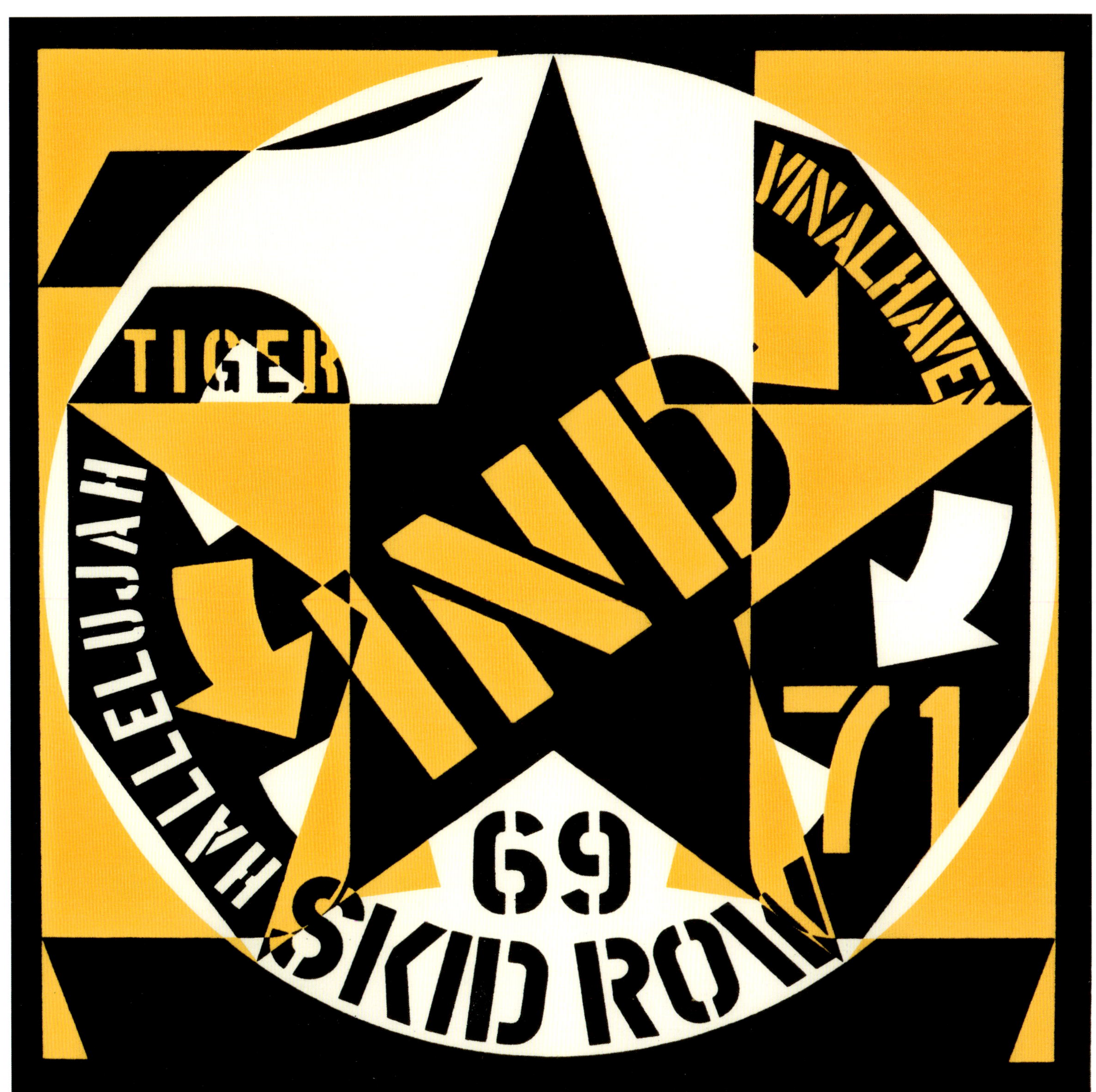

TIGER
HALLELUJAH
69
SKID ROW
71

ART was commissioned by the Indianapolis Museum of Art for the inauguration of its new building in October 1970. The museum already owned Indiana's key *LOVE* painting, 1966, and was soon to become the permanent home of his just-completed twelve-foot-tall Cor-ten steel *LOVE* sculpture. The museum (when known as the John Herron Art Institute) was a place the artist knew from a young age. He had taken Saturday art classes there in 1945 while a student at Arsenal Technical High School and had been offered a scholarship to Herron's art school upon graduation the following year. Intent on moving beyond Indianapolis, however, Indiana joined the Army Air Corps to take advantage of the GI Bill, which enabled him to attend the School of the Art Institute of Chicago.[70] With the exception of going home to bury his mother in 1949, he would not return again until 1966.[71] ● *ART* first appeared in May 1970 as a poster for the exhibition *American Art Since 1960* at the Princeton University Art Museum, and it became a word that occupied Indiana's attention in the early 1970s with variants in oil, print, and sculpture, in typical Indiana fashion.[72] ART and the other brief words in Indiana's lexicon endorsed an observation made many years earlier by one of his favorite authors, Gertrude Stein, which a close colleague, William Katz, cited in reference to Indiana's use of such words in his art: "I began to think then and later more and more that Americans can and do express everything oh yes everything in words of one syllable made up of two letters or three or at most four."[73]

PLATE 28

ART, 1970

screenprint

edition unrecorded

34 ¾ × 25 in. (88.3 × 63.5 cm)

printed for the American Poster Company by Domberger KG, Stuttgart, West Germany

Collection of the Indianapolis Museum of Art, 71.85

70. "Autochronology," in *Robert Indiana* (1968), 51.
71. Ibid., 57.
72. "Autochronology," in *Robert Indiana* (1977), 51.
73. William Katz, "Polychrome—Polygonals: Robert Indiana's New American Geometry," in *Robert Indiana* (1977), 20.

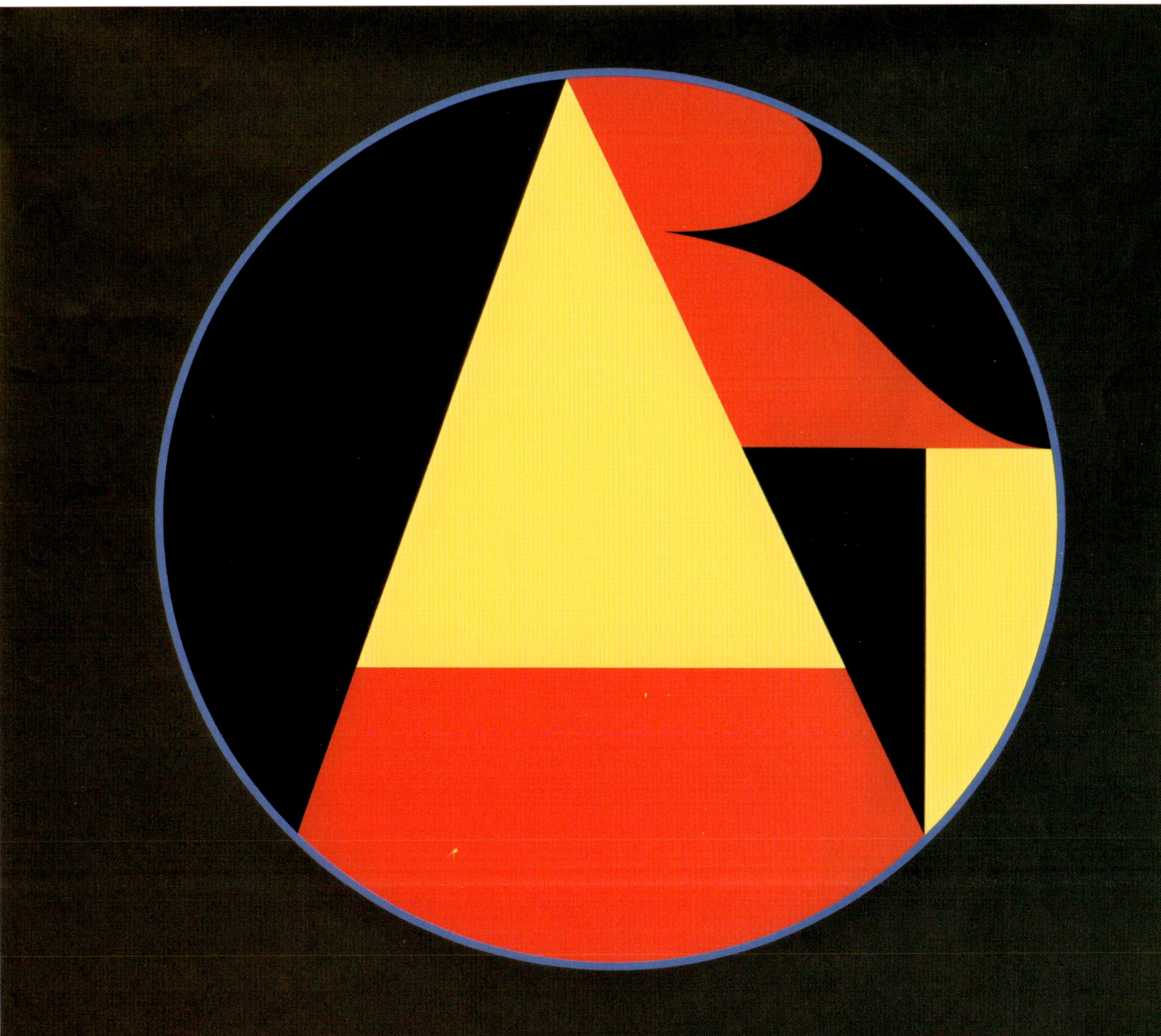
INDIANAPOLIS
MUSEUM
OF
ART
INAUGURAL EXHIBITIONS
25 OCTOBER 1970
For Mrs Samuel R. Harrell
THE AMERICAN POSTER COMPANY
PRINTED IN WEST GERMANY BY DOMBERGER KG
© ROBERT INDIANA 1970

In 1970 Indiana accepted one of his few public commissions. He was to create a seven-foot-square painting to grace the lobby of Indiana National Bank's new thirty-seven-story tower in the artist's hometown of Indianapolis. The subject must have been almost irresistible to the artist. The bank's address was One Indiana Square, which not only seemed to demand representation by a cardinal number but also explicitly suggested a geometrical treatment—two elements highly identified with Indiana's work. The address even included his name (albeit his adopted one). ● This image may be considered a portrait of the place as it shares the format of the *Autoportraits* that Indiana was painting at the same time: a star within a circle over which a number 1 was imposed. But there was also a geographical logic to this format, as Indiana well knew. Indianapolis is the state capital (indicated on maps by a star) and is known as the "Circle City" because of the circular street that runs around the Soldiers' and Sailors' Monument at the heart of the city. This street was the center point of Alexander Ralston's 1821 plat of Indianapolis, which spread out from the circle in a grid of streets that came to mark the area known as "The Mile Square."

PLATE 29

The Diamond ONE (One Indiana Square)

from *The American Dream*, 1997

screenprint

edition of 395

image: 16 × 16 in. (40.6 × 40.6 cm);
sheet: 22 ½ × 17 ½ in. (57.2 × 44.5 cm)

printed and published by Marco Fine Arts
Contemporary Atelier, El Segundo, California

Courtesy of Taglialatella Galleries, New York

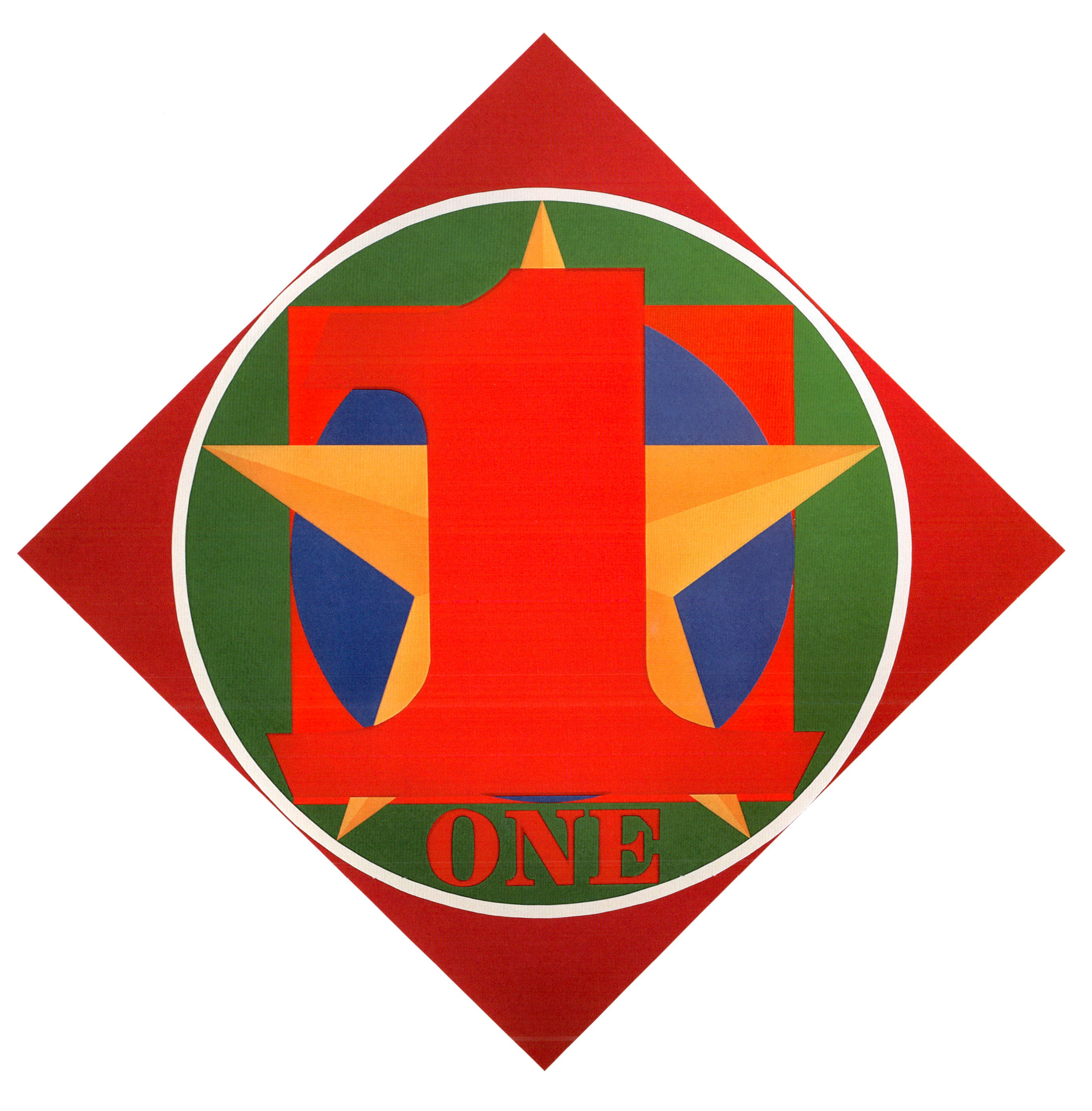
ONE

PLATE 30

PICASSO, 1974

screenprint

edition of 90

image: 24 × 20 in. (61 × 50.8 cm);
sheet: 30 × 22 in. (76.2 × 55.9 cm)

printed by Styria Studio, New York; published by Propyläen Verlag, Berlin, and Pantheon-Presse, Rome

Collection of Morgan Art Foundation, courtesy Marc Salama-Caro

Indiana was delighted to join sixty international artists in honoring Pablo Picasso's ninetieth birthday in 1971 by contributing to a portfolio of prints. For this commission, Indiana reversed his normal practice of having his prints follow from his paintings.[74] Picasso, along with Georges Braque, Fernand Léger, and Joan Miró, shared Indiana's interest in the painted word.[75] But his resultant screenprint portrait of Picasso revealed a deeper fascination, as Indiana explained in 1977:

> But in thrashing around for a theme—I mean, how do you deal with the subject of Picasso? It's so big. I could have done a portfolio on Picasso—what occurred to me was, Picasso was a name changer too, having started out in life as Pablo Ruiz. Some of his early canvases were signed Pablo Ruiz. I can't imagine that a man could have achieved what Picasso achieved with an unpronounceable name, at least for the English, and the change certainly was magical for him. It also was extra magical because the PP, Pablo Picasso, back to back, is a mirror monogram. And, just by coincidence, he was born in 1881, which is one of those rare mirror dates that anyone can be born on, so I would say, somewhere up there the stars were fixed for him.[76]

"He who changes his name is wearing a mask," Indiana said elsewhere in the same interview,[77] and accordingly, in the print, Picasso's mirrored initials form a mask. In the outer circle, starting from the star at the top and rolling in a clockwise direction, are, in chronological order, the place names of Picasso's main residences throughout his life, beginning with his birthplace in Málaga, Spain, and ending with Mougins, France, where he died in 1973. Because Indiana procrastinated, the print was not completed until 1974 and he could therefore include Picasso's death date. Springing off the doubled P are several other alliterative references: the artist's first name, PABLO; the name of his only son, PAULO; the last name of an early friend and studio mate in Barcelona, PALLARES; and the city where the artist settled in 1900, PARIS. In the upper quadrant is a dove echoing Picasso's well-known peace symbol and MA JOLIE, the title of two cubist paintings that Indiana knew well: the first, of 1911–12, was in the collection of the Museum of Modern Art, New York, and the second, of 1913, was at the Indianapolis Museum of Art. The title, which appears in each Picasso painting, has the dual significance of being both a popular song of that era and a pet name for Picasso's lover Marcelle Humbert, a layered meaning much to Indiana's liking.

74. Diamonstein, *Inside New York's Art World*, 156.
75. "Conversations with Robert Indiana," in *Robert Indiana* (1977), 27.
76. Diamonstein, *Inside New York's Art World*, 156–7.
77. Ibid., 163.

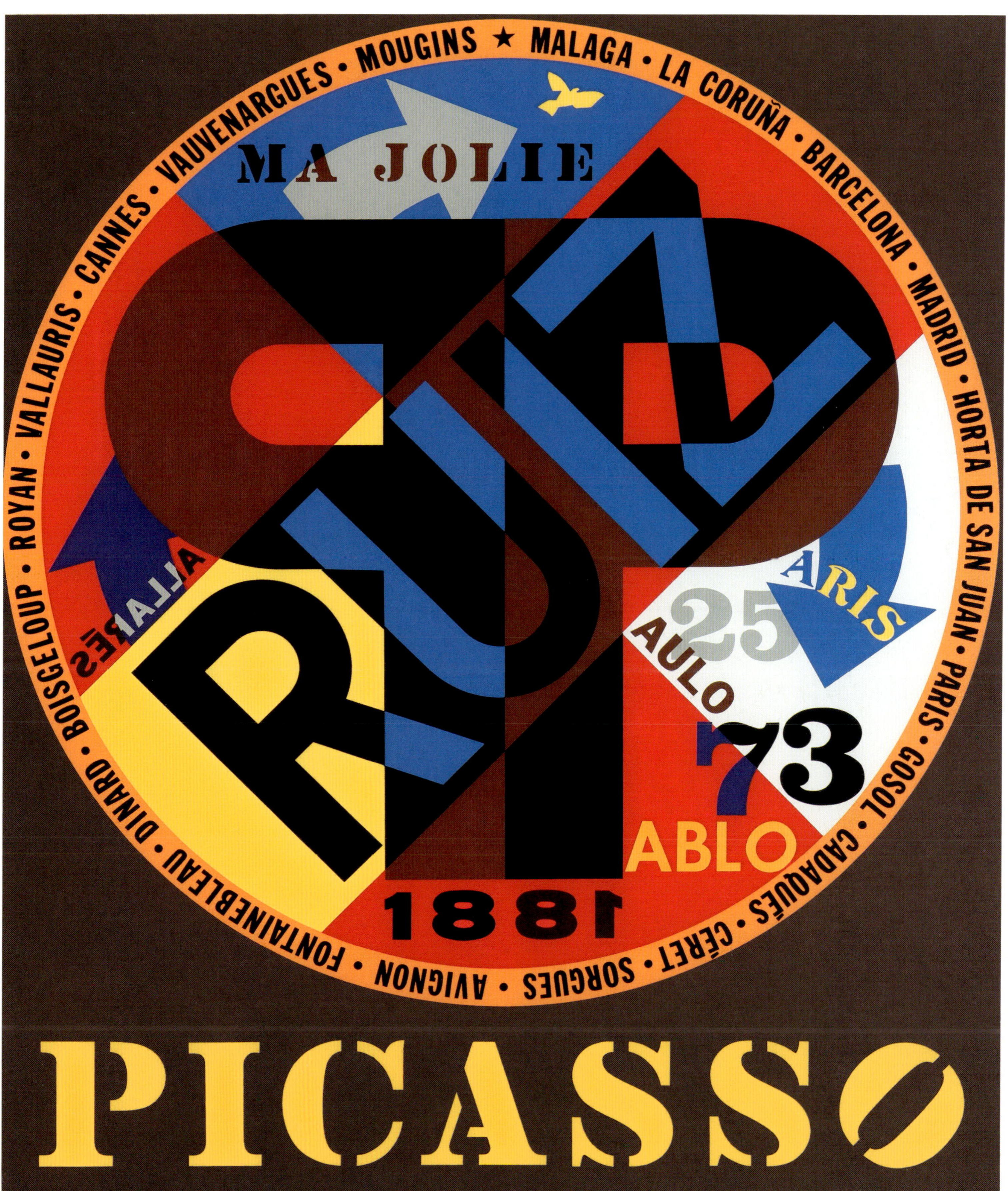
MOUGINS ★ MALAGA • LA CORUÑA • BARCELONA • MADRID • HORTA DE SAN JUAN • PARIS • GOSOL • CADAQUÉS • CÉRET • SORGUES • AVIGNON • FONTAINEBLEAU • DINARD • BOISGELOUP • ROYAN • VALLAURIS • CANNES • VAUVENARGUES
MA JOLIE
PARIS
25
73
ABLO
1881
PICASSO

PLATE 31

Decade: Autoportrait '70, VINALHAVEN

from *Vinalhaven Suite*, 1980

screenprint

edition of 125

image: 24 × 24 in. (61 × 61 cm);
sheet: 26 ¾ × 26 ¾ in. (68 × 68 cm)

printed by Domberger KG, Filderstadt;
published by Multiples, Inc., New York

Collection of Morgan Art Foundation, courtesy Marc Salama-Caro

Indiana's second series of screenprinted *Autoportraits*, covering the decade of the 1970s, repeats the format of the *Autoportraits* for the 1960s: a number 1 (the image of self) superimposed on a star (an American and a personal emblem) within a decagon (for decade) and inscribed in a circle (synonymous in Indiana's work with the eternal cycle of life). In three instances in the series—1970, 1975, and 1979—the palette is the same as its counterpart in the 1960s. Floating around these constants are various names of places, people, or things that were significant to a given year. Anchoring each image is a place on or around the island of Vinalhaven, which Indiana had discovered in 1969 and then visited annually until 1978, when he settled there permanently. ● In the opening print of the series, the 0 for 70 is superimposed on the 1 in overlapping shades of gray, appropriate for the dawn of the decade. EQUINOX reinforces this beginning, with 1970 being Indiana's first season working in VINALHAVEN. In that year, ART became Indiana's new verbal/visual construct, appearing on two posters in 1970 (see Plate 28), a screenprint in 1971, and a painting and a polychrome aluminum sculpture in 1972, reflecting his constant exploration of variation. As he said on the topic in 1981: "I usually work in a series, one suggests the next. Perhaps because I am an only child, I like many progeny."[78] ● On each of the prints of the series, a name preceded by "St." or a variation thereon appears at the lower left. Sometimes these have definable meanings, but sometimes, as in the case of ST. MICHAEL, they do not, recalling Sam Hunter's description of the earlier set of *Autoportraits*: "Their associations are coded in words easily understood on at least one level, though here and there secondary meanings remain stubbornly private and opaque."[79]

78. "Robert Indiana Chats about Life and Painting," *Bangor Daily News*, June 6–7, 1981.
79. Sam Hunter, *Robert Indiana* (New York: Galerie Denise René, 1972), unpaginated.

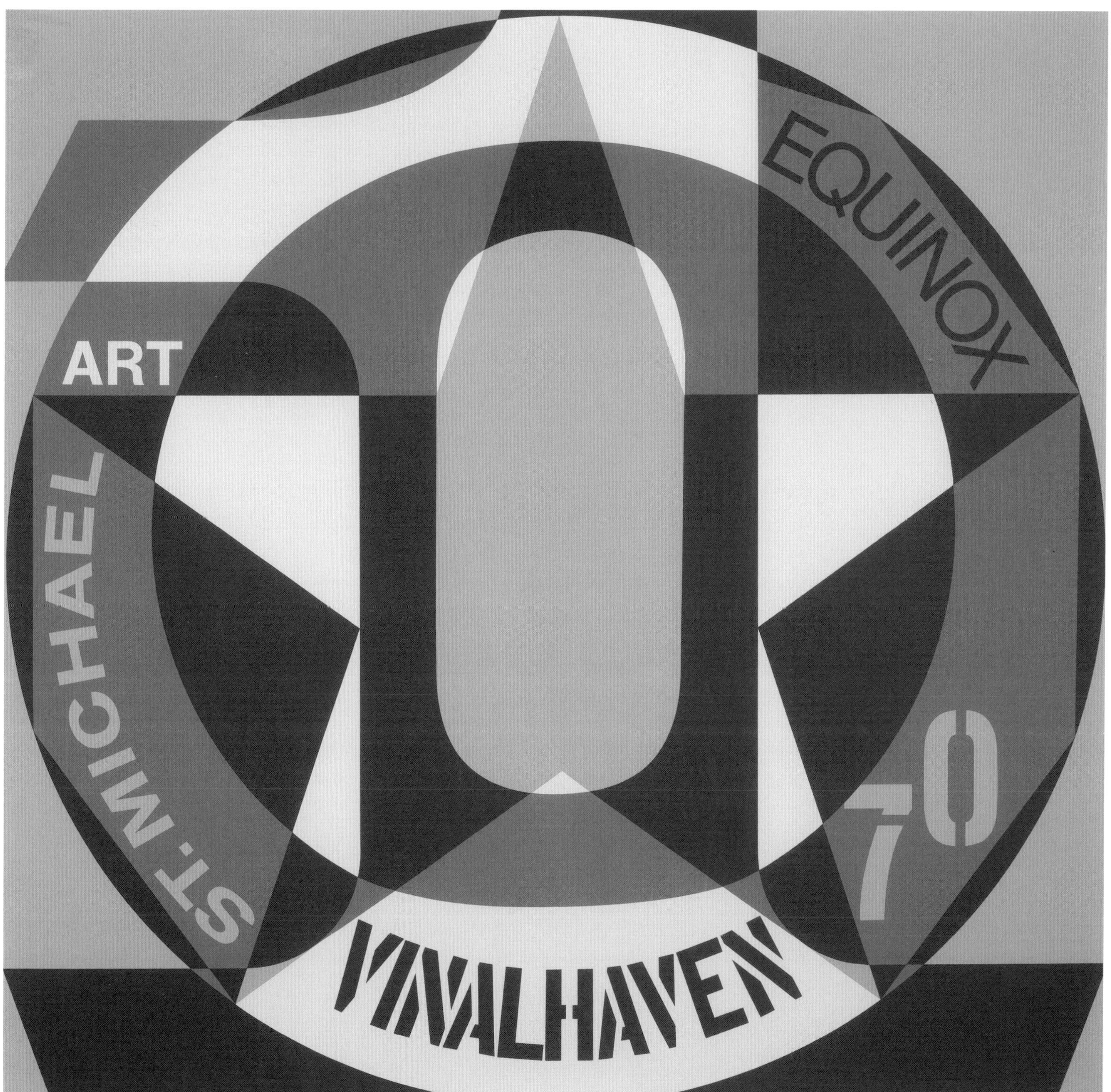
EQUINOX
ART
ST. MICHAEL
70
VINALHAVEN

The preparatory materials for these screenprints were not oil paintings as in the 1960s series but *papiers collés*, collages of paper glued down to form a composition. The medium was pioneered in 1912 by the cubists Picasso and Braque, to whom Indiana admitted his indebtedness. ● ISLE AU HAUT lies to the east of Vinalhaven. APOGEE makes an astronomical mate to EQUINOX, which appeared in the previous print, but here refers also to the title of a painting that Indiana exhibited in 1971 at the Louisiana Museum of Modern Art in Humlebæk, Denmark. LOVE reappears, this time in reference to a three-ton, twelve-foot-tall Cor-ten steel sculpture that was unveiled at the new Indianapolis Museum of Art in a monumental sculpture exhibition titled *Seven Outside*, which opened on October 25, 1970. The work was acquired by the museum at the conclusion of the exhibition in early 1971.

PLATE 32

Decade: Autoportrait '71, ISLE AU HAUT

from *Vinalhaven Suite*, 1980

screenprint

edition of 125

image: 24 × 24 in. (61 × 61 cm);
sheet: 26 ¾ × 26 ¾ in. (68 × 68 cm)

printed by Domberger KG, Filderstadt;
published by Multiples, Inc., New York

Collection of Morgan Art Foundation, courtesy Marc Salama-Caro

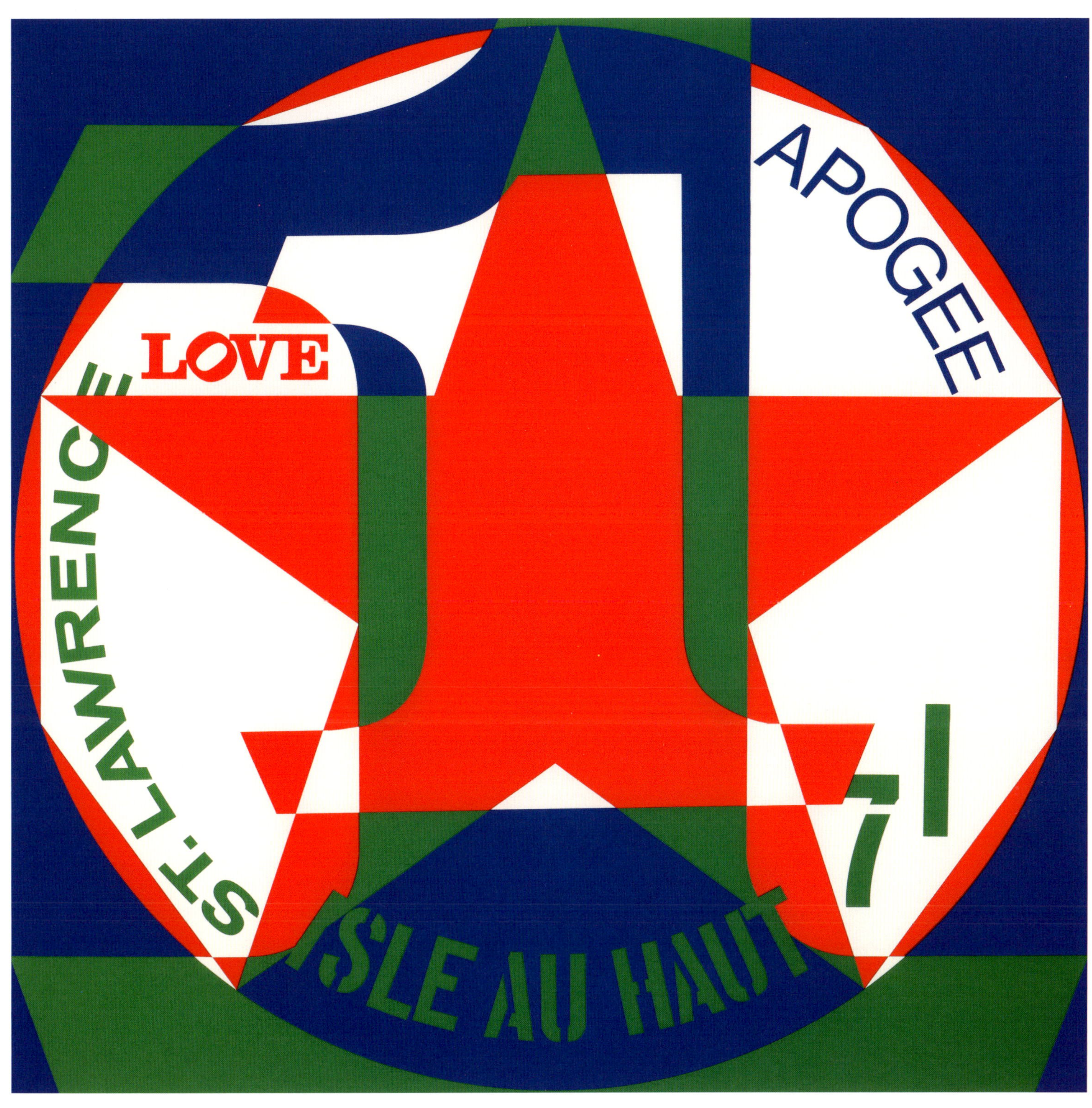
APOGEE
LOVE
ST. LAWRENCE
7
ISLE AU HAUT

Based on a conversation with the artist at Colby College in Waterville, Maine, where this suite was displayed in 1981, a reporter noted that the colors used in the 1972 *Autoportrait* were those of Vinalhaven and the surrounding PENOBSCOT Bay: the intense blue of the sea and sky, the deep green of the spruces, and the white of winter snow.[80] The same reporter cited the references to a 1972 vacation Indiana had taken to SAPPHIRE BAY on the east end of ST. THOMAS in the US Virgin Islands. The final reference point, RENÉ, is a nod to the Galerie Denise René. The gallery, with locations in Paris and Düsseldorf, had opened a new branch in New York, and in November 1972 offered Indiana his fourth New York solo show and his first since the 1966 show at the Stable Gallery. The abrupt closing of Stable in 1970, after a trend-setting seventeen-year run, had left Indiana without New York gallery representation.

PLATE 33

Decade: Autoportrait '72, PENOBSCOT

from *Vinalhaven Suite*, 1980

screenprint

edition of 125

image: 24 × 24 in. (61 × 61 cm);
sheet: 26 ¾ × 26 ¾ in. (68 × 68 cm)

printed by Domberger KG, Filderstadt;
published by Multiples, Inc., New York

Collection of the artist

80. "Robert Indiana Chats about Life and Painting," *Bangor Daily News*, June 6–7, 1981.

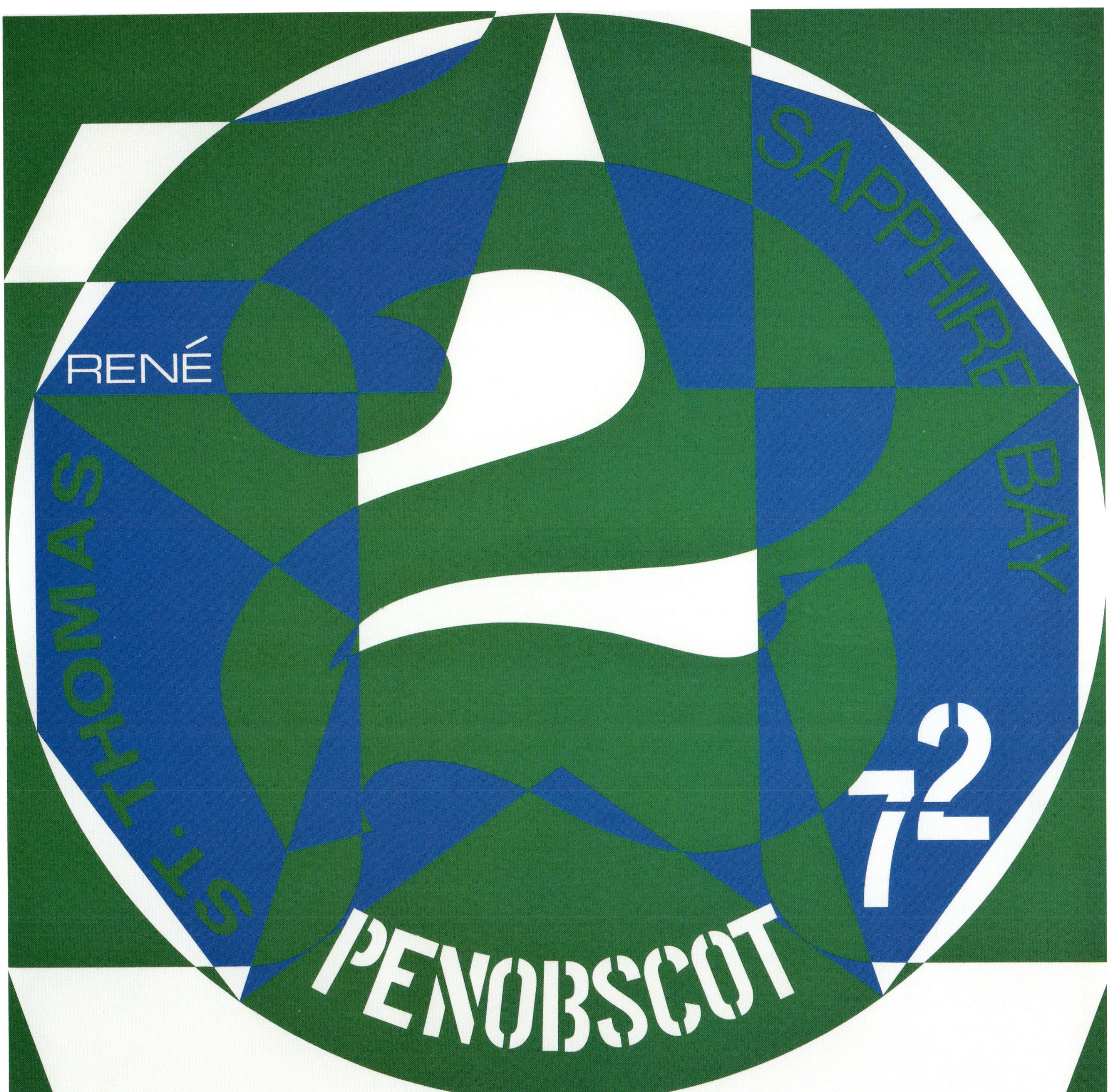
RENÉ
ST. THOMAS
SAPPHIRE BAY
72
PENOBSCOT

As he had in 1972, Indiana here apposes two locales of personal significance, MORNING STAR and CROCKETT COVE. The former was a historically gay-friendly Caribbean beach on the south coast of St. Thomas. The latter was the location on Vinalhaven where photographer Eliot Elisofon had his summer home, to which he first invited Indiana and William Katz in 1969 (see Plate 26). ● The inclusion of US 8¢ in this *Autoportrait* refers to Indiana's $1,000 commission from the US Postal Service to design an 8-cent postage stamp featuring his now universally familiar red, green, and blue *LOVE*. Timed for Valentine's Day, the stamp was issued on January 26, 1973, in the "City of Brotherly Love," Philadelphia. In its combined original issue and 1974 reissue, 330 million *LOVE* stamps were printed, outdistancing any previous commemorative stamp.

PLATE 34

Decade: Autoportrait '73, CROCKETT COVE

from *Vinalhaven Suite*, 1980

screenprint

edition of 125

image: 24 × 24 in. (61 × 61 cm);
sheet: 26 ¾ × 26 ¾ in. (68 × 68 cm)

printed by Domberger KG, Filderstadt;
published by Multiples, Inc., New York

Collection of Morgan Art Foundation, courtesy Marc Salama-Caro

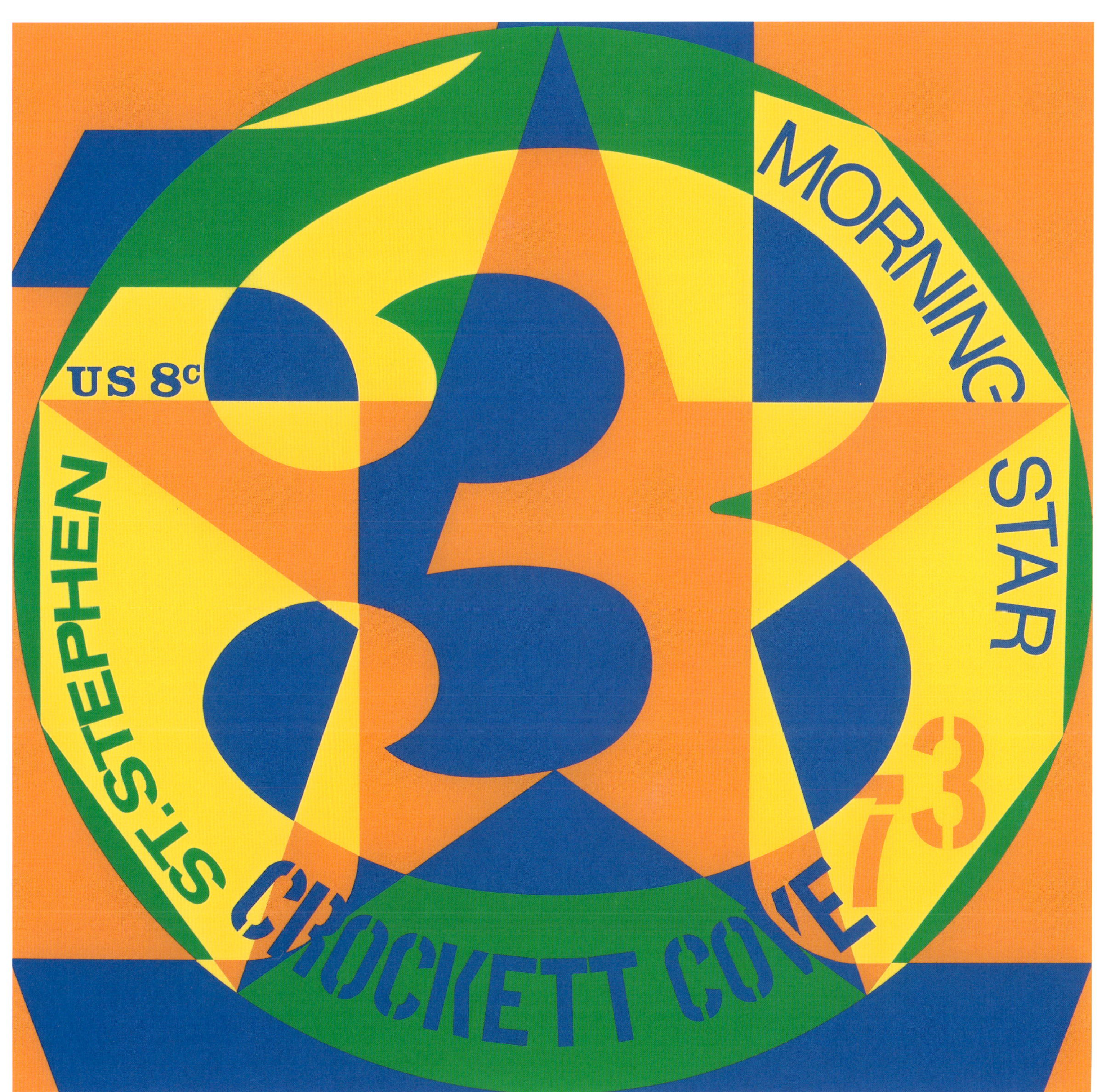
MORNING STAR
US 8c
ST. STEPHEN
CROCKETT COVE
73

The ferry from Rockland, Maine, passes through the many-isled HURRICANE Sound before completing its twelve-mile transit to Vinalhaven. MA JOLIE refers to a cubist painting by Picasso that was cited in Indiana's printed homage, published in 1974, to one of his favorite artists (see Plate 30). VIRGIL is Virgil Thomson, the American composer who had been introduced to Indiana by Andy Warhol ten years earlier and who was again working with Indiana on a new production of the Thomson–Gertrude Stein opera *The Mother of Us All*. When asked about the inclusion of ST. GOODTIME in this *Autoportrait*, Indiana replied that it was the nickname of "a friend," and said nothing more. This same reticence was noted by Richard Brown Baker at the end of his 1963 interview with the artist, which left him feeling that Indiana had not been entirely forthcoming: "I didn't question you about your romantic and emotional life. But I suppose perhaps it's better taste not to," to which Indiana interjected: "No, I don't think that's had very much to do with my development as a painter."[81]

PLATE 35

Decade: Autoportrait '74, HURRICANE

from *Vinalhaven Suite*, 1980

screenprint

edition of 125

image: 24 × 24 in. (61 × 61 cm);
sheet: 26 ¾ × 26 ¾ in. (68 × 68 cm)

printed by Domberger KG, Filderstadt;
published by Multiples, Inc., New York

Collection of Morgan Art Foundation, courtesy Marc Salama-Caro

81. Oral history interview with Robert Indiana by Richard Brown Baker.

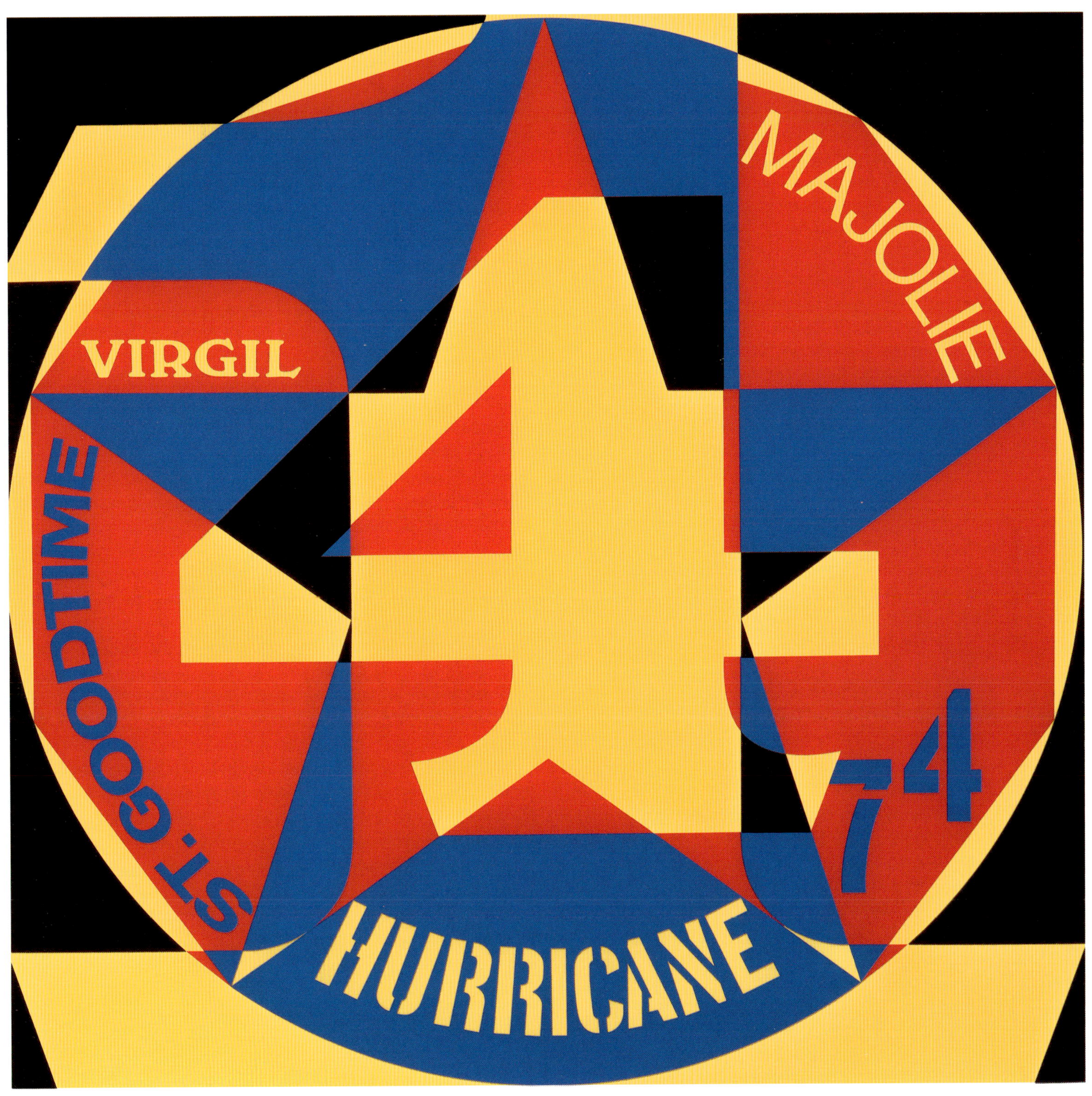
MAJOLIE
VIRGIL
ST. GOODTIME
74
HURRICANE

The red, white, and blue palette for 1975 is a reprise of the 1965 *Autoportrait* (Plate 22), celebrating Indiana's first visit to the White House. That earlier *Autoportrait* was resurrected a decade later for use on the cover of the catalogue for the Corcoran Gallery of Art's *34th Biennial Exhibition of Contemporary American Painting*, which occasioned a return visit to Washington by the artist.[82] TIGER, Indiana's pet cat, also makes a reappearance from the 1969 *Autoportrait* (Plate 27). SHELLEY, "a friend," may be identical to the only person of that name to appear in Indiana's "Autochronology," Shelley Lieberman, who was an assistant working under William Katz on the realization of Indiana's costume and set designs for the 1976 production of *The Mother of Us All*.[83] CARVER'S POND is a tidal basin behind the artist's home in the village of Vinalhaven.

PLATE 36

Decade: Autoportrait '75, CARVER'S POND

from *Vinalhaven Suite*, 1980

screenprint

edition of 125

image: 24 × 24 in. (61 × 61 cm);
sheet: 26 ¾ × 26 ¾ in. (68 × 68 cm)

printed by Domberger KG, Filderstadt;
published by Multiples, Inc., New York

Collection of the artist

82. "Autochronology," in *Robert Indiana* (1977), 53.
83. Ibid., 54.

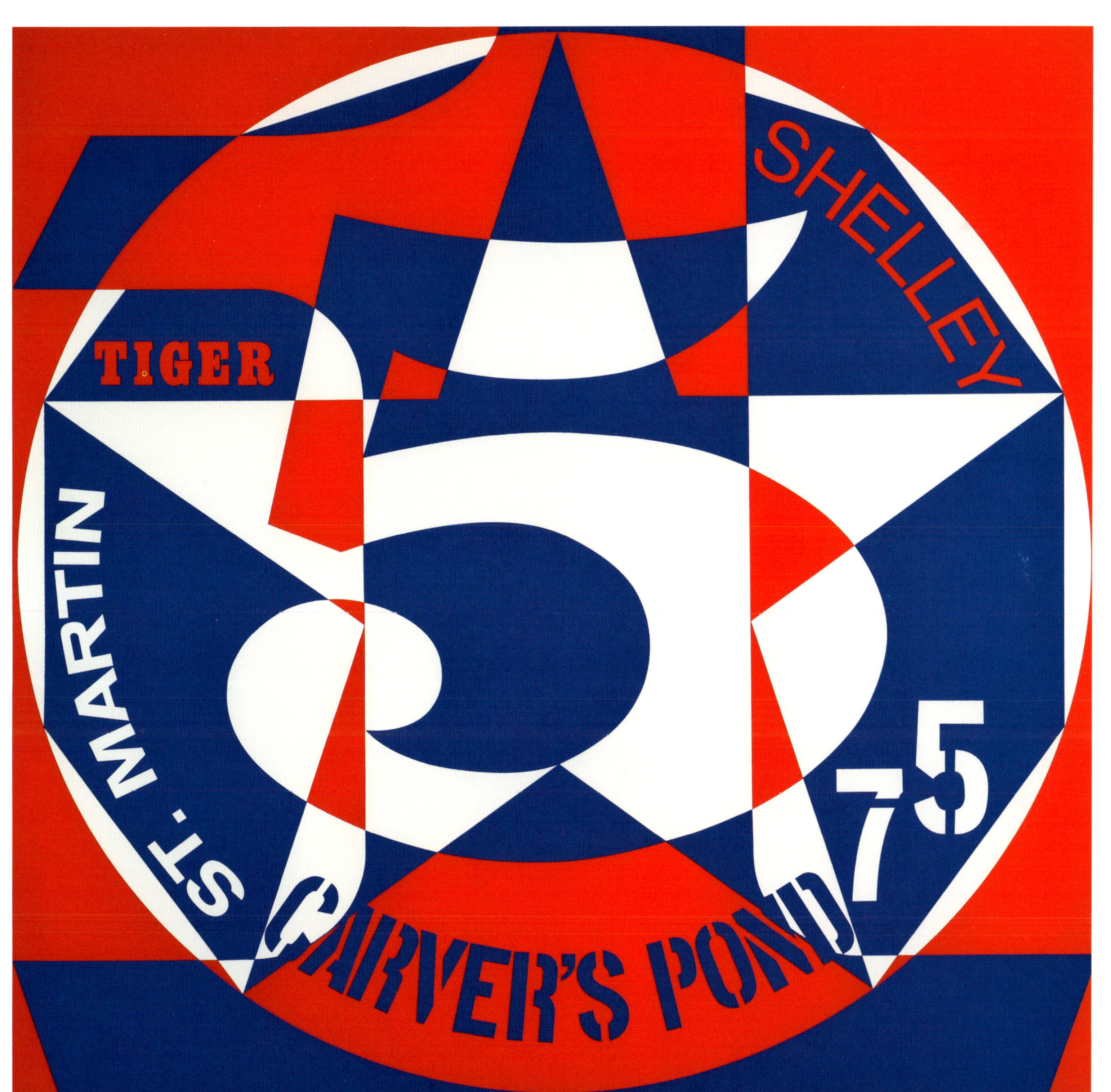
SHELLEY
TIGER
ST. MARTIN
75
CARVER'S POND

Continuing a perambulation around Vinalhaven, Indiana arrives at COOMB'S NECK, the island's easternmost extension. The nation's bicentennial this year is noted with the number 200 at the upper left. As part of the celebration and funded in part by the National Endowment for the Arts, the Santa Fe Opera Company celebrated its twentieth season with a new production of *The Mother of Us All* with new costumes and sets by Indiana, the impact of which the composer Virgil Thomson previewed for the *New York Times*: "The stage will become an enlarged picture—an enormous Robert Indiana painting. If you know what his work looks like, that is exactly what you're going to see."[84] To oversee the production, which opened on August 7, Indiana spent part of the year as an artist-in-residence in SANTA FE.

PLATE 37

Decade: Autoportrait '76, COOMB'S NECK

from *Vinalhaven Suite*, 1980

screenprint

edition of 125

image: 24 × 24 in. (61 × 61 cm);
sheet: 26 ¾ × 26 ¾ in. (68 × 68 cm)

printed by Domberger KG, Filderstadt;
published by Multiples, Inc., New York

Collection of Morgan Art Foundation, courtesy Marc Salama-Caro

84. "Music Notes: Thomson's Opera, Indiana's Painting at Santa Fe," *New York Times*, July 18, 1976.

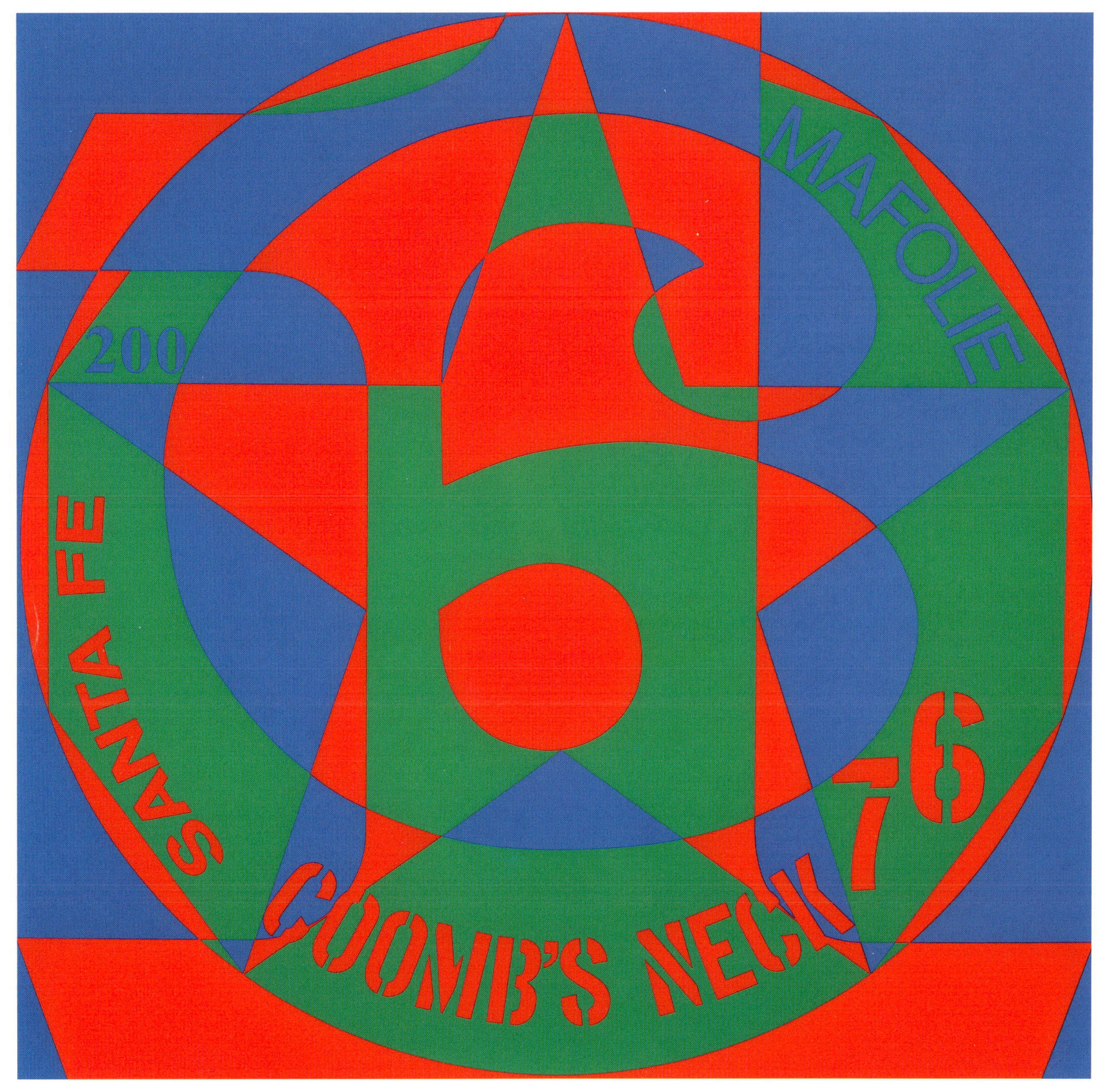
MAFOLIE
200
SANTA FE
76
COOMB'S NECK

The curiously named TIPTOE MT. is a rocky hill overlooking Crockett Cove on the west coast of Vinalhaven. While MECCA and CASABLANCA are two famous destinations in the Islamic world, for Indiana in 1977 they had other meanings. That year he designed the floor for the basketball court shared by the Milwaukee Bucks and the Marquette Warriors in the MECCA (Milwaukee Exposition Convention Center and Arena). CASABLANCA was Indiana's code name for the White House (*casa blanca* in Spanish), to which Indiana was twice invited in 1977: on January 29 to witness the inauguration of President Jimmy Carter, whose campaign Indiana had aided with the design of a poster titled *VOTE*, and later that year in preparation for a symbolic portrait of the president, *AN HONEST MAN HAS BEEN PRESIDENT*, commissioned as a screenprint by the Democratic National Committee and published in 1980 as a fundraiser for Carter's unsuccessful reelection campaign. ● SAN ANTONIO was the ultimate destination for the thirty-two paper-collage costume designs and the twenty-eight Pentel-ink set designs that Indiana made for *The Mother of Us All*; these were given in 1977 to the Marion Koogler McNay Art Institute by local collector Robert L. B. Tobin. That same year, Tobin also served as guest curator for *Robert Indiana*, a large traveling retrospective exhibition that opened at the University of Texas at Austin on September 25.

PLATE 38

Decade: Autoportrait '77, TIPTOE MT.

from *Vinalhaven Suite*, 1980

screenprint

edition of 125

image: 24 × 24 in. (61 × 61 cm);
sheet: 26 ¾ × 26 ¾ in. (68 × 68 cm)

printed by Domberger KG, Filderstadt;
published by Multiples, Inc., New York

Collection of the artist

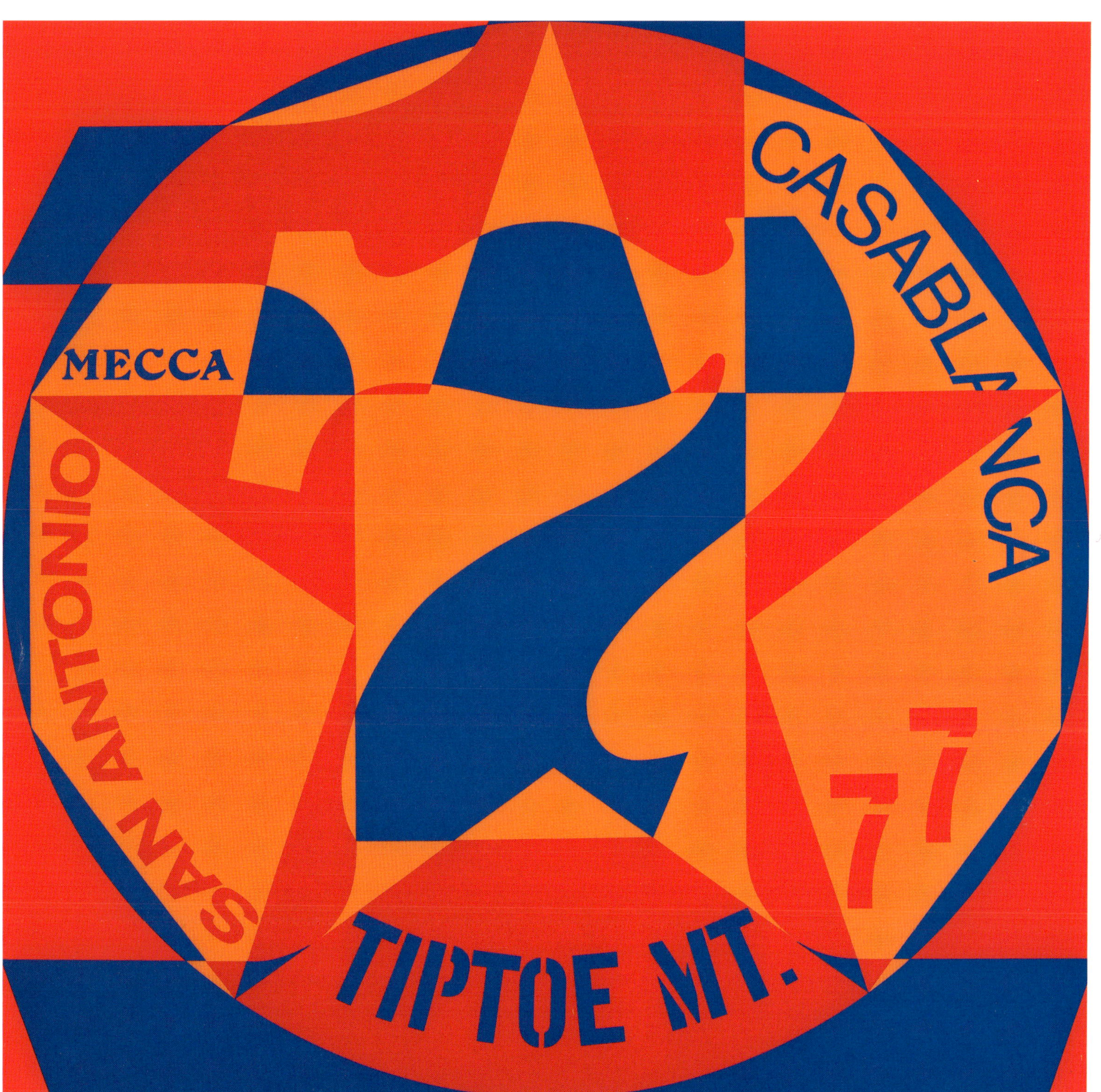
MECCA
CASABLA
NCA
SAN ANTONIO
TIPTOE MT.
7
7

In 1978 Indiana moved permanently into the STAR OF HOPE, the lodge built in 1874 for the Odd Fellows of Vinalhaven, and bid ADIEU to New York. SOUTH BEND, the city in northern Indiana, had personal and professional associations for the artist. It was there, in 1938, that his step-grandmother on his mother's side was shot to death "because she was so mean" by her daughter-in-law Ruby Watters.[85] In 1969 St. Mary's College in South Bend had organized *Robert Indiana Graphics*, the first exhibition devoted to this branch of Indiana's art, and in June 1978 the Art Center in South Bend was the final venue for the traveling retrospective exhibition *Robert Indiana* (see Plate 38). The show was hung in the center's new downtown location in the Century Center, a move for which Indiana produced *SOUTH BEND*, a celebratory color lithograph in the form of an emblematic city map.

PLATE 39

Decade: Autoportrait '78, STAR OF HOPE

from *Vinalhaven Suite*, 1980

screenprint

edition of 125

image: 24 × 24 in. (61 × 61 cm);
sheet: 26 ¾ × 26 ¾ in. (68 × 68 cm)

printed by Domberger KG, Filderstadt;
published by Multiples, Inc., New York

Collection of the Indianapolis Museum of Art, Gift of the Print, Drawing and Photography Study Group in memory of Dr. Thomas Kuebler, 2012.124

85. "A MOTHER IS A MOTHER AND A FATHER IS A FATHER," in *Robert Indiana* (1968), 36.

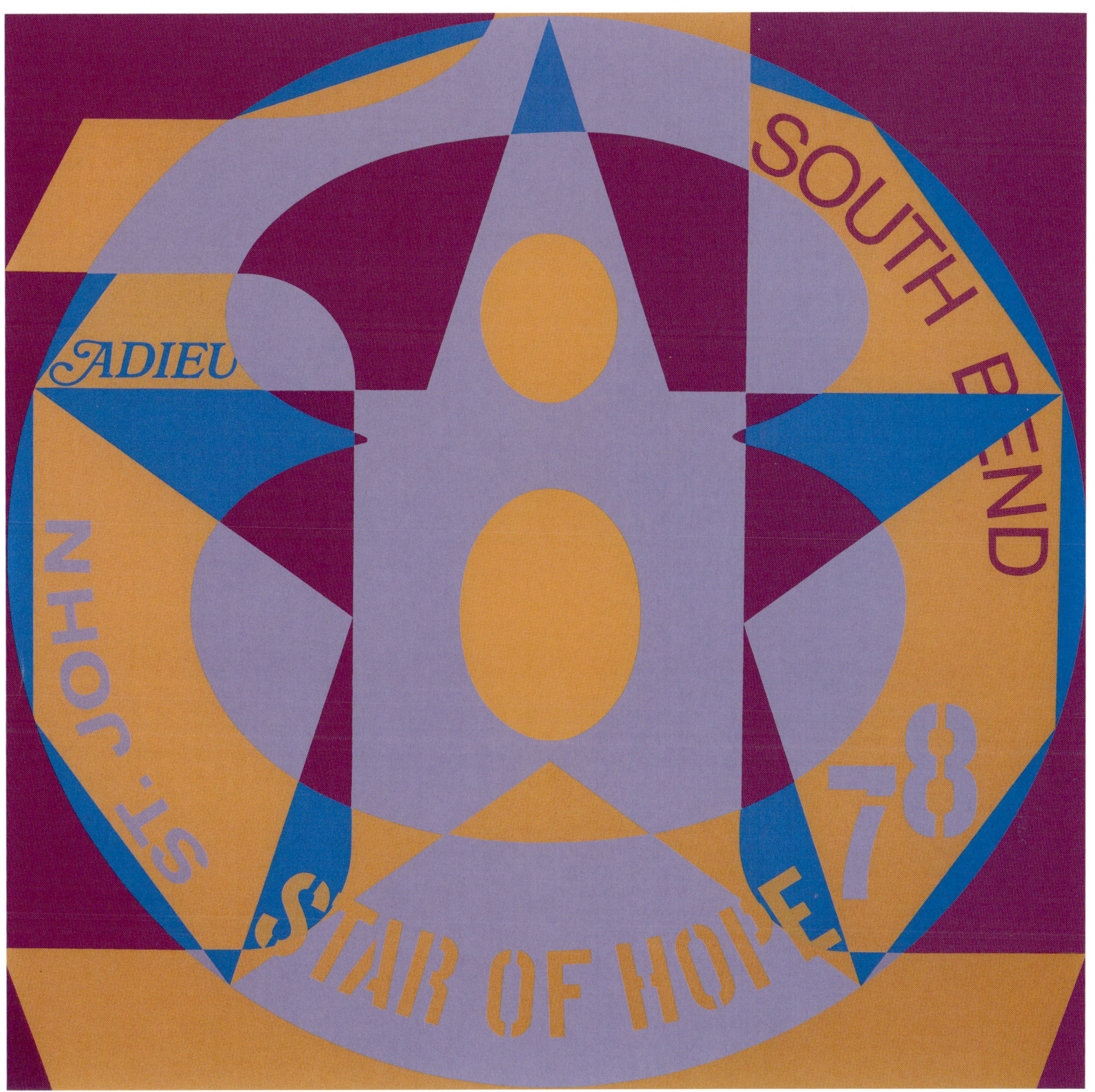
SOUTH BEND
ADIEU
ST. JOHN
78
STAR OF HOPE

Aptly named, BRIMSTONE is one of North America's few volcanic islands. It lies five miles southeast of Vinalhaven. Maine is the United States' "land's end" (FINIS TERRE), just as Land's End is England's and Finisterre is Spain's on the opposite side of the Atlantic. The 1979 *Autoportrait* is printed in the same "winter" palette of yellow and black used in the 1969 versions (Plates 26 and 27), bringing to an end both series. ● AHAVA refers to Indiana's Hebrew version of his 1970 *LOVE* sculpture, constructed to the same twelve-foot scale and likewise fashioned in Cor-ten steel at Lippincott in North Haven, Connecticut. In early 1979, two years after it was completed, *AHAVA* arrived at its final destination in the art garden of the Israel Museum in Jerusalem. As Indiana explained (in the third person) in his "Autochronology," the sculpture had a personal connection that tied it to Israel:

> For the artist, it is in memory of the priest who had much to do with his involvement in the concept of love in the first place and who died in the Israeli desert—Bishop [James A.] Pike, for whom he worked at the Cathedral of St. John the Divine.[86]

Though Indiana performed only clerical jobs at the Cathedral in Manhattan's Morningside Heights district in 1958, the liberal Episcopal bishop's views on civil rights and planned parenthood resonated with the young artist. The Bishop James Pike is doubtlessly the ST. JAMES of the *Autoportrait*.

PLATE 40

Decade: Autoportrait '79, BRIMSTONE

from *Vinalhaven Suite*, 1980

screenprint

edition of 125

image: 24 × 24 in. (61 × 61 cm);
sheet: 26 ¾ × 26 ¾ in. (68 × 68 cm)

printed by Domberger KG, Filderstadt;
published by Multiples, Inc., New York

Collection of Morgan Art Foundation, courtesy Marc Salama-Caro

86. "Autochronology," in *Robert Indiana* (1977), 55.

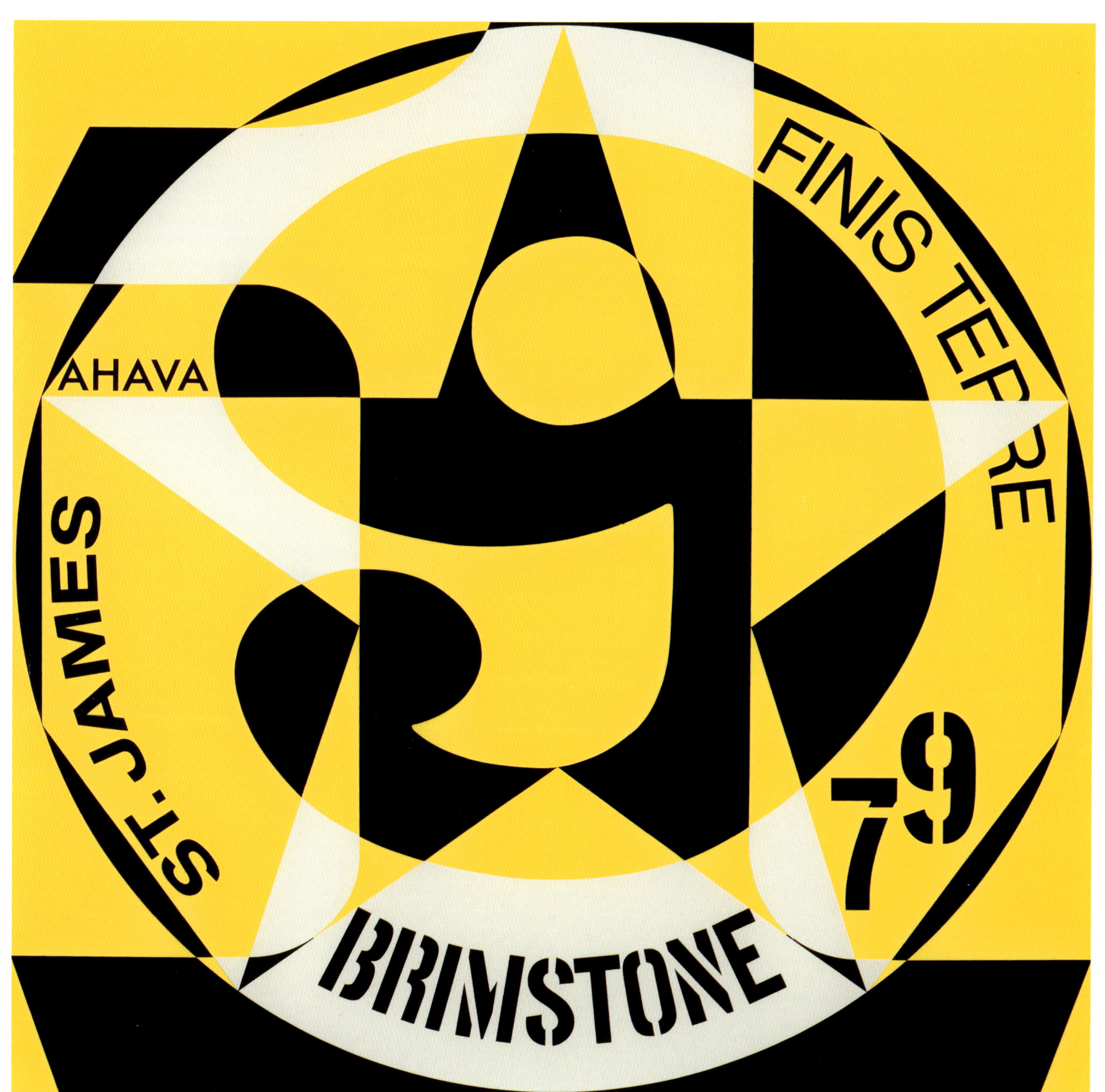

FINIS TERRE
AHAVA
ST. JAMES
79
BRIMSTONE

Indiana was one of eight artists commissioned to celebrate the city in print form for a portfolio titled *New York, New York*. Then no longer a resident, he revisited the theme of the Brooklyn Bridge, which had been in daily view from his studio on Coenties Slip. He again quoted Joseph Stella's fragmented depiction of the bridge, as he had in 1964 (Plate 7). But here, his subsequent move to Vinalhaven and its connection back to the bridge are expressed in the text that runs along the circumference of the surrounding circle: FROM THE VOWELS [read: bowels] OF VINALHAVEN TO THE CONSONANTS OF BROOKLYN AND MANHATTAN. In a reversal of Indiana's migration, granite blocks quarried on Vinalhaven had been transported to New York for the base of the bridge precisely a century before the screenprint's publication. And, reinforcing Indiana's sense of an almost predestined connection to the island, the eight monolithic granite columns in the nave of the Cathedral of St. John the Divine, where Indiana had worked in 1958, had likewise come to Manhattan from Vinalhaven, in 1899.

PLATE 41

THE BRIDGE

from *New York, New York*, 1983

screenprint

edition of 250

image: 31 7/8 × 23 in. (81 × 58.4 cm);
sheet: 35 3/8 × 24 3/4 in. (89.9 × 62.9 cm)

printed by Alexander Heinrici, New York;
published by The New York Graphic Society, Greenwich, Connecticut

Collection of the artist

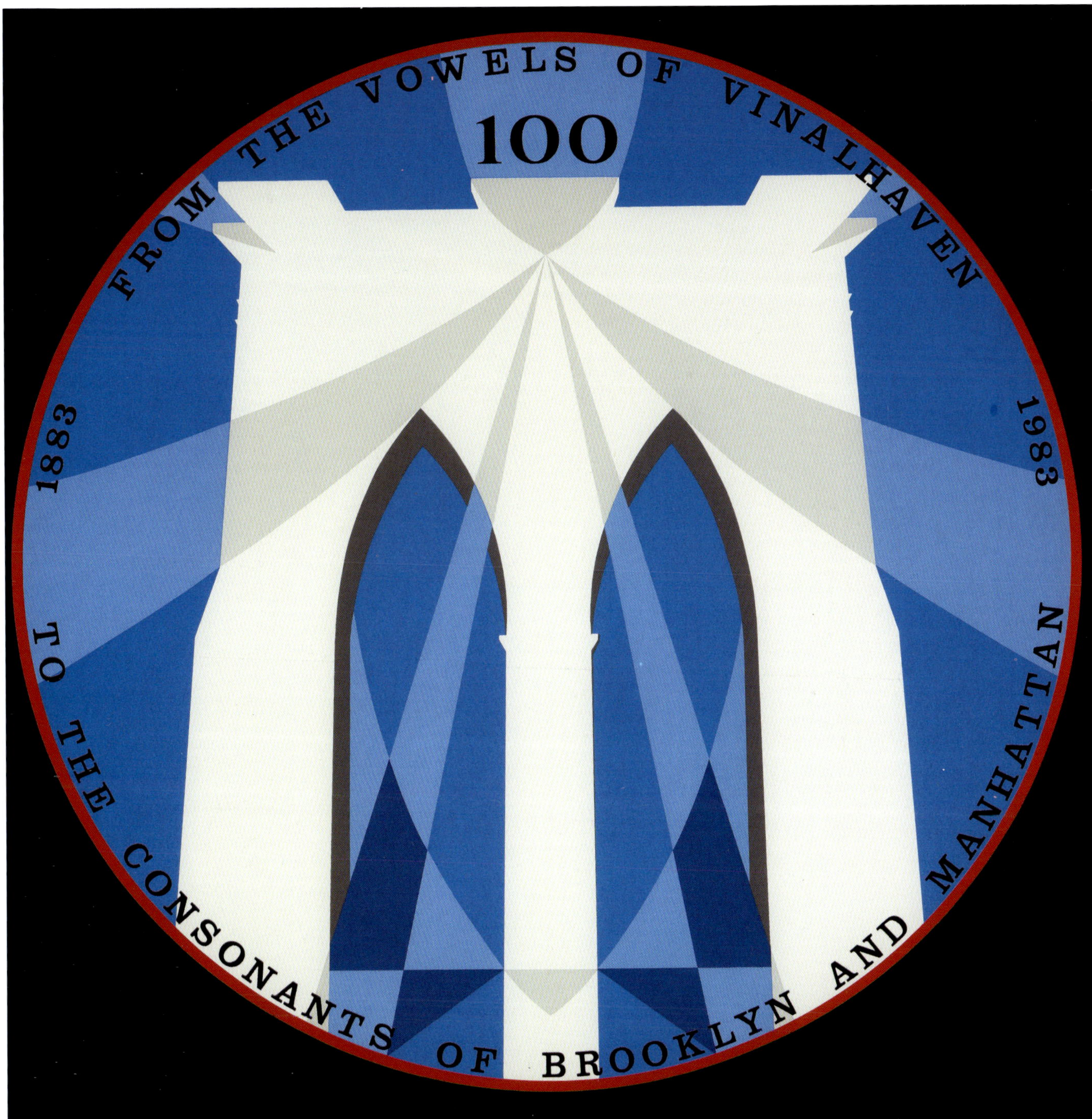
FROM THE VOWELS OF VINALHAVEN
100
1883
1983
TO THE CONSONANTS OF BROOKLYN AND MANHATTAN

THE BRIDGE

PLATE 42

MOTHER OF EXILES, 1986

hard-ground etching and aquatint

edition of 41

image: 35 ¼ × 23 ¾ in. (89.5 × 60.3 cm);
sheet: 47 ½ × 31 ½ in. (120.7 × 80 cm)

printed and published by Vinalhaven Press, Vinalhaven, Maine

Collection of the artist

In 1984 Pat Nick founded her Vinalhaven Press in the old school building on the island, and Indiana used this neighborly intaglio shop to make his first etchings since his days at the Art Institute of Chicago. In June 1986 he began work on *MOTHER OF EXILES*, which celebrates the centennial of the Statue of Liberty's completion on Bedloe's Island in New York Harbor. It was a hollow celebration in Indiana's opinion, given increasingly restrictive government policies toward immigration and the conservatism of the current Reagan administration. "Immigrants are no longer freely welcomed into this country, as recent history and legislation have aptly demonstrated," Indiana opined. "The loss of this vital meaning has turned Lady Liberty into an empty and over-exposed public icon, and her animate sadness on this turn of events is fully appropriate for a celebration of her hundredth birthday."[87] ● The title, *MOTHER OF EXILES*, comes from Emma Lazarus's sonnet "The New Colossus," immortalized within the statue's pedestal, which exhorts: "Give me your tired, your poor, / Your huddled masses yearning to breathe free, / The wretched refuse of your teeming shore." In the poem, Lazarus anthropomorphized the bronze colossus as a "Mother of Exiles," and Indiana likewise maternalized her as teary-eyed and bare-breasted. The latter fact, somewhat camouflaged by the lettering, is almost certainly an allusion to his own mother, whom he portrayed in similar undress in the *Mother and Father* diptych, 1963–67 (page 28). Indiana saw himself as a political exile in late 1980s America and, even more personally, as a refugee from the New York art scene, his decampment from which he described in 1994 as "my exile to Maine."[88]

87. Aprile Gallant and David Becker, *In Print: Contemporary Artists at the Vinalhaven Press* (Portland, Maine: Portland Museum of Art, 1997), 32–34.

88. Michael Plante, "Truth, Friendship, and Love," in *Dictated by Life: Marsden Hartley's German Paintings and Robert Indiana's Hartley Elegies* (Minneapolis: Frederick R. Weisman Art Museum, University of Minnesota, 1995), 57.

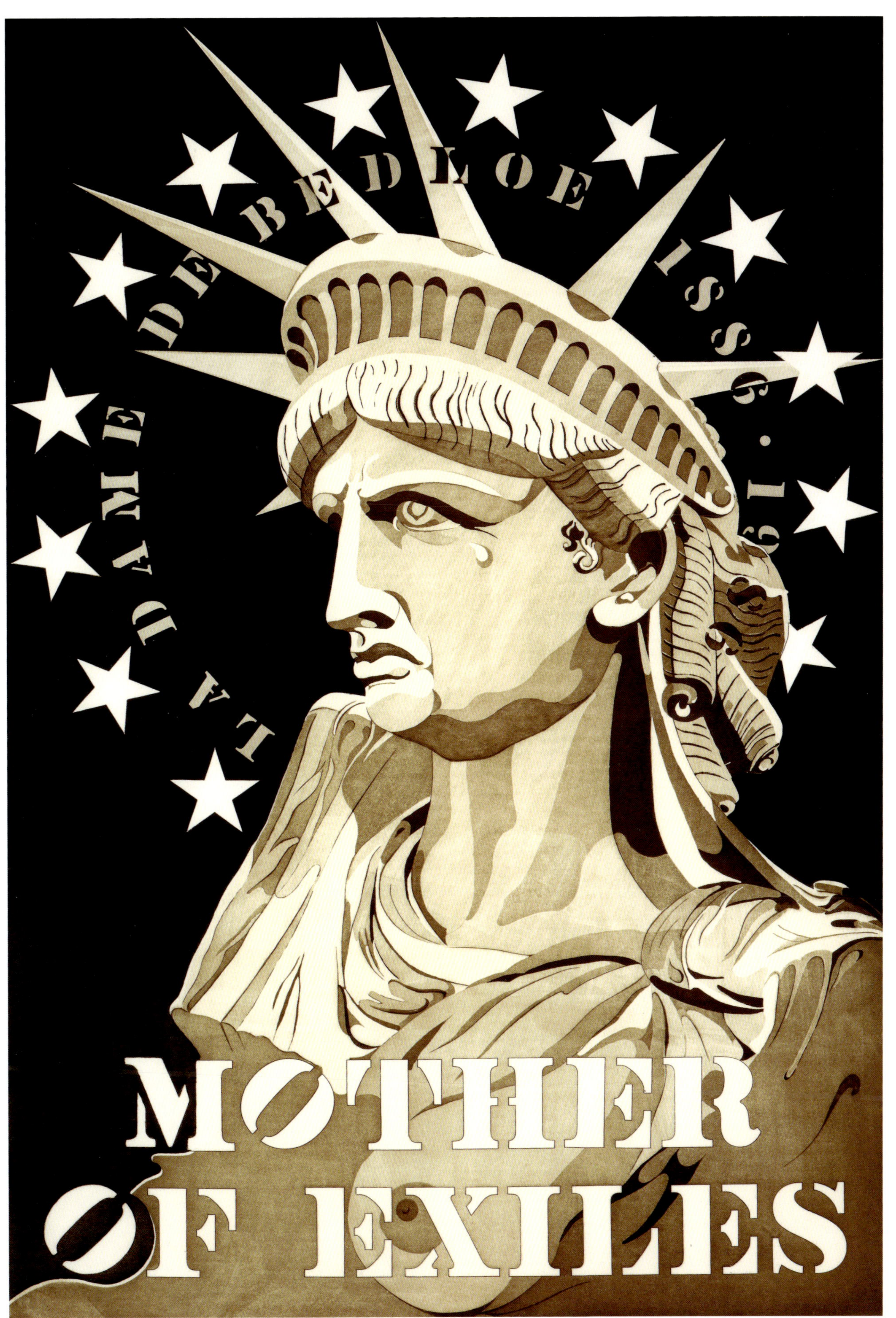
LA DAME DE BEDLOE 1886 · 19
MOTHER
OF EXILES

When the artist moved to Maine in 1978, it took him twelve vanloads and then two years of stowing things away before he started painting again. ● By April 1980 he had decided to paint a series in tribute to Marsden Hartley, the pioneering American modernist painter who had been born in Maine. Indiana wrote to former Indianapolis Museum of Art director Carl Weinhardt: "I feel an homage to this artist, particularly in relation to his Berlin period, is in order and very much in the offing."[89] In actuality, it would be nearly a decade before Indiana would produce this series of ten screenprints and related paintings that take as their point of departure Hartley's *Portrait of a German Officer* (Metropolitan Museum of Art), painted in Berlin in 1914. ● *KvF I* is a distillation of that painting, containing in simplified form the same bits of military panoply that had so impressed Hartley when he was in Germany in the months preceding the outbreak of World War I. Though Hartley denied the presence of any symbolic content in his painting, his friend Arnold Rönnebeck, who had seen it being painted, knew it to be a symbolic portrait, which he decoded for the collector Duncan Phillips in a letter written after Hartley's death in 1943:

> There is a very personal and emotional connection between this picture and myself, because I am partly symbolized in it. I am one half of the Prussian officer. The other half is a cousin of mine. . . . Rather dominating is the Iron Cross. My cousin was killed in action in France on the 24th of October, 1914 (24). [He actually died on October 7 at the age of 24. —Ed.] He was an active officer in the 4th regiment of the Kaiser's guards (center) 4 on blue ground (of shoulder straps). He received the Iron Cross a day before his death. Next to the 4 is an E and I am certain that it is in red on yellow ground which stands for Queen Elisabeth of Greece or the patroness of the third regiment of the grand-grenadiers in which I then served. The E appears again in the lower middle right on my "full dress epaulettes" and the long tassels next to 24 represent the heavy silver-wire tassels I wore as an aide-de-camp in the guards. In the lower left corner we distinguish the initials K.V.F. My cousin's name was Karl von Freyburg.[90]

Though Hartley had decided not to reveal his intimate friendship with the deceased von Freyburg, Rönnebeck did so in writing and Indiana makes it manifest in the ring surrounding the subject, which includes 7 October 1989—the date Indiana chose to begin *The Hartley Elegies*, seventy-five years to the day of von Freyburg's death.

PLATE 43

KvF I

from *The Hartley Elegies: The Berlin Series*, 1990

screenprint

edition of 50

image: 75 7/8 × 53 1/4 in. (192.7 × 135.3 cm);
sheet: 79 7/8 × 55 1/2 in. (202.9 × 141 cm)

printed by Brand X Editions, Ltd., New York;
published by Park Granada Editions, Tarzana, California

Collection of the Indianapolis Museum of Art,
Martha Delzell Memorial Fund, 2010.120

89. Weinhardt, *Robert Indiana*, 211.
90. Gail Levin, "Hidden Symbolism in Marsden Hartley's Military Paintings," *Arts Magazine* 54, no. 2 (October 1979): 155–56.

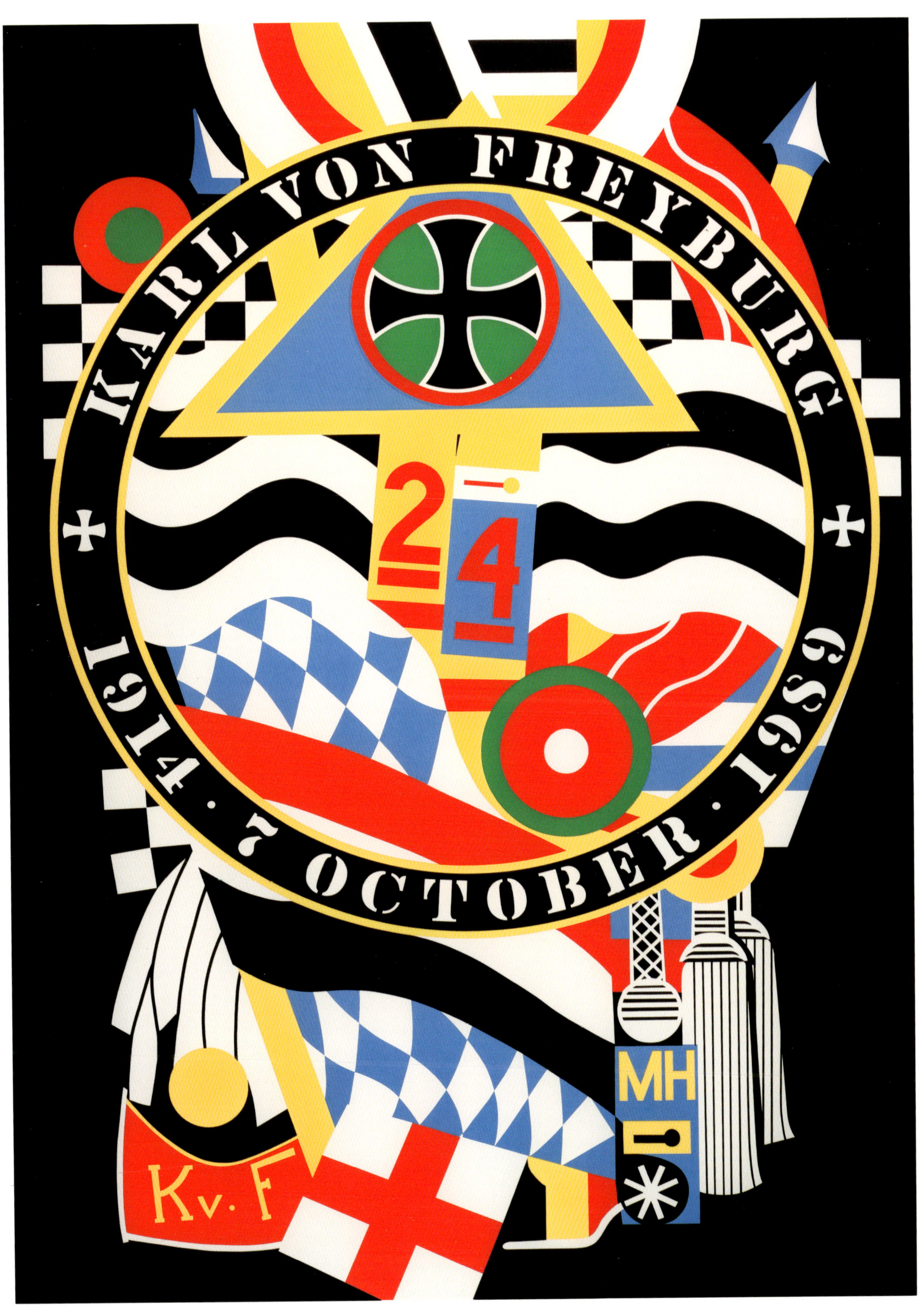
KARL VON FREYBURG
1914 · 7 OCTOBER · 1989
24
MH
Kv. F

KvF I morphs into *KvF II*, with Indiana giving Hartley center stage in place of his friend and perhaps lover Karl von Freyburg. The Stars and Stripes replaces the array of German flags that appear in the preceding screenprint as well as in Hartley's painting: the Prussian black-and-white stripes, the Bavarian blue-and-white diamond pattern, and the black-over-red-over-white stripes of the pre-1918 German national flag. The black-and-white checkerboard is carried over from Hartley's *Portrait of a German Officer*, where, according to Rönnebeck, it was included to reflect von Freyburg's love of chess—a love shared by Indiana.[91] Freyburg's age at death (24) and the year (14) appear, as does Hartley's death date (1943). The figure 8 looms up and, though it did not appear in the keynote painting, it does appear in other related paintings of the era. Hartley wrote to Alfred Stieglitz in 1913 of his "spiritual enthusiasm" for a painting he was working on containing a "mystical presentation of number 8," which he saw, he wrote, everywhere in Berlin.[92] Indiana, too, had a fascination with numbers, and they exemplified "the magic of coincidence" by which the artist said he worked.[93]

PLATE 44

KvF II

from *The Hartley Elegies: The Berlin Series*, 1990

screenprint

edition of 50

image: 76 5/8 × 53 in. (194.6 × 134.6 cm);
sheet: 79 7/8 × 55 1/2 in. (202.9 × 141 cm)

printed by Brand X Editions, Ltd., New York;
published by Park Granada Editions, Tarzana, California

Collection of the Indianapolis Museum of Art,
Delavan Smith Fund, 2010.121

91. Ibid., 156; Paul Taylor, "Love Story," *Connoisseur* 221, no. 954 (August 1991): 97.
92. Levin, "Hidden Symbolism in Marsden Hartley's Military Paintings," 158.
93. Edgar Allen Beem, "Robert Indiana: At Home in Penobscot Bay," *Down East Magazine*, August 1982, 77.

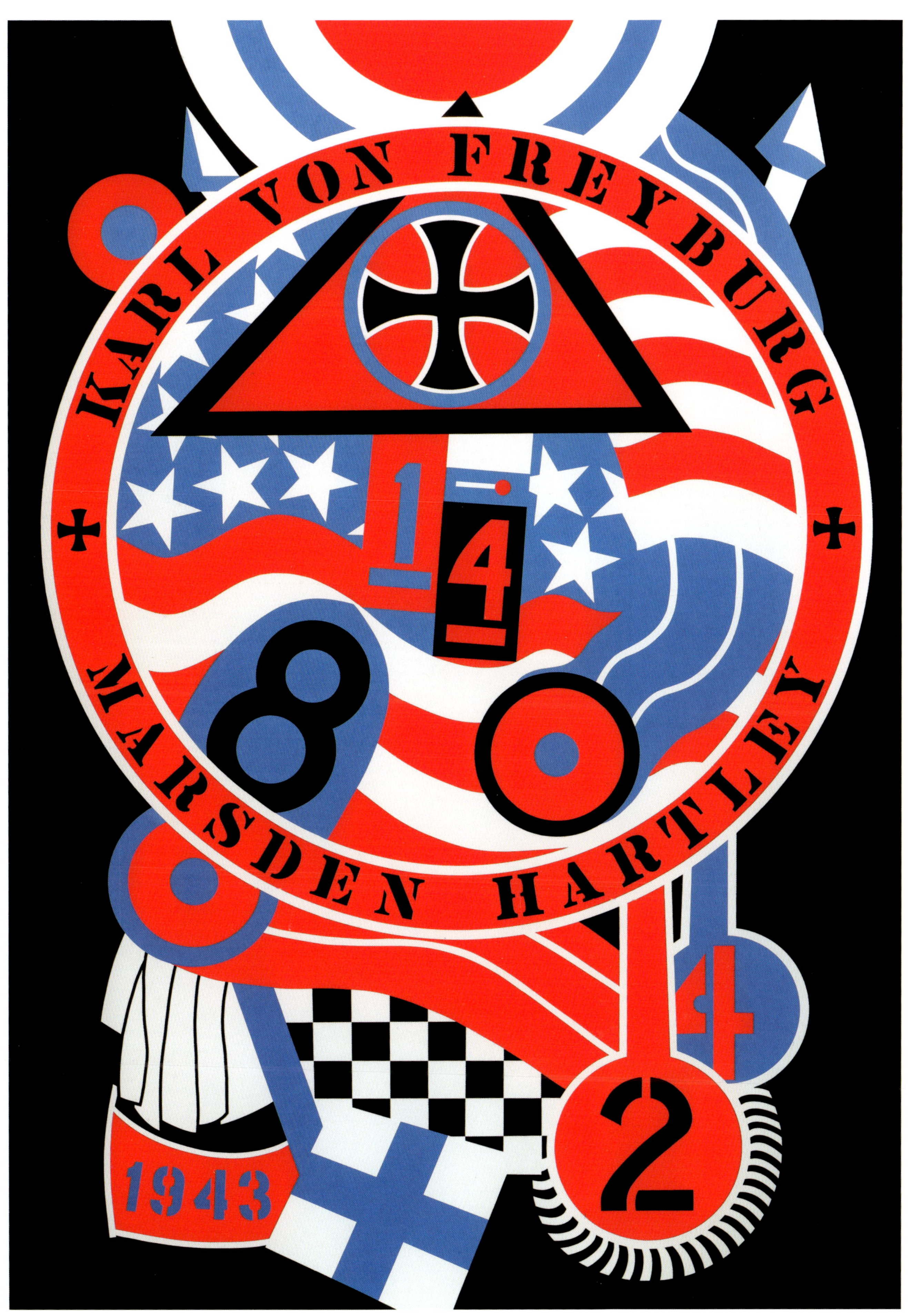
KARL VON FREYBURG
MARSDEN HARTLEY
14
8
2
4
1943

KvF III is a simulacrum of Hartley's *Painting No. 47, Berlin* (Hirshhorn Museum and Sculpture Garden). As Indiana knew, Hartley produced some fifty paintings in Berlin in 1914–15 memorializing von Freyburg and known collectively as the *War Motifs*. Indiana drew upon three of these paintings for his *Hartley Elegies*. Indiana, too, had always worked serially and though he had been criticized for repetitiveness, he was unapologetic about conceiving his work this way:

> I go on working with my words and numbers and their endless variations like Mr. Albers' squares or Mr. Monet's haystacks. It would be very nice if Americans could stop equating artists with Detroit, expecting new models every year. That concept has just about buried this country now, and it certainly exhausts artists![94]

Certain insignia and other bits of uniform appear and reappear throughout both Hartley's and Indiana's series, and here the figure 9 shows up for the first time, silhouetted against the white ostrich plumes that adorned the ceremonial helmets of the Kaiser's Guard to which von Freyburg belonged. In occultism, to which Hartley subscribed, the number 9 stands for the highest possible spiritual and mental achievement, which is how Hartley described von Freyburg in a letter to Alfred Stieglitz: "in every way a perfect being—physically, spiritually, and mentally perfectly balanced."[95] ● Indiana's main departures from the Hirshhorn painting are the addition of the initials for Hartley and von Freyburg, which are flanked by their respective ages at death, 66 and 24. Indiana also alters the colors of the central waving flag from Hartley's black, white, and red to black, yellow, and red, reflecting the change in the German national flag post–World War II. Such an updating accords with the German phrases that surround the image: DER AMERIKANISCHE MALER (The American Painter), an appropriate designation for the Germanophile Hartley and an echo of Indiana's own aspiration as expressed in his 1961 artist's statement for the Museum of Modern Art: "Not wishing at all to unsettle the shades of Homer, Eakins, Ryder, Sheeler, Hopper, Marin et al., I propose to be an American painter."[96] ICH BIN EIN BERLINER (I am a citizen of Berlin) is not only akin to a 1913 caricature of Hartley (Beinecke Rare Book and Manuscript Library, Yale University) inscribed "Marsden adopts Germany! to the tune of 'Ich bin ein Preusser'" (I am a Prussian), but famously echoes President Kennedy's words in Berlin on June 26, 1963, where the divisive Wall would fall in November 1989, a month after *The Hartley Elegies* were begun.

PLATE 45

KvF III

from *The Hartley Elegies: The Berlin Series*, 1990

screenprint

edition of 50

image: 76 5/8 × 52 7/8 in. (194.6 × 134.3 cm);
sheet: 79 7/8 × 55 1/2 in. (202.9 × 141 cm)

printed by Brand X Editions, Ltd., New York;
published by Park Granada Editions, Tarzana, California

Collection of the Indianapolis Museum of Art,
Jane Weldon Myers Acquisition Fund, 2010.122

94. Mary Trasco, "The Most American Painter: Robert Indiana," *Indiana Alumni Magazine* 42, no. 9 (July 1980): 11.
95. Roxana Barry, "The Age of Blood and Iron: Marsden Hartley in Berlin," *Arts Magazine* 54, no. 2 (October 1979): 171.
96. Susan Elizabeth Ryan, "Robert Indiana and Marsden Hartley: The Hartley Elegies," in *Robert Indiana: The Hartley Elegies* (Lewiston, Maine: Bates College Museum of Art, 2005), 17.

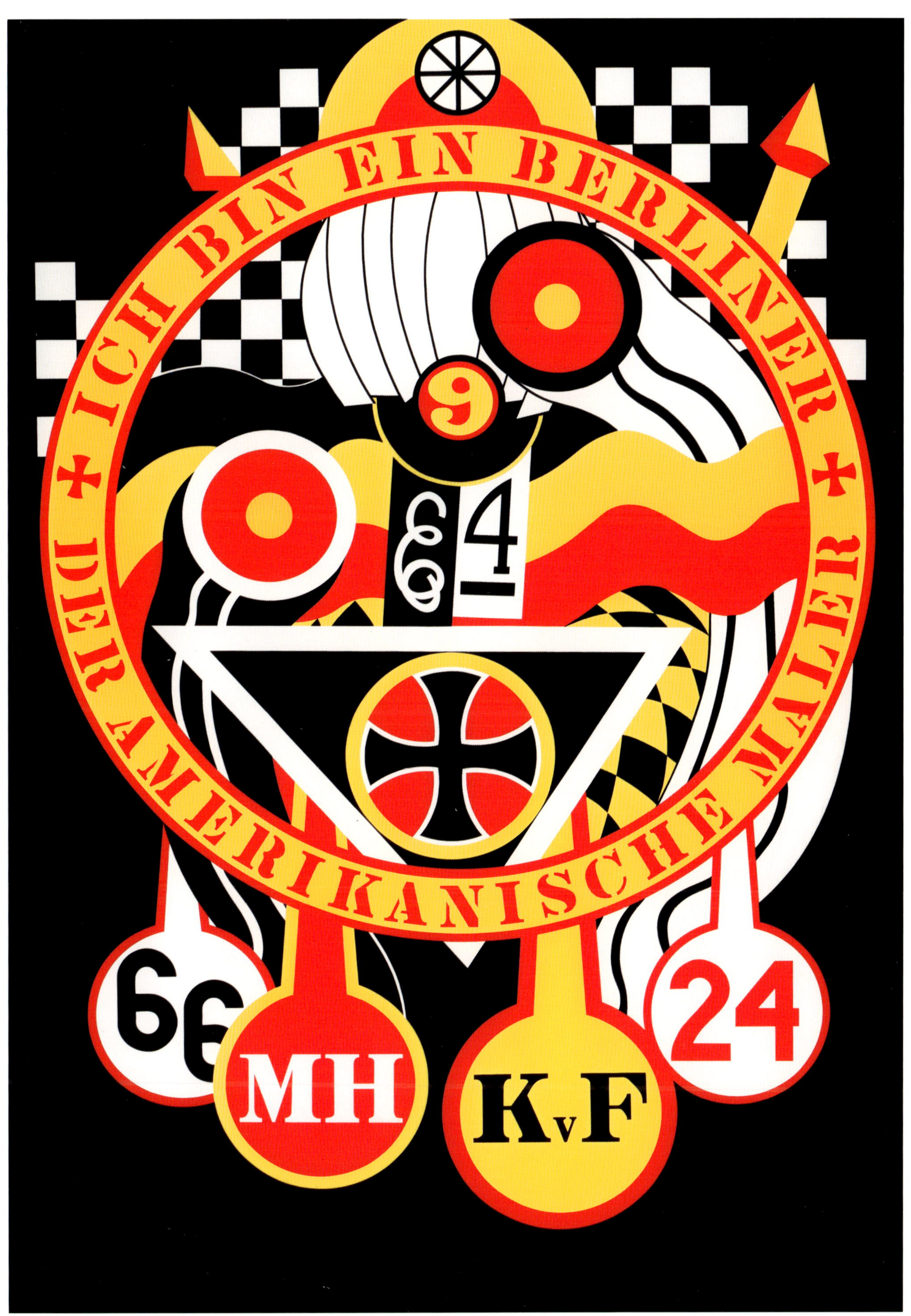

ICH BIN EIN BERLINER
DER AMERIKANISCHE MALER
9
64
66
MH
KvF
24

Hartley's *Painting, Number 5* is the obvious source for *KvF IV*. It is in the collection of the Whitney Museum of American Art, New York, which rescued Hartley from oblivion with a retrospective exhibition in 1980, mounted at the very moment that Indiana was conceiving his homage to the artist. It was the fifth of Hartley's series of *War Motifs* painted in 1914–15, and is less three-dimensional and more abstract than the two previously cited works. Though still filled with flags, medals, epaulettes, and circular cockades of military regalia, the painting makes no direct allusion to Karl von Freyburg. Similarly, Indiana's references here are to Hartley alone, with his life dates, 1877–1943, at the base and significant places in his life in the embracing ring. Joining NEW YORK and BERLIN are three towns in Maine: LEWISTON, where Hartley was born; VINALHAVEN, where he summered in 1938; and ELLSWORTH, where he died. All five are lettered in green on white, the colors that Indiana most associated with Maine. For Indiana, Vinalhaven provided a link to Hartley, with whom he felt "a distinct relationship."[97] And the coincidence of the town of Ellsworth sharing the first name of Indiana's early friend and mentor Ellsworth Kelly was certainly not lost on the artist.

PLATE 46

KvF IV

from *The Hartley Elegies: The Berlin Series*, 1990

screenprint

edition of 50

image: 77 1/8 × 53 1/8 in. (195.9 × 134.9 cm);
sheet: 79 7/8 × 55 9/16 in. (202.9 × 141.1 cm)

printed by Brand X Editions, Ltd., New York;
published by Park Granada Editions, Tarzana, California

Collection of the Indianapolis Museum of Art,
Martha Delzell Memorial Fund and Delavan Smith Fund, 2010.123

97. Plante, "Truth, Friendship, and Love," 81.

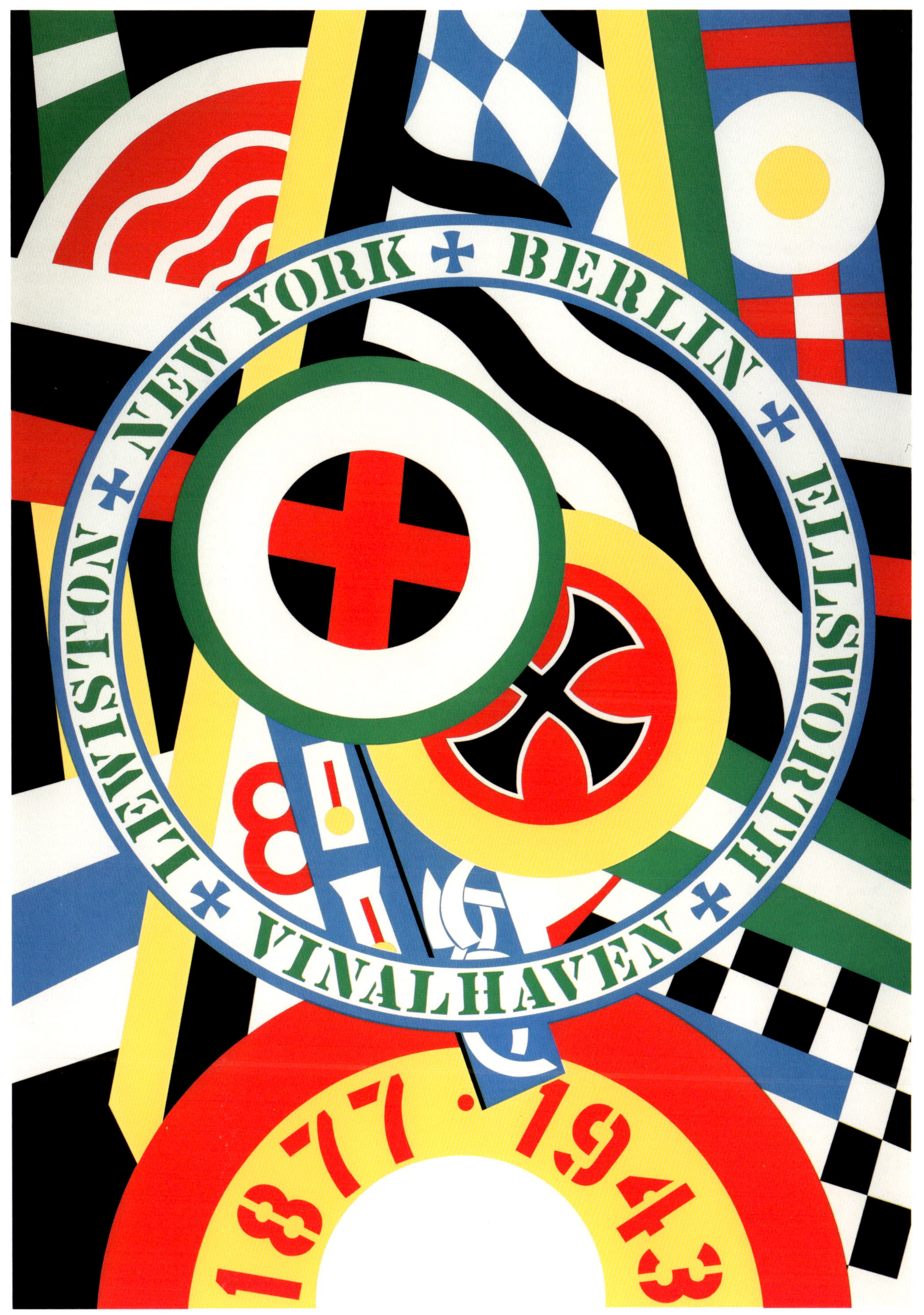
NEW YORK + BERLIN + ELLSWORTH + VINALHAVEN + LEWISTON
1877 · 1943

In the last of the rectangular screenprints, Indiana reconnects Hartley, von Freyburg, and, obliquely, himself. He adopts certain elements from the *War Motif* paintings, but the synthesis is Indiana's. The central field is dominated by the juncture of the pre-1918 German flag and the American flag, symbolizing the union of von Freyburg and Hartley, which was physically broken when von Freyburg died in 1914 but immediately reconnected spiritually through Hartley's paintings. The year 1914 is memorialized by Indiana on the fringed epaulettes silhouetted against the yellow and red rays of the setting or rising sun, a motif encountered in Hartley's Berlin paintings.[98] The bond between the two men was defined by the words TRUTH LOVE FRIENDSHIP. These same three words in inverse order were the central ideals that bound together the fraternity of the Independent Order of Odd Fellows, in whose former Star of Hope Lodge on Vinalhaven *The Hartley Elegies* were created.[99] Indiana found these symbols and other pieces of Odd Fellow regalia after occupying the abandoned lodge. He described them as possessing "all the ceremony and pomp, and a touch of the military—all that stuff that Hartley loved."[100]

PLATE 47

KvF V

from *The Hartley Elegies: The Berlin Series*, 1990

screenprint

edition of 50

image: 77 1/16 × 53 1/2 in. (195.7 × 135.9 cm);
sheet: 79 7/8 × 55 1/2 in. (202.9 × 141 cm)

printed by Brand X Editions, Ltd., New York;
published by Park Granada Editions, Tarzana, California

Collection of the Indianapolis Museum of Art, Martha Delzell Memorial Fund and Jane Weldon Myers Acquisition Fund, 2010.124

98. See, for example, Hartley's *Himmel*, 1914–15 (Nelson Atkins Museum of Art, Kansas City), and *Painting No. 49, Berlin*, 1914–15 (Seattle Art Museum).
99. Komanecky, *Robert Indiana and the Star of Hope*, 48.
100. David Colman, "At Home with Robert Indiana," *New York Times*, February 6, 2003.

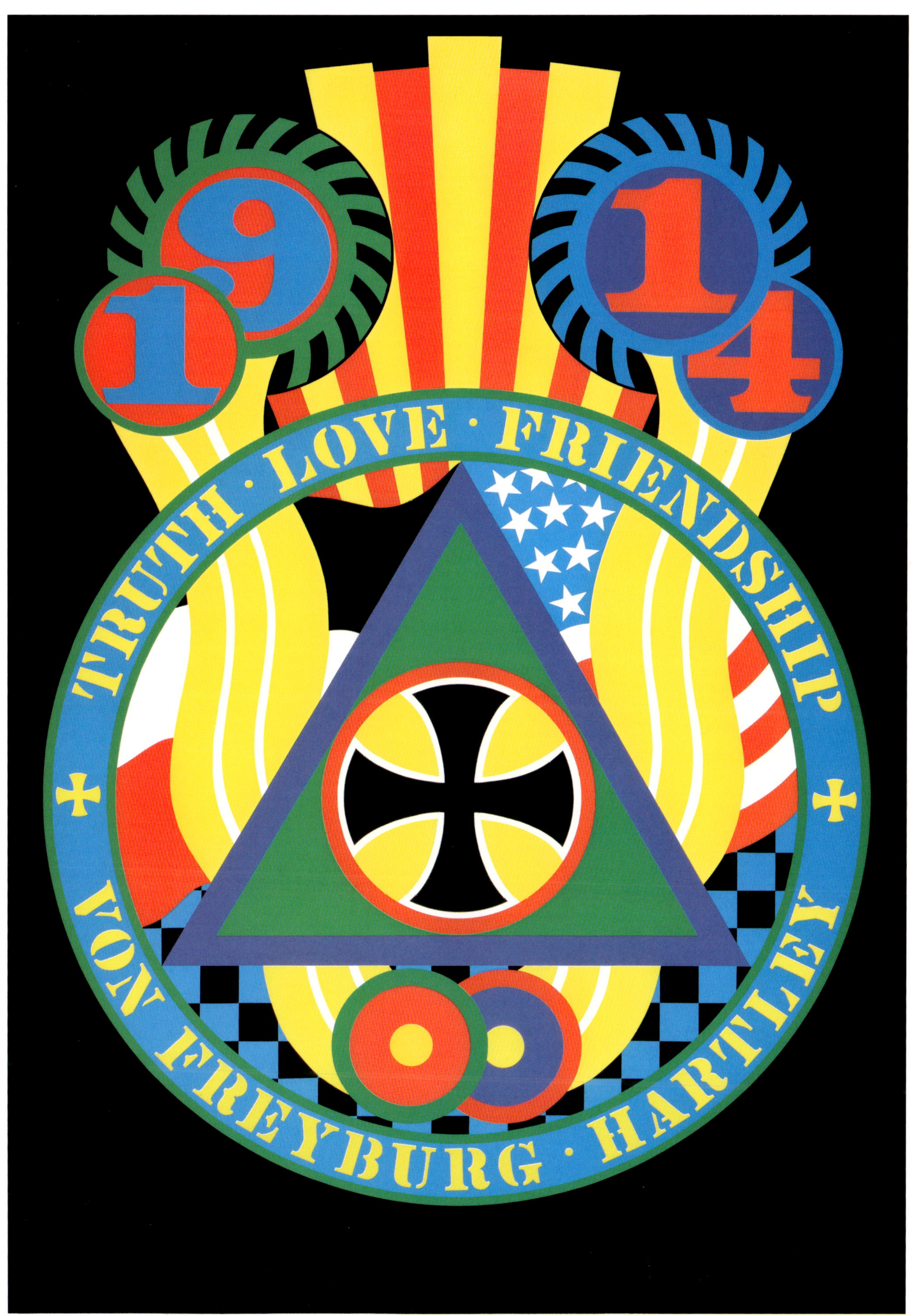
1914
TRUTH · LOVE · FRIENDSHIP
VON FREYBURG · HARTLEY

The second five *Hartley Elegies* abandon the upright, rectangular "portrait" format for a diamond shape, which had nothing to do with Hartley, but which Indiana had been using since 1962. Although the superimposed lettering from *KvF I–V* is repeated in *KvF VI–X* (if not in the same order), the second half of Indiana's *Berlin Series* screenprints show a reduced allegiance toward the elements that Hartley had used to compose his collaged Berlin "portraits." In *KvF VI*, for instance, the central black-and-white striped Prussian flag of *KvF I* becomes red and blue, and both the black-and-white checkerboard and the blue diamonds of the Bavarian flag are newly rendered in blue and green. Whereas the Hartley originals with their heraldic spirit and imagery of circles, triangles, numbers, and letters "could almost be Indiana's," as critic Paul Taylor observed in 1991, the diamond-shaped *Elegies* could hardly be Hartley's.[101] As if to make this implicit, Indiana gives central place to 75, the number of years separating the first of Hartley's symbolic portraits and the inception of Indiana's elegiac series. ● This kind of evolution as a series developed was standard procedure for Indiana, as he explained in 1976:

> It was almost a kind of process of elimination, and that is, that with my work and particularly my early work, it's almost like the architectural dictum that less is more and in a sense I got down to the subject matter of my work, to its bare bones. . . . It was really a matter of distillation.[102]

PLATE 48

KvF VI

from *The Hartley Elegies: The Berlin Series*, 1991

screenprint

edition of 50

image: 57 7/16 × 57 7/16 in. (145.9 × 145.9 cm);
sheet: 59 7/8 × 59 3/8 in. (152.1 × 150.8 cm)

printed by Brand X Editions, Ltd., New York;
published by Park Granada Editions, Tarzana, California

Collection of the Indianapolis Museum of Art, Martha Delzell Memorial Fund and Martha M. Shertzer Art Purchase Fund in memory of her Nephew, Charles S. Sands, 2010.125

101. Taylor, "Love Story," 97.
102. "Conversations with Robert Indiana," in *Robert Indiana* (1977), 36.

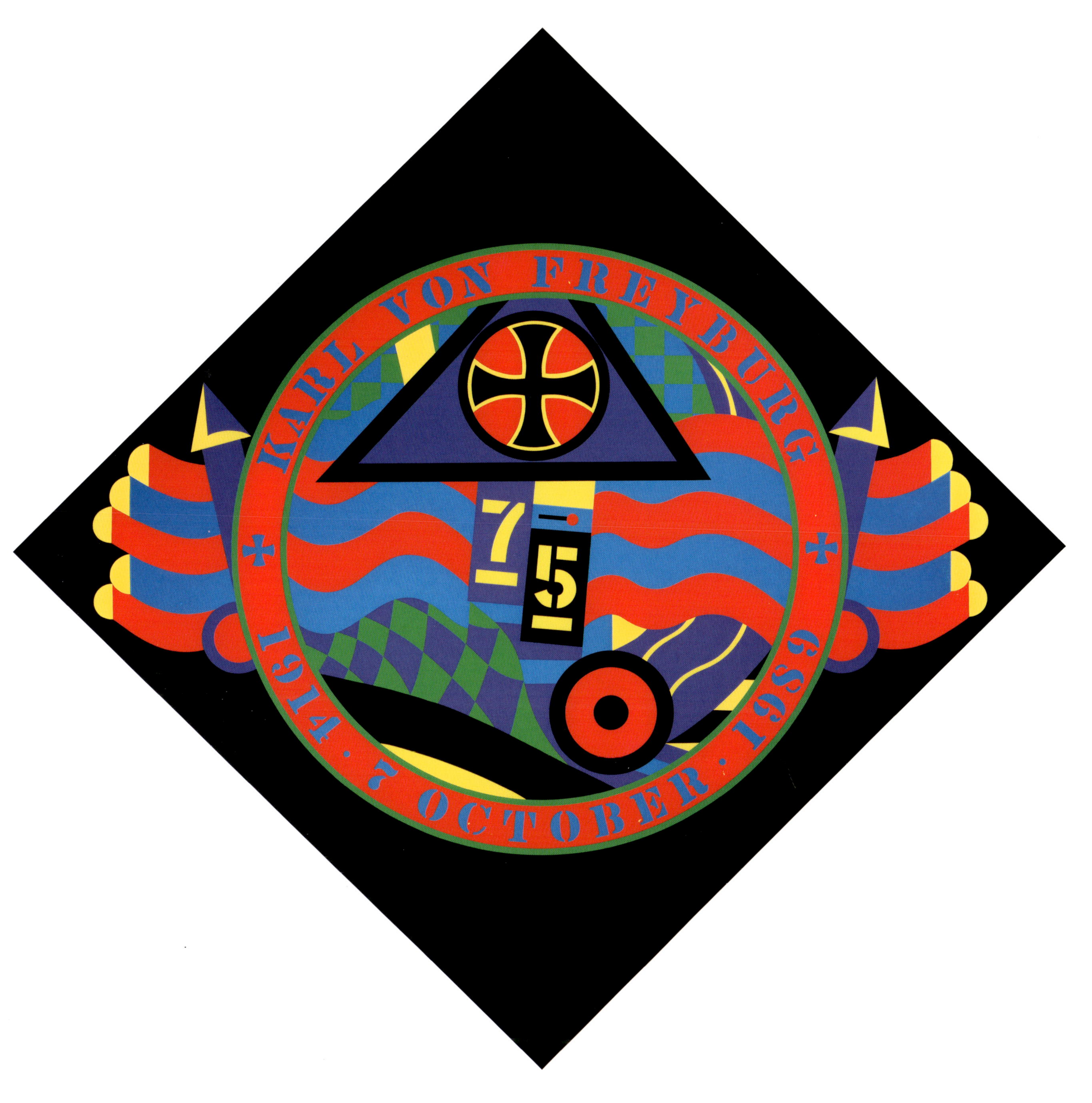
KARL VON FREYBURG
75
1914 · 7 OCTOBER · 1989

KvF VII borrows the elements from *KvF II* but reduces and regiments them. Part of the initial attraction of Hartley's originals for Indiana had been the rather freewheeling abandon by which they had been constructed: "They're a natural for me," Indiana said in 1991. "They liberate me from the symmetry and strict formalism that I had been rather stuck in for some time."[103] But Indiana had no interest in imitating Hartley and felt that their respective approaches to painting differed: "My manner is different from Hartley's. I'm hard edge coming from a geometric background; but our works deal with the same thing—the fabric of people's lives."[104] This personally felt kinship with and sympathy for Hartley became ultimately more important to Indiana than the similarities between their art, which had attracted his attention years before:

> This isn't touched upon too frequently, but know that for me the artist is probably about two or three times as interesting as his art. I'm fascinated by the lives of artists and I have tried to design my own life so that it is a little bit more interesting than my mother and father's, shall we say.
> It is Hartley's life and his tragedy which caught my attention.[105]

PLATE 49

KvF VII

from *The Hartley Elegies: The Berlin Series*, 1991

screenprint

edition of 50

image: 57 1/2 × 57 3/4 in. (146.1 × 146.7 cm);
sheet: 59 7/8 × 59 1/2 in. (152.1 × 151.1 cm)

printed by Brand X Editions, Ltd., New York;
published by Park Granada Editions, Tarzana, California

Collection of the Indianapolis Museum of Art, Martha Delzell Memorial Fund and Martha M. Shertzer Art Purchase Fund in memory of her Nephew, Charles S. Sands, 2010.126

103. Taylor, "Love Story," 97.
104. Beem, "Robert Indiana: At Home in Penobscot Bay," 77.
105. Sheehan, *Robert Indiana Prints*, 14.

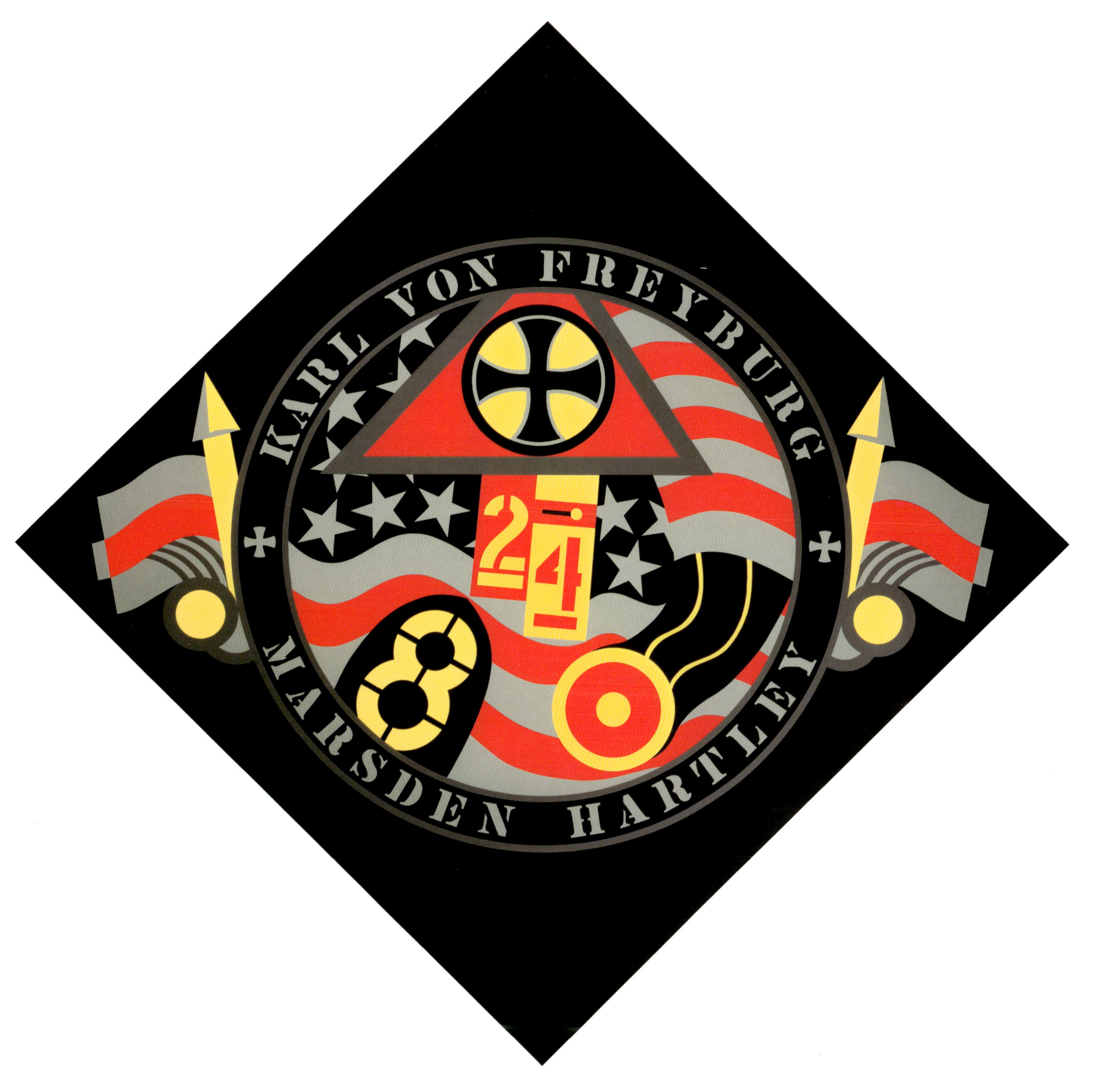
KARL VON FREYBURG
24
8
MARSDEN HARTLEY

The Hartley Elegies occupied Indiana from 1989 to 1994. There were thirty in all: ten screenprints, eighteen paintings (six rectangles, six diamond-shaped, and six tondos), and two new herms, *KvF* and *MARS* (Marsden). For Indiana, it was a period of intense work with unusual cross-fertilization among genres, as he admitted in 1991:

> And with the Hartley series it has been a very different process because the prints have been an incentive and very instrumental in my complete involvement with *The Hartley Elegies*. The paintings are feeding on the prints as much as the prints are feeding on the paintings. That is about the first time that has happened.[106]

The thread tying the works in the series together is a shared elegiac mood, which is more palpable in the more formal, hieratic, emblematic, and restrained diamond-shaped prints than in the more exuberant portrait rectangles. In these, with their emptier backgrounds, the black core is more insistent, which carries forward, sympathetically, the mood with which Hartley invested his painted memorials to Karl von Freyburg. "These paintings, with one or two exceptions, are all black," Indiana remarked while at work on the homages. "These are paintings in the nineteenth-century concept of mourning. I am mourning the situation just as Hartley did at the time that he did them."[107]

PLATE 50

KvF VIII

from *The Hartley Elegies: The Berlin Series*, 1991

screenprint

edition of 50

image: 57 ½ × 57 ½ in. (146.1 × 146.1 cm);
sheet: 59 ½ × 59 ½ in. (151.1 × 151.1 cm)

printed by Brand X Editions, Ltd., New York;
published by Park Granada Editions, Tarzana, California

Collection of the Indianapolis Museum of Art, Martha Delzell Memorial Fund and Mr. and Mrs. Theodore P. Van Vorhees Art Fund, 2010.127

106. Ibid., 12.
107. Plante, "Truth, Friendship, and Love," 84.

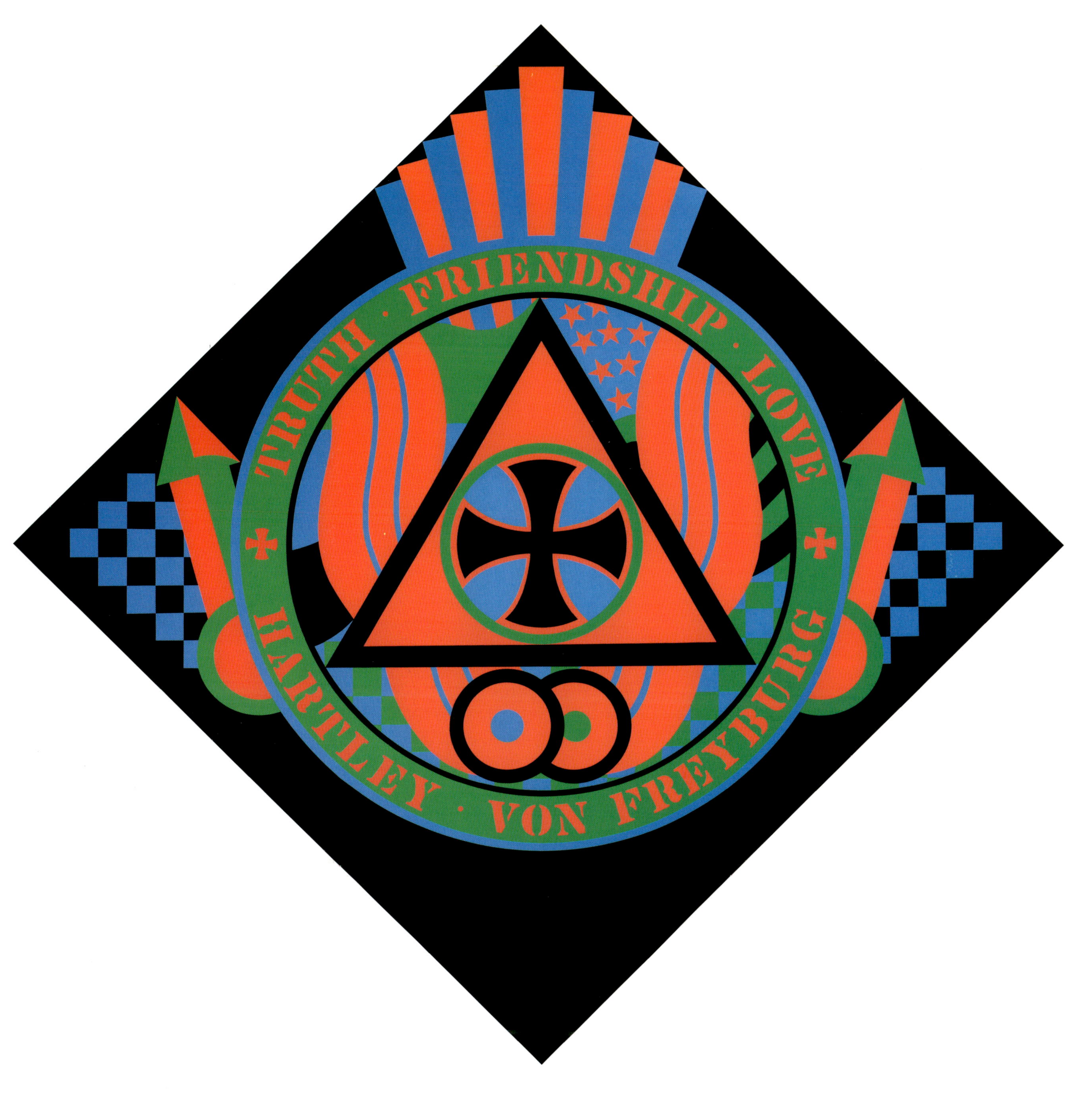
TRUTH · FRIENDSHIP · LOVE
HARTLEY · VON FREYBURG

In the exhibition catalogue that first paired Hartley's paintings with Indiana's tributes, art historian Michael Plante wrote, "Hartley avoids direct sexual references in *Portrait of a German Officer*, and so, too, does Robert Indiana in his homages. Yet, if the context is not always a sexual one, it is at least a *homosocial* one."[108] Because such decorum has marked Indiana's career, it seems highly imaginative that for one writer the number 69 in *KvF IX* "retains its sexual connotation with the presence of phallic canons above."[109] These elements can be read otherwise, with 69 marking the year of Indiana's arrival on Vinalhaven; that number is in fact paired in one of the *KvF* paintings with 38, the year of Hartley's single visit to the island. The "phallic canons" are the descendants of spiked projections appearing in Hartley's symbolic portraits of von Freyburg, where they might represent the finials on flagpoles or the "pickelhelm" that jutted from the top of German helmets. Yet, sexual overtones do seem to have been on Indiana's mind, according to an interview with *Connoisseur* he gave at the time of this print's creation. "I had for a long time wanted to bring the LOVE from the spiritual into the erotic," he said, and Hartley's work, particularly a portrait of a male model in a G-string, "suddenly spurred me to get back to drawing. I have always loved that painting because it was one of the first Hartleys that I ever experienced in person. I would love to redo that nude as an homage to Hartley and remove Mr. Hartley's inhibitions—and the G-string." He began a series of phalluses drawn from life. "And that," said Indiana, "is where the recent difficulties came from."[110] He was falsely charged in 1990 by two of his paid models of engaging in prostitution, of which he was acquitted in 1992.

PLATE 51

KvF IX

from *The Hartley Elegies: The Berlin Series*, 1991

screenprint

edition of 50

image: 57 7/16 × 57 7/16 in. (145.9 × 145.9 cm);
sheet: 59 3/8 × 59 3/8 in. (150.8 × 150.8 cm)

printed by Brand X Editions, Ltd., New York;
published by Park Granada Editions, Tarzana, California

Collection of the Indianapolis Museum of Art, Martha Delzell Memorial Fund and Elizabeth S. Lawton Fine Art Fund, 2010.128

108. Ibid., 85.
109. Liz Kelton Sheehan, "Decoding the Elegies," in *Robert Indiana: The Hartley Elegies*, 45.
110. Taylor, "Love Story," 97.

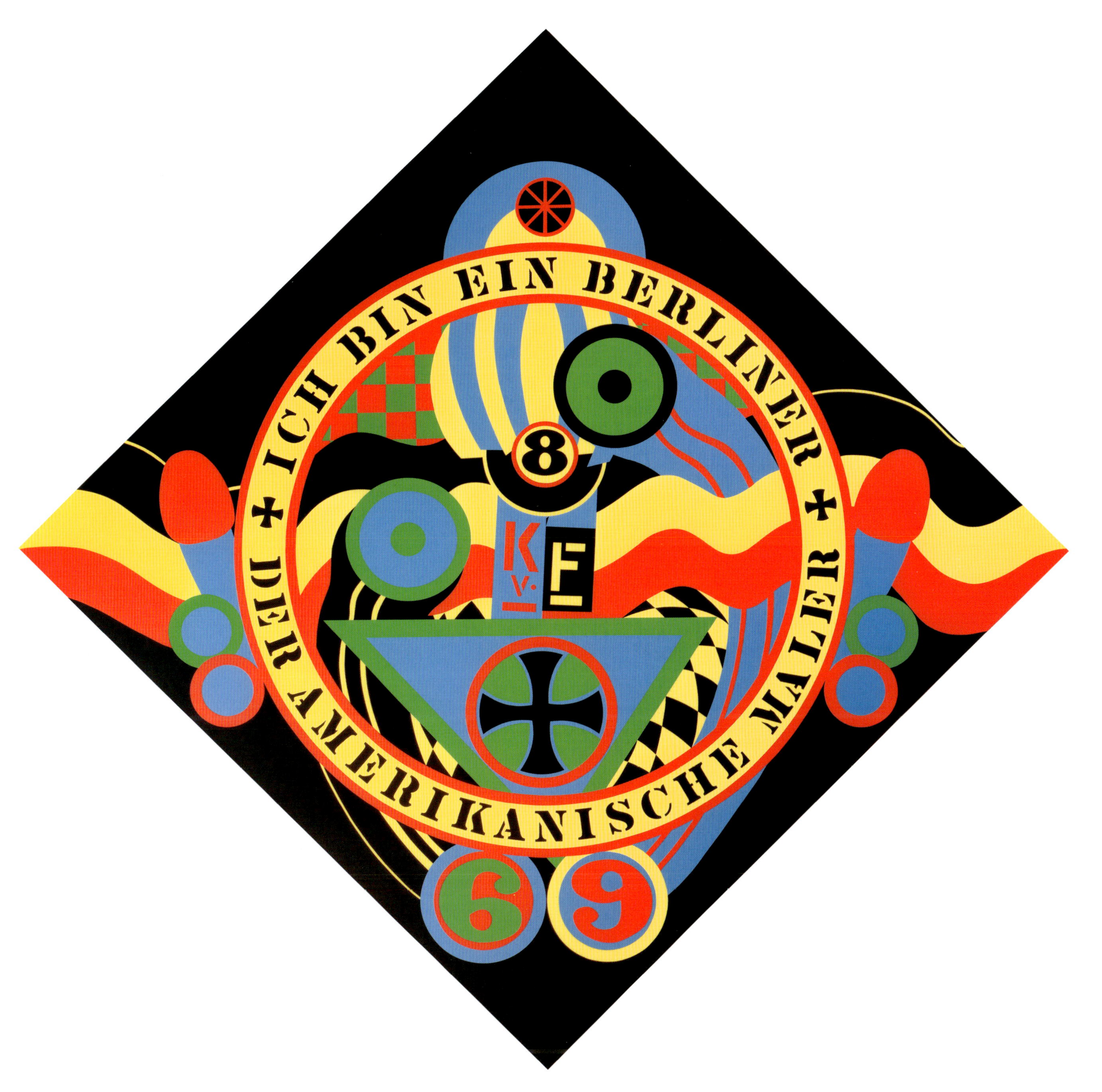

ICH BIN EIN BERLINER
DER AMERIKANISCHE MALER
8
K
v.
E
69

In his first fifteen years of residence on Vinalhaven, Indiana was involved in many personal and artistic projects: restoring the Star of Hope, making prints at the Vinalhaven Press until its closure in 2002, and manufacturing a set of ten eight-foot-high painted aluminum numbers destined for the Indianapolis Museum of Art. But he was most consumed by his Hartley project, conceived in 1980, begun in 1989, and finished in 1994. *The Hartley Elegies* were executed in a spirit of near collaboration, with Hartley supplying the imagery and Indiana modifying it. "Hartley had a very loose edge," Indiana said in 1989. "I'm going to straighten him up, clarify him, and strengthen him."[111] ● Just as Hartley, in the subsequent paintings of his *War Motif* series, mined his own *Portrait of a German Officer* for elements symbolizing his deceased friend Karl von Freyburg, so Indiana borrowed first from Hartley and then from himself as the *Elegies* metamorphosed from Hartley's into Indiana's. Akin to his various homages to Charles Demuth, cited by Indiana as the precedent for his Hartley series, the *Elegies* allowed Indiana to portray himself through the lens of Hartley's memorialization of his friend using remnants of his life. The tripartite bond between Hartley, von Freyburg, and Indiana is expressed by the three linked words TRUTH · FRIENDSHIP · LOVE appearing in both *KvF V* and *VIII*, which express the ideals of fraternity. The depth of this kinship was revealed in the artist's concluding statement from a 1991 interview: "'The only thing I'm worried about,' says Indiana, casting his eyes heavenward, 'is, what is Marsden thinking?'"[112]

PLATE 52

KvF X

from *The Hartley Elegies: The Berlin Series*, 1991

screenprint

edition of 50

image: 57 ½ × 57 ⅜ in. (146.1 × 145.7 cm);
sheet: 59 ¾ × 59 ⅝ in. (151.8 × 151.4 cm)

printed by Brand X Editions, Ltd., New York;
published by Park Granada Editions, Tarzana, California

Collection of the Indianapolis Museum of Art, Martha Delzell Memorial Fund and General Art Fund, 2010.129

111. Carl Little, "Robert Indiana at the Portland Museum of Art," *Art in America* (October 1991): 162.
112. Taylor, "Love Story," 97.

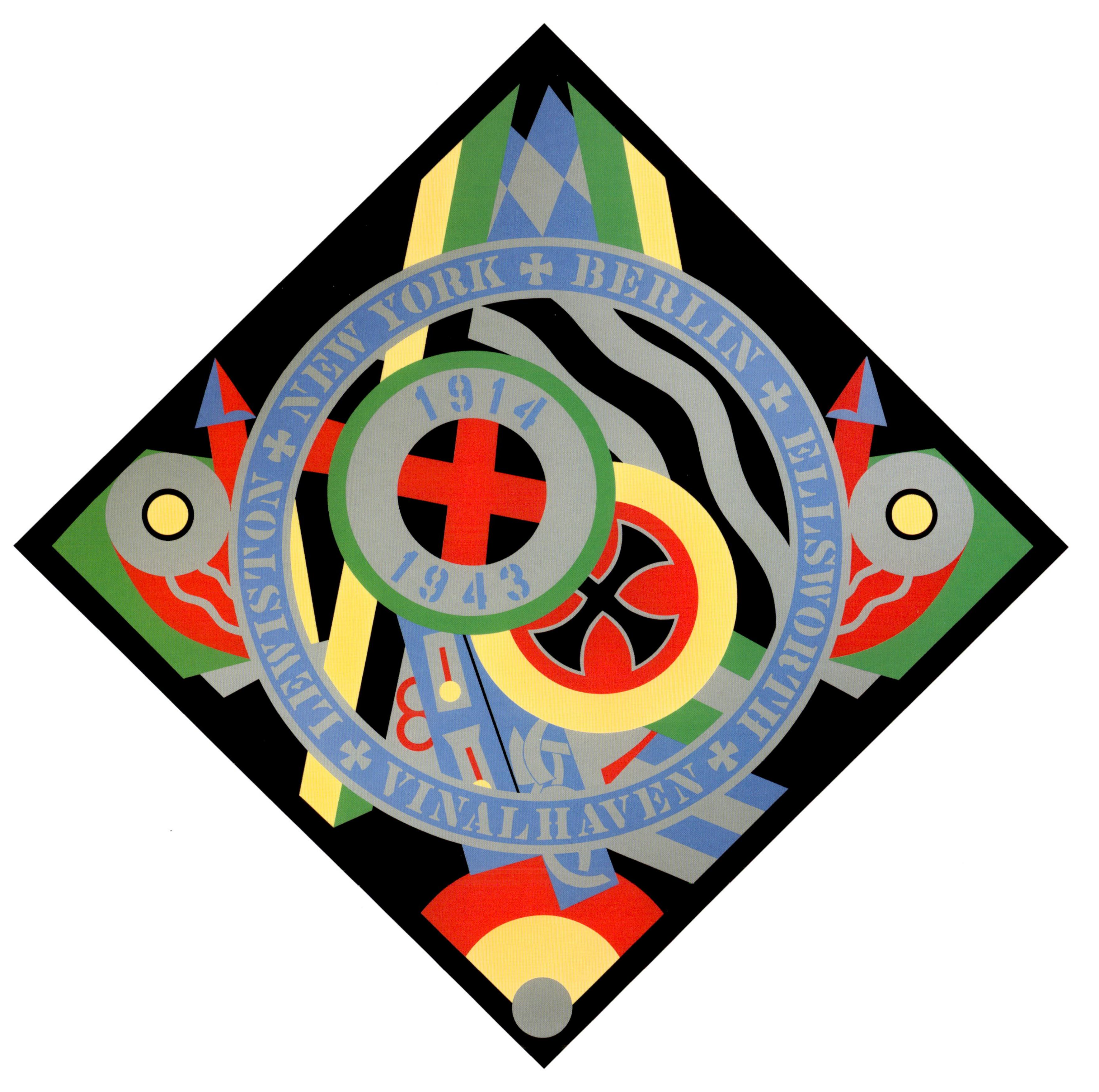
NEW YORK
BERLIN
ELLSWORTH
VINALHAVEN
LEWISTON
1914
1943

HOPE is one of those universal human aspirations that was bound to intrigue Indiana's sensibilities, particularly after his acquisition of the Star of Hope Lodge. Visually, like *LOVE*, *HOPE* had the requisite number of letters. The idea of turning the concept into an image gestated until 2006, when Indiana learned of Barack Obama's new book *The Audacity of Hope: Thoughts on Reclaiming the American Dream*. "Hope" and "Change" became the clarion calls of Obama's 2008 presidential campaign, and HOPE had already appeared graphically in Shepard Fairey's iconic Obama campaign poster. Indiana's version was likewise made to benefit the Democratic candidate. He remarked later in 2008: "There might be a chance that we survive eight years of [President] Bush, I don't know. That's where the hope comes in."[113] ● His *HOPE* debuted as a six-foot-tall aluminum sculpture at the Democratic National Convention in Denver in August 2008. It soon appeared as screenprints and on T-shirts, key chains, and bumper stickers, the proceeds from which put more than $1 million in the coffers of the Obama for America campaign. Indiana, who had been involved in Democratic politics since the Johnson administration, fashioned his *HOPE* in the manner of his *LOVE*, just as he had done with *VOTE*, which was made to benefit the Carter campaign in 1976 (see Plate 38). Referring to *HOPE*, Indiana said, "It's really a brother to *LOVE*, or a sister or a very close family member."[114]

PLATE 53

HOPE, 2009

screenprint on canvas

uneditioned

image and sheet: 36 × 36 in. (91.4 × 91.4 cm)

Collection of the artist

113. "Maine Artist Finds HOPE after LOVE," *USA Today*, August 30, 2008.
114. Ibid.

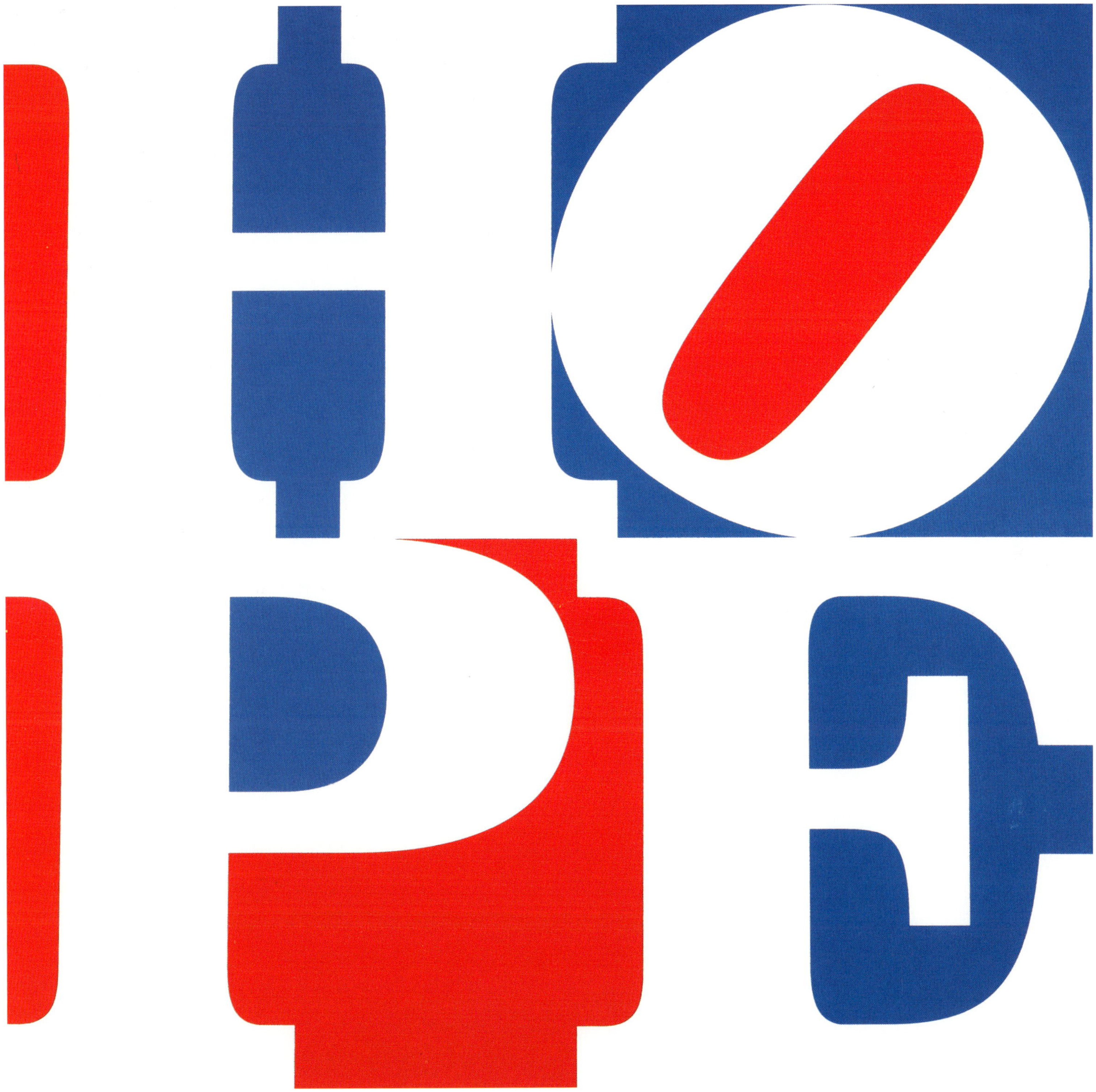

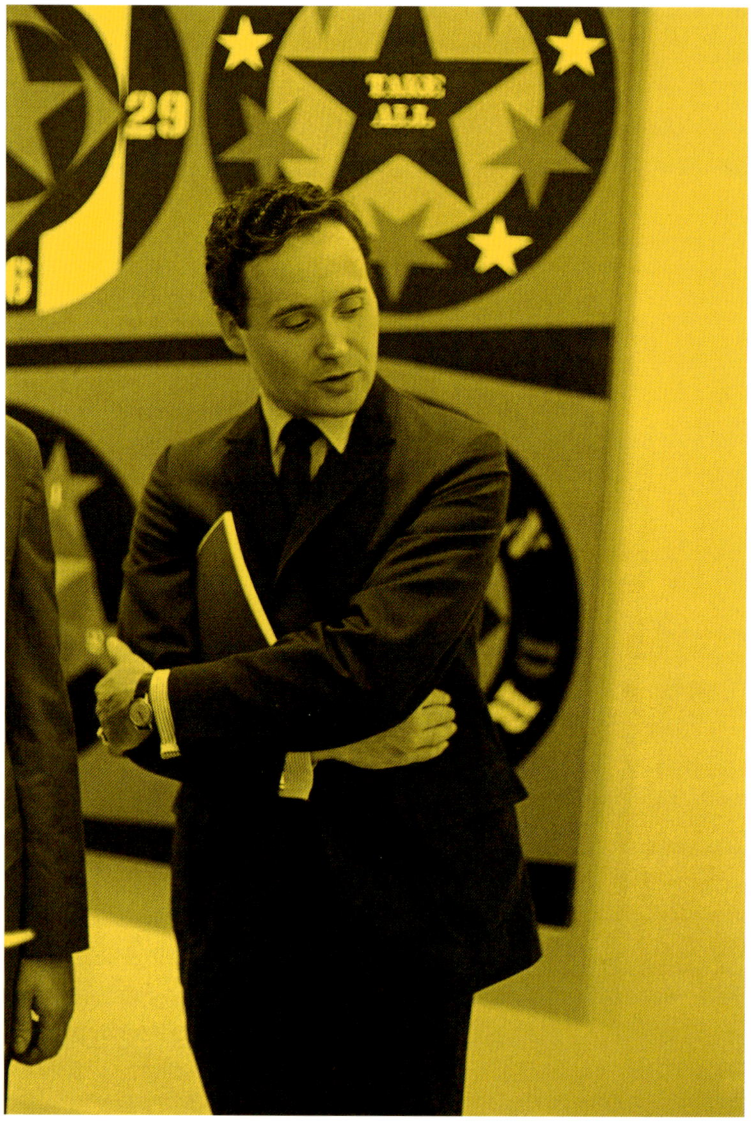

29
TAKE ALL

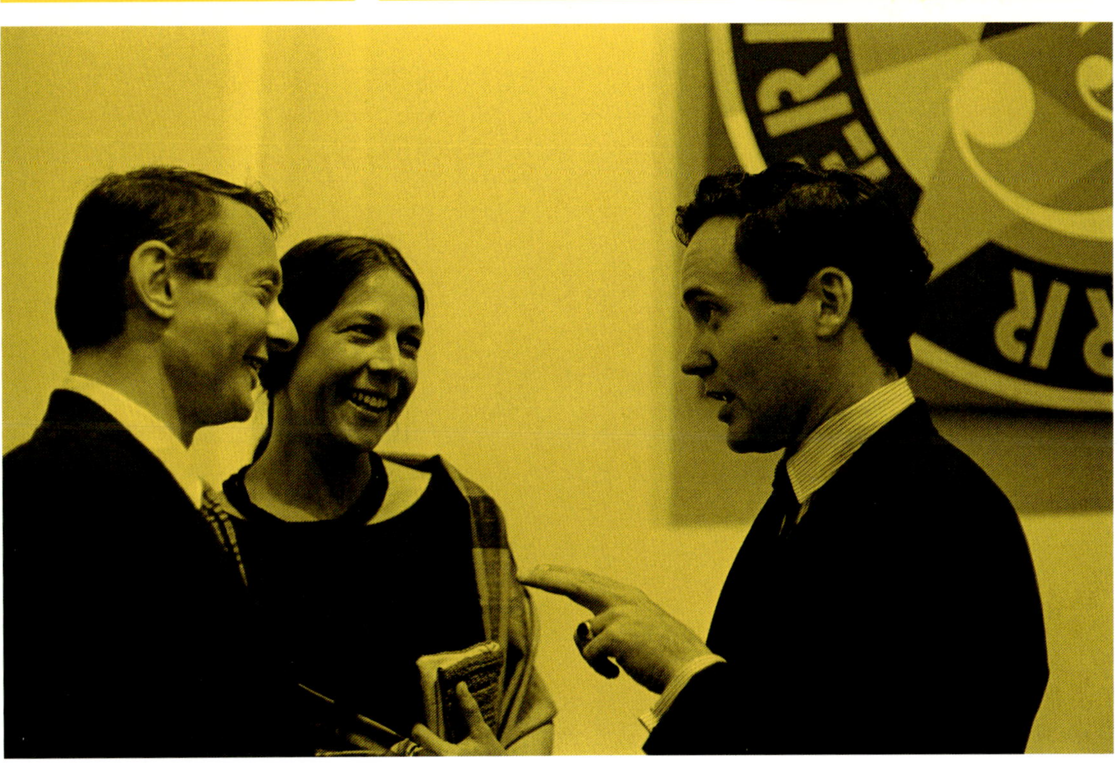

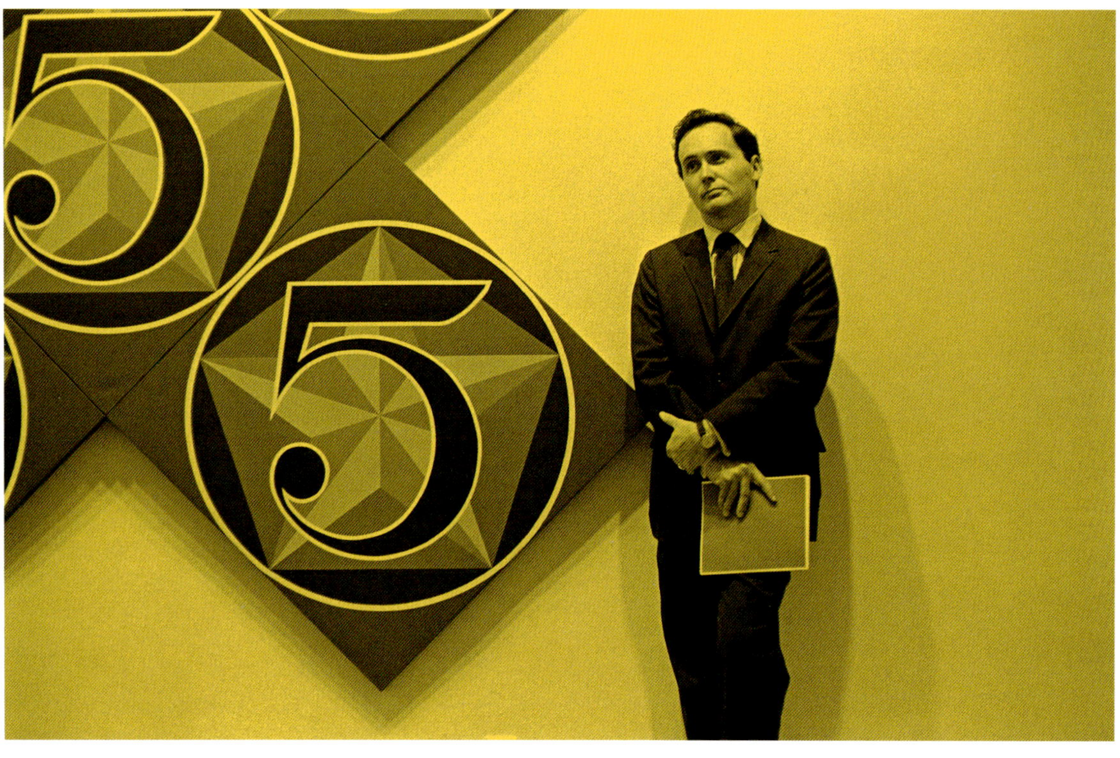

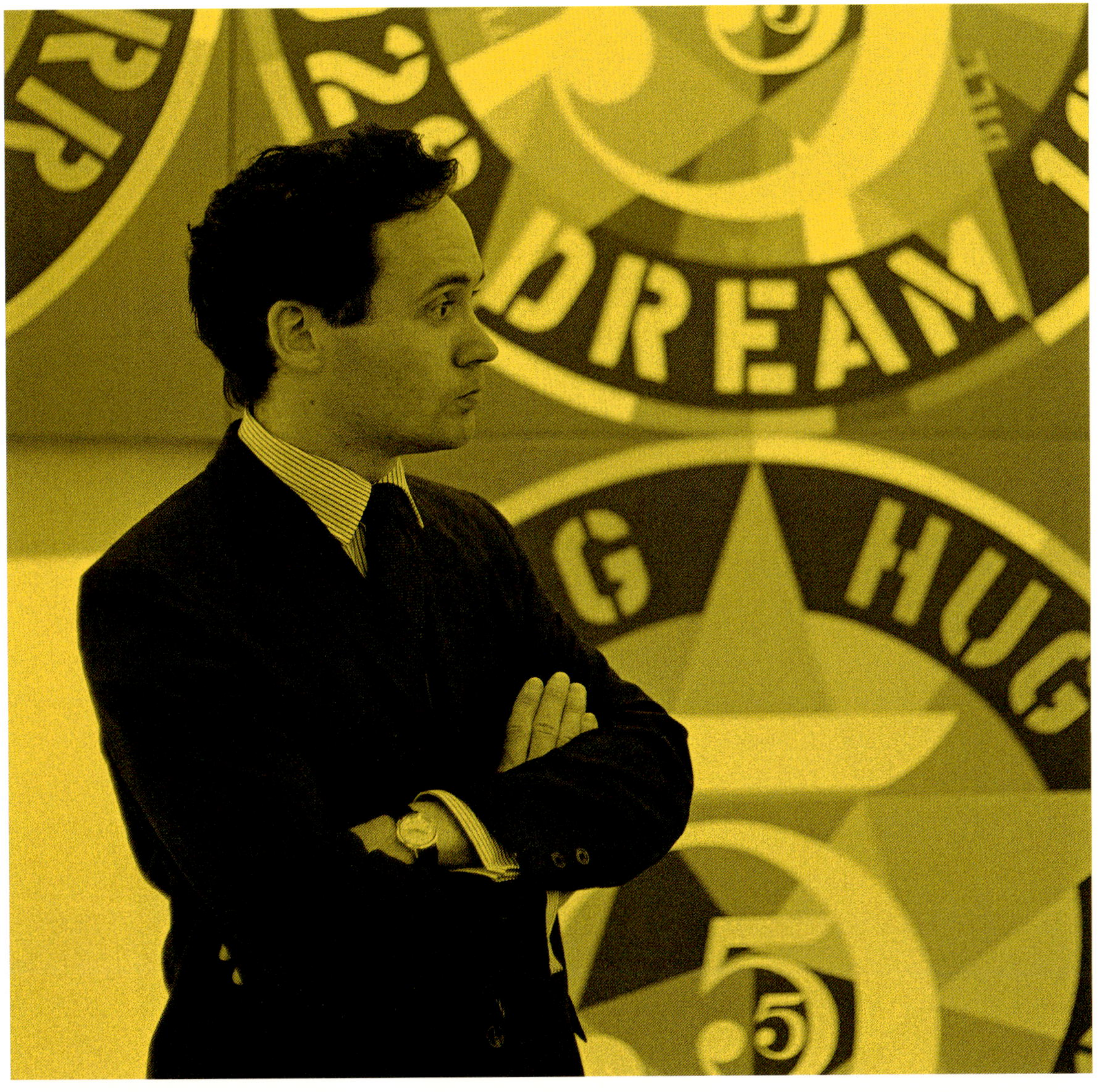
DREAM
HUG

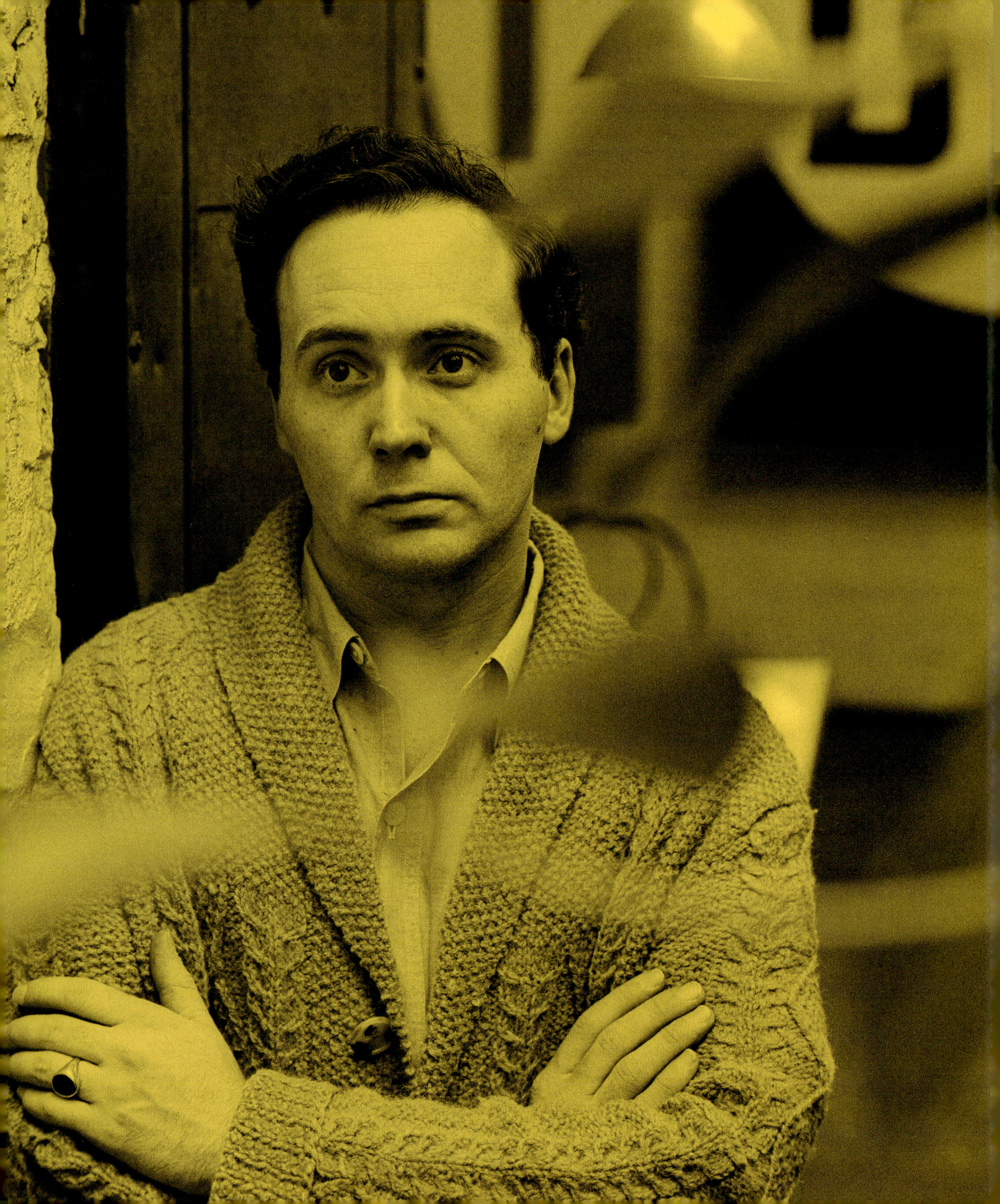

REPRODUCTION CREDITS

Unless otherwise noted, plates photography by Hadley Fruits, Indianapolis Museum of Art

The Diamond ONE (page 95) and *HIGH BALL on the REDBALL MANIFEST* (page 67) photos courtesy of Taglialatella Galleries

Photo of Robert Indiana, Martin Krause, and John Wilmerding (page 152) courtesy of Robert Indiana Studio

PAGE 2: Robert Indiana holding his cat at his Coenties Slip studio, 1963

PAGE 10: Robert Indiana holding an ampersand stencil at his Coenties Slip studio, 1963

PAGE 11 (TOP): Robert Indiana with his cat sitting on his shoulder at his Coenties Slip studio, 1964

PAGE 11 (BOTTOM): Robert Indiana holding his cat at his Coenties Slip studio, 1964

PAGE 12: Robert Indiana standing in the plant room at his Coenties Slip studio, 1964

PAGE 14: Eleanor Ward and Robert Indiana at the *Americans 1963* exhibition at the Museum of Modern Art, 1963

PAGE 16: Profile of Robert Indiana at his Coenties Slip studio with his 1961 painting *YEAR OF METEORS* in the background, 1963

PAGE 36: Robert Indiana at the *Americans 1963* exhibition at the Museum of Modern Art with his 1963 painting *The Demuth American Dream No. 5* in the background, 1963

PAGE 144: Robert Indiana at the *Americans 1963* exhibition at the Museum of Modern Art with his 1961 painting *The American Dream, I* in the background, 1963

PAGE 145: Roy Lichtenstein, Isabel Lichtenstein, and Robert Indiana at the *Americans 1963* exhibition at the Museum of Modern Art, 1963

PAGE 146: Robert Indiana at the *Americans 1963* exhibition at the Museum of Modern Art with his 1963 painting *X-5* in the background, 1963

PAGE 147: Robert Indiana at the *Americans 1963* exhibition at the Museum of Modern Art with his 1963 painting *The Demuth American Dream No. 5* in the background, 1963

PAGE 148: Robert Indiana at his Coenties Slip studio with his 1962 diptych *EAT/DIE* on the wall, 1963

BACK COVER: Robert Indiana standing in the plant room at his Coenties Slip studio, 1964

INDEX

Note: Page numbers in italics indicate illustrations.

CONTRIBUTORS

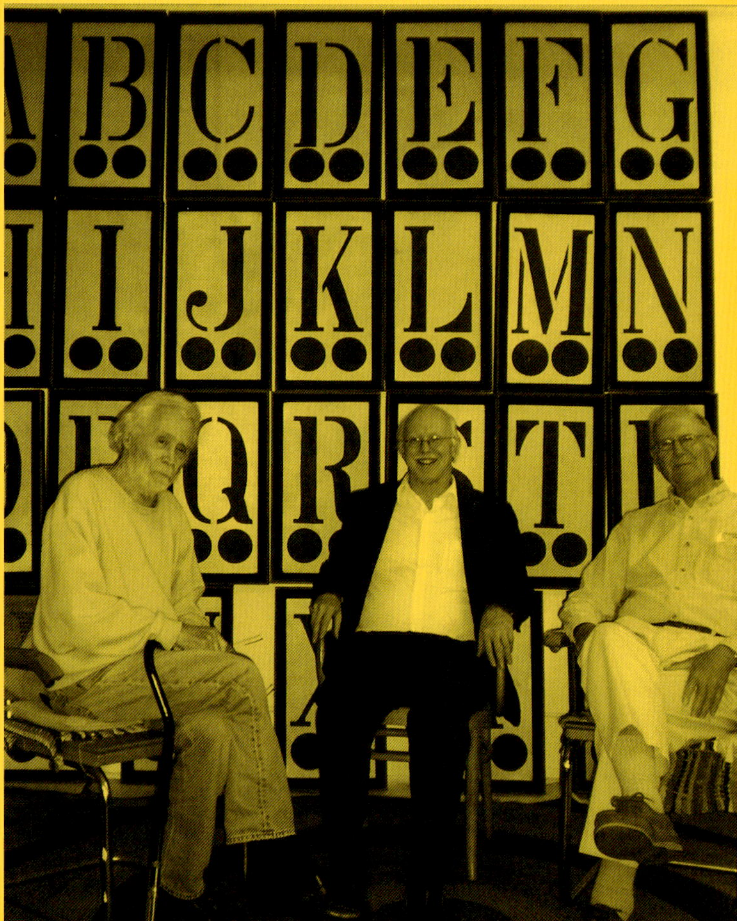

Left to right: Robert Indiana, Martin Krause, and John Wilmerding

Since 1979, Martin Krause has served as curator of prints, drawings, and photographs at the Indianapolis Museum of Art, a major repository of Robert Indiana's prints, paintings, and sculptures. Krause has written or coauthored twelve books on aspects of nineteenth- and twentieth-century European and American graphic arts, including monographs on J. M. W. Turner, Gustave Baumann, and Garo Antreasian, as well as on the history of art in Indiana.

John Wilmerding is the Sarofim Professor of American art, emeritus, at Princeton University. Formerly, he was a visiting curator in the department of American art at the Metropolitan Museum of Art, New York, and has also served as senior curator and deputy director of the National Gallery of Art in Washington. A noted scholar of American art and cultural studies, he is the author of monographs on Fitz Henry Lane, John F. Peto, Winslow Homer, and Thomas Eakins. More recently, he has written books on Richard Estes, Robert Indiana, Tom Wesselmann, Roy Lichtenstein, and Wayne Thiebaud.